JUXTA CRUCEM

*The Life of
Basil Anthony Moreau*

BASIL ANTHONY MOREAU, C.S.C. FOUNDER AND FIRST SUPERIOR GENERAL OF THE CONGREGATION OF HOLY CROSS AND OF THE MARIANITE SISTERS OF HOLY CROSS.

JUXTA CRUCEM

The *Life* of
Basil *Anthony Moreau*
1799—1873

Founder of the Congregation of Holy Cross
and of the
Marianite Sisters of Holy Cross

BY

GERALD M. C. FITZGERALD, C.S.C.

P. J. KENEDY & SONS · NEW YORK

Imprimi Potest
JAMES A. BURNS, C.S.C.
July 14, 1937.

Nihil Obstat
ARTHUR J. SCANLAN, S.T.D.
Censor Librorum.

Imprimatur
✠ PATRICK CARDINAL HAYES
Archbishop, New York.
November 5, 1937.

COPYRIGHT, 1937,
GENERAL ADMINISTRATION CONGREGATION OF HOLY CROSS
NOTRE DAME, INDIANA
MADE IN U.S.A.

TO
THE HOLY FAMILY
of
NAZARETH AND HEAVEN
whom
FATHER MOREAU
served
so faithfully
and
so earnestly desired
should be imaged
in
his own
Family of Holy Cross.

DECLARATION

I hereby declare that, in conformity with the decrees of Urban VIII respecting the Canonization of Saints and the Beatification of the Blessed, I do not intend to give to facts or expressions contained in this book, particularly such expressions as "saint," "sanctity," "miracle," any other sense than that authorized by the Church, to whose judgment I gladly submit in advance.

THE AUTHOR.

WORKS CONSULTED

Annales de la Congregation, Saint-Laurent, 1930.
A Story of Fifty Years, Ave Maria, Notre Dame.
Basile-Antoine Moreau, par L'Abbé Charles Moreau, Finnin-Didot, Paris, 1898.
Blessed Mary of St. Euphrasia Pelletier, Burns Oates, 1934.
Brothers of Holy Cross, Trahey, C.S.C., University Press, Notre Dame, 1904.
Dom Guéranger, Mame, Paris, 1924.
Histoire de Père Moreau, Montiligeon (Orne), 1923.
Life of Mother Pelletier, A. M. Clarke, Burns Oates, 1895.
Méditations Chrétiennes, Moreau, Oratoire St. Joseph, Montreal, 1932.
Mémoire, Frère Marie-Antoine, C.S.C., Saint-Laurent, 1920.
Moreau et Mollevaut, Scolasticat Sainte-Croix, Quebec, 1923.
On the King's Highway, Sr. M. Eleanore, C.S.C., Appleton, 1931.
Our Light and Our Way, Sr. M. Eleanore, C.S.C., Bruce, 1936.
Three-Quarters of a Century, Thebaud, S. J., United States Catholic Historical Society.
Vie de M. Mollevaut, Lecoffre, Paris, 1875.
Sermons—P. Basile A. Moreau, Montreal, Oratoire St. Joseph, 1923.
Church History, Poulet-Raemers, B. Herder, 1935.
General Archives, C.S.C., Notre Dame, Indiana.

TABLE OF CONTENTS

		PAGE
ACKNOWLEDGMENTS		xii
INTRODUCTION		xiii
PREFACE, THE MOLD		xvii

CHAPTER
I.	A CENTURY OF CONFLICT	1
II.	THE WINE MERCHANT'S SON	5
III.	BASIL LEAVES HOME	10
IV.	THE DESIRED GOAL	13
V.	PARIS AND ST. SULPICE, 1821-22	16
VI.	ISSY AND MOLLEVAUT, 1822-23	22
VII.	THE TEACHING YEARS, 1823-35	31
VIII.	THE GOOD SHEPHERD OF LE MANS	44
IX.	THE AUXILIARY PRIESTS	55
X.	THE BROTHERS OF ST. JOSEPH	61
XI.	OUR LADY OF HOLY CROSS—THE ASSOCIATION	75
XII.	THE MARIANITE SISTERS	93
XIII.	THE CALL OF THE MISSIONS, 1840-50	99
XIV.	HOME FIRES, 1840-50	111
XV.	ROME	123
XVI.	ROUGH SEAS, 1851-55	136
XVII.	OUT OF THE DEPTHS, 1855	159
XVIII.	SAFE ANCHORAGE, 1856-57	166
XIX.	THE FINISHED TEMPLE, 1857	177
XX.	AMERICA, 1857	192
XXI.	FATHER MOREAU'S TESTAMENT, 1858	199
XXII.	RAIN AND SUNSHINE, 1858-61	208

TABLE OF CONTENTS

CHAPTER		PAGE
XXIII.	RESIGNATION, 1862-66	221
XXIV.	DEEPENING SHADOWS, 1866-67	240
XXV.	LIGHT IN DARKNESS, 1866-68	247
XXVI.	BLACK HORIZONS, 1867-68	254
XXVII.	CONSUMMATION, 1869	262
XXVIII.	WINTER SUNSET, 1869-72	267
XXIX.	WAITING FOR THE MASTER, 1872	273
XXX.	THROUGH THE GATES, 1873	278
XXXI.	A PRECIOUS HERITAGE	283
	EPILOGUE	291
	APPENDIX	293

LIST OF ILLUSTRATIONS

FATHER MOREAU, C.S.C.	*frontispiece*
	FACING PAGE
FATHER DUJARIÉ	62
MOTHER MARY OF THE SEVEN DOLORS	94
NOTRE DAME DE SAINTE-CROIX	182
NOTRE DAME DU LAC	194
ORATORY OF SAINT JOSEPH	218
FATHER SORIN, C.S.C.	256
FRÈRE ANDRÉ, C.S.C.	288

ACKNOWLEDGMENTS

THE author wishes to express his gratitude to the many friends both within and without Holy Cross who have assisted him in the progress of his work. In particular he wishes to acknowledge his indebtedness to the researches of the Reverend William H. Condon, C.S.C., of Notre Dame, the Reverend Edward L. Heston, C.S.C., of Notre Dame, and of the Reverend Philias Vanier, C.S.C., Superior at Le Mans, France. Acknowledgment is also due to the able work of Sister M. Eleanore, C.S.C., of St. Mary's College, Notre Dame, Indiana, and to D. Appleton for the use of copyrighted matter. Nor can the author forgo the addition of a word of appreciation for the encouragement and helpfulness of his former Superior, the Reverend Joseph Metivier, C.S.C., of the Canadian Province, to the Reverend Francis E. Gartland, C.S.C., for proof-corrections, and to his colleagues, past and present, of the Seminary of Our Lady of Holy Cross, North Easton: the Reverend Vincent J. McCauley, C.S.C., the Reverend Robert Woodward, C.S.C., the Reverend Paul D. Doherty, C.S.C., A.M., the Reverend George P. Benaglia, C.S.C., A.M., the Reverend Charles A. Lee, C.S.C., A.M., and the Reverend John P. Whelly, C.S.C., A.M.

Finally he wishes to express his deep gratitude to his Provincial Superior, the Reverend James A. Burns, C.S.C., and most particularly to the Very Reverend James W. Donahue, C.S.C., Superior General of the Congregation of Holy Cross, both for the obedience which is herein fulfilled and for the abiding inspiration which has so lightened the task.

THE AUTHOR.

INTRODUCTION

IN the Encyclical Letter addressed to the members of Religious Institutes, on the Feast of St. Joseph, March 19, 1924, by our illustrious Pontiff, Pius XI, now gloriously reigning, we read:

> We exhort, in the first place, all religious to take pattern after their Father Founder and Lawgiver if they would become sure and abundant sharers in the graces which are bound up with their vocation. For what else did these illustrious men do than obey Divine inspiration when they founded their Institute. Therefore, every Founder wished that something distinctive might characterize his Institute and assuredly those among his followers in whom this character is found are not wandering from the primitive foundation. Hence, let religious like the best of sons take every care to safeguard the honor of their Father Lawgiver by observing his precepts and counsels and absorbing his spirit; nor will they go astray as long as they walk in the footsteps of their Founder. "And their children for their sakes remain forever" (Eccl. XLIV., 13). May they obey with such humility the laws of their Institute and maintain so well the manner of life observed from the beginning that daily they may be more worthy of the religious state!

It is in this spirit and in obedience to his Religious superiors that the Reverend Gerald M. C. Fitzgerald, C.S.C., presents to American readers for the first time the story of the Founder and first Superior General of the Congregation of Holy Cross, the Very Reverend Basil Anthony Moreau. This is the biography of a faithful disciple of Christ Crucified, a devoted son of the Mother of Sorrows to whom was granted the sublime but painful privilege of standing beside her on Calvary's hill.

One hundred years ago, March 1, 1837, Father Moreau founded the Congregation of Holy Cross by uniting the Auxiliary Priests of Le Mans, France,—a society organized by himself—to the Brothers of St. Joseph, founded by a fellow-priest of Le Mans Diocese, the Reverend James Dujarié. The union received definitive Papal approval in 1857. As a result of the religious persecution at the beginning of the present century, the international headquarters of the Congregation were transferred from Paris, France, to Notre Dame, Indiana, the Congregation's best known American establishment, which was founded in 1842 by the Reverend Edward Sorin, C.S.C., and six Brother companions whom the Founder of Holy Cross sent to Indiana at the request of His Excellency, Celestin de la Hailandière, Bishop of historic Vincennes.

The Sisters of Holy Cross, whose American Generalate is at St. Mary's, Notre Dame, Indiana, were founded by Father Moreau in 1841. This chapter of Father Moreau's life has been delightfully told by Sister Eleanore in "On the King's Highway."

A life of Father Moreau by his nephew, the Reverend Charles Moreau, was written in French some years after the Founder's death. Though admirable in many ways, it was marked by a tone of resentment, easily understandable in the circumstances, by reason of the close ties which united the author and his subject. Notwithstanding this defect, Father Charles Moreau's biography remains a source book of great and unquestioned value as the author of the present work has found it to be. Father Fitzgerald has thought it best, however, wherever possible, to find the true Father Moreau in the latter's own words; and the materials he has drawn from the French biography are, in large measure, but the express thoughts of the Founder himself.

"The Life of Basil Anthony Moreau" admirably combines scholarly accuracy and literary charm. The result is a biography both trustworthy and readable. It is based on authentic documents and archival matter to which the author has had free access and which he has used with fine historic sense. Decisions of the Roman Congregations, letters from officials of the Roman Curia and hierarchy, Chapter and Council rulings, the circular and private letters of Father Moreau, his sermons and conferences, the writings of his contemporaries, constitute the warp and woof of Father Fitzgerald's weaving. The result is history in the best sense of the word. The filial piety towards his "Father Founder and Lawgiver," so highly recommended to all Religious by His Holiness and which breathes from every page of this book, never betrays its author into overstatement or unwarranted conclusion. Whenever in the course of his work the argument so demands, reference is given to the proper authorities.

In telling his story the author reveals the same Salesian charm and optimism which has endeared him under the name of Father Page to a host of souls whom he has helped to grow in the knowledge and love of God in Christ Jesus, Our Lord. That this volume will continue this meritorious and much needed work is our hope and prayer. May the story of the heroic Founder of Holy Cross encourage many souls in their efforts to belong completely to God. Strengthened by Father Moreau's example may they stand with him and the Mother of Sorrows close to the Cross of Christ in the steadfast performance of duty.

> Juxta Crucem tecum stare
> Et me tibi sociare,
> In planctu desidero.

JAMES W. DONAHUE, C.S.C.
Superior General.

Feast of the Seven Sorrows of the Blessed Virgin
September 15, 1937
The Generalate
Notre Dame, Indiana

PREFACE
THE MOLD

*But to me thy friends, O God,
are made exceedingly honourable.*
—PS. 138-17.

THERE are many definitions of sanctity, but all contain the same essential note. There are a multitude of saints whose names are inscribed on the calendar of Mother Church, and still others whose lives remain hidden in God, yet in all these holy ones will be found the same essential characteristics and but one fundamental mode of life. Nor is the reason of this truth hard to find. From the beginning there has been only One Exemplar, One Supreme Model of Holiness whom the patriarchs visioned and prefigured dimly and whom the saints of these later times have had ever before their eyes. This Model is and can be none other than Jesus Christ, Who is "yesterday, today, and the same, forever." He it is Who is the First-born of every creature, the Spiritual Rock whence all must draw the waters of grace, the Unique Mold in which all His brethren must be fashioned that they may come to the fullness of His likeness upon earth and of His glory in eternity.

It is in this Unique Mold of Jesus Christ that all the saints and servants of God have been shaped, and if they vary, as indeed they do, this is not because of any difference in the Mold, but rather by reason of the diversity of the material placed therein; and more profoundly because of the secret designs of that Heavenly Father who governs all by the breath of His Spirit and the touch of His Son's riven hands till all things shall be completed and the number of His elect shall have been made up.

Jesus Christ is, therefore, the Mold of His Saints, and that is why in authentic sanctity we find the marks of His holy wounds. Jesus in His Saints is always, at least eventually, Jesus Crucified. There can be no real sanctity without conformity to this Crucified Model. We cannot reach Christ on the heavenly Tabor except by way of Calvary. We cannot take place on His right hand and on His left in the kingdom of His Father until we have shared the chalice of His Passion.

The life of a saint of our own day, Saint Therese of the Child Jesus, illustrates very beautifully this truth. Not in the roses with which she loved to cover her crucifix, but in the thorns which she held so bravely against her own innocent heart is to be sought the secret of her influence over the Heart of God and in God over the hearts of men. The roses for Christ, the thorns for self, that has been always and everywhere the program of "God's heroes," the saints of His eternal reign.

In the month of January, 1873, while the Little Flower lay cradled a new-born babe in her mother's arms, not far distant at Le Mans a venerable priest lay dying; Basil Anthony Mary Moreau was his name, the Congregation of Holy Cross and the Marianite Sisters of Holy Cross had been the fruit of his virginal life-long love for God and souls. Like the Master he died cradled on the Cross; like the Master also there stood at the foot of that cross with the holy women only one of his disciples. The Mother of Jesus we may be sure was there, and after all it is that which truly matters. For where Mary stands there will be Jesus, and where Jesus is there will be life—life in death, the fruit of death in life.

One of that valiant host raised up by God for the spiritual restoration of France in the last century, Basil Moreau had ever been conscious of his heritage and faithful to his election. He merited well of God and his fellowmen. Destined to lay the foundation of two religious congregations consecrated to the

Sorrowful Mother of the Redeemer, it was necessary that both founder and foundations should be sealed by the sacred emblem of Salvation. Well versed in the verities of the spiritual life and the lives of the saints, Father Moreau was aware of the price that must be paid for success. He paid that price to the last farthing. He lived and died a soldier of Mary beneath the shadow of the Cross. Few more pathetic and at the same time inspiring pictures of heroic resignation will be found in the lives of God's servants than the one of this venerable priest in the evening of his years bravely continuing his apostolic ministry amid the apparent ruin of his lifework.

"You are of Holy Cross? What a holy man you had for a founder!" exclaimed a Jesuit missionary at a later period when meeting some Brothers of the Congregation.

"But, Father, where have you known him?" responded the pleased Brothers.

"I was the first of our Society who went to Holy Cross after the misfortunes of the Very Reverend Father Moreau," replied the Jesuit.[1]

That Father Moreau may be better known and consequently better loved by the members of the great family of Holy Mother Church whose needs were ever so close to his priestly heart, as well as by the members of his own spiritual family whom he loved so greatly, is the purpose and earnest prayer of

THE AUTHOR.

[1] Conference, Saint-Laurent, August 3, 1920—by Frère Marie Antoine, C.S.C.

I
A CENTURY OF CONFLICT

> *God has made the nations of the earth curable and He puts them into the wine-press only to make them worthy of His mercy.*
> —FATHER MOREAU.

TO grasp properly the story of a life we must know something of the time and place in which that life was lived. Environment is the stage of each life-drama and a just appreciation of the actor demands a study of his stage. This truth will appear even more clearly, when, as in the present instance, the story is that of a soul destined to defend and advance the old ideals amid new philosophies of life and changing fashions of government. During the life-span of Father Moreau, France witnessed nine different civil governments. When he was born the Directory was still in power, when he died the Third Republic had begun the restoration of a nation humiliated by the fortunes of war. Thus for even a partial understanding of his life and work we must glance at the Europe of his day and more especially at the France in which he lived.

The 19th Century found the peoples of Europe in ferment. The infiltration of republican ideas, aided by the vastly improved methods and means of communication, had made the masses painfully aware of the limitations of their rulers. Inventions in the field of manufacture were paving the way for the advance of the middle class. Men were questioning the validity of older institutions. The taste for civil liberties had been whetted but not satisfied, and the resultant stirrings within the hearts of men were accompanied by a perceptible growth in the spirit of national consciousness.

Against these growing forces in the political blood stream of European life moved the countercurrent of the old regime. Royalty, despite its failings, still struck responsive chords in the life of the masses, while the aristocracy was not prepared to yield its position of ascendancy without a struggle. It was this conflict between the new and the old in almost every phase of human society that the 19th Century witnessed.

Of this popular ferment France was the center. From her capital in the last decade of the previous century had come the first impulse of change. Thereafter her assemblies, her academies, her courts, the very streets of her cities [1] became the battleground where these conflicting ideas and principles clashed.

But if France was the heart of the new unrest she did not thereby cease to be the eldest daughter of the Church. Her soul was Catholic, and remained so, purified by a baptism of blood. Though her Emperor imprisoned Pius VII, her soldiers defended Pius IX, a Montalembert challenged the sons of Voltaire, Jean de Lamennais atoned for his brother Felix's apostasy, while a de Quelen and an Affre showed the world how nobly spiritual shepherds could live, how bravely die. The very battle cry of Republican France—Liberty, Equality, Fraternity—became the standard of the champions of the Church in their fight for freedom of education and administration. Thus this Century which saw the rise of some of the Church's bitterest enemies witnessed as well the careers of some of her most illustrious defenders. The spirit of evil had moved over the land sowing cockle. Yet the wheat had been planted also, and, in God's own good time, would be ready for His harvesting.

[1] Vide, for intimate picture, Thebaud, S. J., "Three-Quarters of a Century," U. S. Cath. H. S., Vol. I.

The toxic elements of Gallicanism and Jansenism were still discernible in the blood stream of the nation's life, but God had prepared the necessary antitoxins. Not a rank within the Church, not a class of society, not a way of Christian living that did not make notable contributions to this end. What memories of spiritual achievement an even partial listing of these Catholic forces awakes! Beside the names already mentioned let us place those of Cardinals de Bonald and Donnet, Archbishop Dupanloup, Bishops Gerbet and Rohrbacher, and Monseigneur de Segur.

This, too, was the century of Lacordaire and Ravignan, of Mollevaut, of Monsieur Dupont, Jean-Baptiste Dumas, Falloux, Pasteur, Le Vernier, Veuillot and Villefranche! This the moment Mazenod, Colin, Libermann, and Mother Couderc consecrated their companies to the service of Heaven's Queen. This the hour Saint Madeleine Barat gave her daughters to the Sacred Heart. This the time Abbé Debrabant dedicated his daughters to the Holy Union, while Abbé Dujarié confided his Sisters to Providence and his Brothers to St. Joseph. This the period in which Blessed Mother Pelletier consolidated and extended the Apostolate of the Good Shepherd, and before its close Blessed Eymard had inaugurated his Triple Guard of Honor for the Eucharistic King. This the epoch of Ozanam and his work of social charity, saw as well Pauline Jaricot and Madame Petit organize the material support for Catholic Missions, and Cardinal Lavigerie and a host of others enlist in the noblest of Crusades. Nor must we forget that least of parish priests, St. John Mary Vianney, whose life was so vivid and forceful a proof of the reality of the things of the spirit, nor the little Rose of Carmel whose passing sounded a fitting and heavenly benediction over the closing years of the age—the bugle call of the victorious spirit of Christian faith.

Thus this Century in France represents a hundred years

of conflict. Not without purpose did God assemble this host which we have so hurriedly reviewed. It has been said that the devil never sleeps, but let us remember that God is Eternal Act. He is ever guiding His children; His hand is ever raised in benediction above them, and though at times it may seem to be withdrawn or appear to cast a shadow yet in its shade there is always to be found peace—peace and strength for men of good will.

II

THE WINE MERCHANT'S SON

> *—we too have received our consecration in the waters of baptism that marked us all with the seal of the children of God. See to it, then, that nothing soiled approach . . .*
>
> —FATHER MOREAU.

NINE miles out of the city of Le Mans, in the Northwestern part of France, sleeps the little village of Laigné-en-Belin. It was there Basil Anthony Moreau was born February 11, 1799. The ninth of the fourteen children of Louis and Louise Pioger Moreau, the boy grew up amid the simple pleasures and humble duties of the French countryside. The business of his father, that of a wine merchant, often necessitated his absence, and the management of the home and modest farm fell largely on the shoulders of the mother. It would seem that God had fitted the back to the burden. The unselfish industry of both parents left an indelible impression on the mind of their little son. Years later we find the expression of this memory in his letters and in his loving solicitude for their remembrance at God's altar.

Before a child newly born thoughtful Christians pause in reverence. Here Nature knows a resurrection, and Faith finds an immortal soul, naked and shivering, to be cleansed and clothed in a garment of grace by water and the Holy Ghost. The baptism of Basil Moreau was delayed for ten days, a sufficient indication of the troubled state of the times.

The Directory was still in power and the harassed priests of the countryside might well echo the words of their Master, "the birds of the air have their nests, the foxes have their holes, but the Son of Man has not even so much as whereon to lay His head!" Napoleon's vigorous hand was soon to be felt at the helm of the Government, and brighter, though far from cloudless days dawn for the Church in France.

From earliest childhood the boy gave earnest indications of his future career. Bright, friendly, pious with that simple directness of character that so often disarms criticism, young Moreau was not long in assuming a natural leadership among his companions in the things that pertained to God. He taught them to serve Mass, erecting for this purpose a tiny altar in his own home. He organized their play, disciplining, by exclusion, those who had failed in proper respect at the little presbytery school that Father Le Provost, the Curé of Laigné-en-Belin, had established. He even attempted to preach at home to his mother and his sisters, and when the latter failed in proper decorum the youthful preacher would appeal to the maternal authority of his good mother, "Mama, make them keep quiet, I do not wish them to laugh."

Thus it was not difficult to discern the attractions of this youthful Samuel of the Moreaus. Some the Lord of the Vineyard calls only at the eleventh hour. The little son of Louis Moreau He called in the first blush of life's morning, and the wonder of that spiritual sunrise was destined to abide in the boy's soul; it was to enlighten more than sixty years of his life, and became in life's evening a golden sunset.

When under the Consulate the Church in France was restored some measure of freedom, the Parish of Laigné-en-Belin received for its spiritual shepherd, Father Julien Le Provost. The choice was a singularly happy one. The new pastor, formerly an assistant in the neighboring canton of Bouloise, had distinguished himself during the terror-years of the Revolution by his courageous pursuit of his priestly ministry at Le Mans.

This zealous shepherd was not slow in recognizing the needs of his new flock, and set himself with characteristic energy to supply them. At that period in France, almost everywhere woeful ignorance of Christian truths prevailed—the black ruins in the wake of the red flame of revolt. On all sides existed coldness and indifference to the things of God, the natural fruit of materialistic philosophy and misdirected liberty. The work, therefore, of Christian instruction was of paramount importance, and to this task Father Le Provost gave himself. He opened a school in his own rectory for the boys and the young men of the parish. Many of the latter, though twenty years of age, had not made their First Holy Communion.

The work of the good pastor for his boys was ably seconded by a devout lady of the parish, Miss de Boismont. She undertook the instruction of the girls and, besides, contributed generously to the expense of the education of seminarians. Basil Moreau cherished grateful remembrance of both these benefactors, and when years later a letter from his sisters informed him of the grave illness of the former, he replied as follows: "I am most anxious to receive news from the presbytery. Oh, what reason you have to express your sorrow over so great a loss! I share your tears and your affliction. He is my father, she is my mother; I am their son in Jesus Christ."

The good priest on his part was not slow in discerning the gifts of mind and heart of his pupil. With that clear vision that God gives to His servants Father Le Provost was looking to the future, and his grace-illumined soul read in Basil Anthony's the uprightness, the generosity and the reverent interest in the things of God, that are characteristic of priestly vocation.

At twelve Basil had completed his primary education and the zealous pastor spoke to Louis Moreau of the boy's future. The wine merchant listened respectfully to the priest whom he and all the parish were coming to revere. Father Le Provost was convinced of Basil's vocation to the priesthood, the need of apostolic priests was great, everywhere the work of spiritual renovation awaited workers. Yet the elder Moreau hesitated. Some youths of the parish had but lately made use of the sacrifices of their parents and of their pastor for their higher education only to abuse them. Now they were a source of scandal. In the end, however, the faith and conviction of the good priest carried the day. His words awoke echoing chords in the faith-guided soul of his parishioner. Little Basil might continue his studies, might commence the study of Latin, might prepare himself for the Priesthood since God willed it so. Nevertheless there was to be no shirking of home duties. The boy must continue to share in the labor of the farm. Thereafter when the weather was fine in the Moreau pasture one might observe the bowed form of a shepherd lad seated on a bench, a Latin grammar on his knee, his lessons intermingled with pleasant reveries of the future in which the gentle tinkling bells of his leisurely feeding flock became strangely interwoven with Mass chimes, and himself a priest, bowed before the Lamb of God.

Presently the sharp staccato of his dog's bark would break the boyish dreaming, and the lengthening shadows give notice of the approach of eventide. The little shepherd of the Moreaus would rouse himself, call his dog, and lead his flock homeward, Tricot's Rudiments in his hand, the little bench on his shoulder, and himself unmindful of the chill of the evening because of the love of the good God which was already burning steadily in his heart.

How often the past is the mirror of the future! The shepherd boy of Laigné-en-Belin was to be the good shepherd of Le Mans leading his Father's flock, still in old age devoted to education, still with God's love guiding his steps aright. Only the bench on his shoulder would by then have become strangely heavier and very similar to the crook of the Good Shepherd, very much like the Holy Cross! Thus does Jesus love to reproduce in His servants the characteristics of His own life upon earth. He wishes them to be mirrors holding His image and reflecting His eternal love.

III

BASIL LEAVES HOME

> *For what is more delicate and more sacred than a vocation? And of what a terrible crime would he be guilty who would seek to destroy it or even to influence it wrongly.*
> —FATHER MOREAU.

ON a morning in early October, 1814, a man and a boy might be seen walking along the hard dirt road that left the village of Laigné-en-Belin for Le Mans and the great outer world. Possibly the boy's eyes were misty, his heart pounding beneath his stiffly-starched blouse and the muscles of his throat strangely taut. They would walk briskly and in silence, as men walk who share a sorrow and have a definite object to their journeying. The village housewives would have identified them: "Behold M. Moreau, the wine merchant and his son, Basil. He takes the boy to the college at Chateau-Gontier. The Moreaus will presently have a priest among them."

What was passing meanwhile in the youthful heart of Basil Moreau? Those who have shared such a journey need not be informed. For the rest, a letter written to Basil's sister Victoria from Chateau-Gontier some time after will withdraw the veil.

"I have been deeply moved," he writes, "by the proofs of affection you have shown me, and can in all truth say that if you shed tears when we parted, I was almost overcome with grief, and am not yet consoled."

The letters of the youthful seminarian reveal the inner workings of a tender and unselfish heart, a heart devoted to parents, brothers and sisters, yet already dominated by faith and the grace of his priestly vocation. Almost overcome with grief he yet goes on; and what afflicts him most is that he sees "a very hard winter ahead for mother."

Thus at a time of life when selfishness is proverbial we find in Basil Moreau, a youth whose affections are sweetly spiritualized and who grieves more over the burdens that fall on the shoulders of others than for those he must bear himself. We will find generosity and magnanimity in the natural order brought to heroic perfection by an all-pervading spirit of supernatural faith, the life-story of Basil Moreau.

A fragrant sense of gratitude pervades his letters of this period as well as those of his maturer years. From childhood he was of the number of rare souls who find God's ministering love in all things and are humbly appreciative of the ever-present touch of their Heavenly Father's hand. A quotation from a letter of the young seminarian to his good parents will illustrate this engaging trait of his character.

> My dear Father and Mother:
> If I write you today, it is not to fulfill a duty required by ordinary civility and imposed upon me at such a time [his father's patronal feast], nor to give you praise, which is so often but deceitful and vain flattery. Surely not. Guided by a motive which is purer and listening only to the voice of gratitude, which animates me, as well as my brothers and sisters, I speak to you the simple truth.
>
> How many are the interesting objects that rise before my imagination at this happy moment! How many precious souvenirs retrace themselves in my memory! With what transports of joy do I celebrate what is for you and for us all a day of feast and of solemnity! If I recall the days of my childhood, what powerful motives of gratitude do I not discover! If I consider the lovely days of innocence I spent with you, if I reflect on the early education and proficiency of each of my brothers and sisters, I see you in the tumult of confining busi-

ness procuring for us the necessaries of life and striving to bring us up in a becoming manner. Here I see a hard-working father hurrying through the town and countryside; there a watchful mother guarding her children and anxious about their future welfare. In truth, what care, what anxieties, what pain, and what labor, has our training cost you! Up to the present your life has been but a tissue of worries; up to the present you have spent your days in business difficulties, and now you can say with a feeling of deepest gratitude, "Behold, O my God, those whom Thou hast given me for the comfort of my old age. I thank Thee for having preserved them to me, while so many families have been broken up by the loss of children who died on the field of battle."

A letter such as this would be noteworthy even if dictated by the mature reflection of age; but let us remember it came from the youthful heart and reflective mind of a youth, a youth who already gave signs of possessing the wisdom that God alone can give. "Where the Spirit wills, He breatheth."

IV
THE DESIRED GOAL

> *Let us remember that from all eternity we have been called to fill a place in the sanctuary or in the world, for "He chose us in Him before the foundation of the world."*
> —FATHER MOREAU.

LIKE many another youth, before and since, Basil Moreau left home and dear ones in October, 1814, to become a priest. Only God knows fully what it means to be a priest! Yet from the hour of the Last Supper till that of the Last Judgment, despite all opposition diabolical as well as mundane, the Divine Master shall have His servants, His priests: shall have other hands to lift Him to His Heavenly Father and give Him to His people; shall have other lips to utter His truth, breathe His praises, declare His mercies, and convey His benedictions; shall have other hearts to love with, other wills to do His will; other selves to reveal unto men the height and the depth and the breadth of His Eternal love.

To one who was truly such a priest, Louis Moreau confided his son at the end of the memorable journey to Chateau-Gontier. The director of the little seminary was at this time Father Basil Horeau, a venerable confessor of the Faith, and a friend of the Pastor of Laigné-en-Belin. The latter had already informed Father Horeau of Basil Moreau's qualities of mind and heart. Accordingly the director received the boy with open arms, and assured the elder Moreau that he would make a first-class seminarian of his son. The confidence was to prove well founded.

From the first Basil Moreau revealed himself both to his superiors and to his companions as an earnest, honorable, intelligent student, a lively companion, and a devout seminarian whose eyes were ever fixed upon the goal of his ambition, the priesthood of Jesus Christ. Nothing shows more clearly the impression Basil Moreau left behind him at Chateau-Gontier when in due time he passed on to the Major Seminary of St. Vincent at Le Mans, than the hope entertained by Father Horeau that Basil might return as his assistant, and, when God so willed it, become his successor as superior at the little seminary. The director even wrote of this desire to Bishop Pidoll. But God had other designs for Basil's future.

In September, 1818, young Moreau entered the Major Seminary of St. Vincent at Le Mans. In the private chapel of Bishop Pidoll on the 18th of the same month, he received the Tonsure, the first formal step toward the priestly consecration. If hitherto he had walked in the way of the Lord, henceforth he would run. Less than a year later, on July 30, 1819, he received Minor Orders. The Subdiaconate followed on the 27th of May, 1820; the Diaconate, April 7, 1821. Basil Moreau was but one step from his goal, and here a difficulty intervened.

The canonical age for ordination to the priesthood is twenty-four years completed. Basil was only twenty-two. Yet he had made so favorable an impression upon the faculty of St. Vincent's and upon Monseigneur de la Myre, who had succeeded Monseigneur Pidoll as Bishop of Le Mans, that a dispensation from this impediment was sought from Rome, and upon its reception Basil was ordained to the Priesthood in the chapel of the old Visitation Convent, Le Mans, August 12, 1821. Basil Anthony Moreau was at last a priest.

Even before the vision of religious life as such had cast its light across the soul-path of the young priest, even before binding himself to the relentless obligation of the Subdiaconate, young Moreau had seen the glory of Christ's Priesthood, had sensed the dignity of priestly consecration and the consequent obligation of unworldly living. In life's morning he had realized what some have known only in its evening—that to be a true priest one must follow closely in the footsteps of the Master, one must be crucified with Christ and in Christ.

We find this entry in his spiritual diary:

VOWS WHICH I MADE BEFORE RECEIVING THE SUBDIACONATE

First, a vow of perpetual chastity; second, a vow of obedience, that is to say, a vow never to solicit and never to refuse any appointment; third, a vow of poverty, that is to say, I will never set my heart on money and I will wear clothing of the commonest quality; fourth, a vow to fast as well as to abstain on Fridays, and to drink water only at the collation as long as I reside in the seminary (in order to save myself embarrassment during vacation time). The prime motive of this mortification is to do penance for my sins; the second, to grow more and more in the love of Jesus Christ.

What light these last words of Basil throw upon his spiritual state at this critical period of his seminary days. Motives are the hidden, mysterious forces that direct our lives. How difficult to analyze our own, how well-nigh impossible to ascertain with surety those of others! Yet in this severe yet prudently circumscribed program of the ardent seminarian, closing with the humble avowal that it is undertaken primarily as means of penance for his sins, there is a ring of sincerity, a note of convincing truth. The soul of Basil Moreau lies revealed before us, earnest, humble, holy, reaching out for God.

Moreover, what Basil Moreau was on the day he received the accolade of the Priesthood kneeling before Bishop de la Myre, he would be fifty years later when he received from Pius IX, the crowning benediction of his priestly life on the occasion of the golden jubilee of his ordination.

V

PARIS AND ST. SULPICE. A LIGHT AT THE WINDOW—1821-22

> *Hence, laying aside the burden of sin—let us run with constancy in the career which is opened to us, our eyes ever fixed on Jesus, the Author and Rewarder of our faith.*
>
> —FATHER MOREAU.

IT was a day never to be forgotten by the villagers of Laigné-en-Belin, and above all by the worthy pastor and the Moreau family, when a few days after his ordination, Basil returned to celebrate his First Solemn Mass in their midst. The preacher for the occasion was the venerable Father Huard, pastor of Notre Dame de la Couture at Le Mans, a dear friend of Father Le Provost and like the latter a kindly benefactor of the newly ordained priest. Did the elder priest dream as he warmed to the glorious theme of Christ's Priesthood, that the frail, white-faced young levite who listened so earnestly to his words, would many years later be called upon to preach the eulogy of his own priestly life? As for the rest, no one but a priest can sound the depths of joy, the heights of exultation of a priest's First Mass.

That morning on the golden paten a second host rested with the Host Divine; the second was the virginal soul and body of Basil Anthony Moreau. The Master accepted the oblation. He took it in His hands but it would be more than fifty years later before the second host should be consumed. Meantime the mystical Mass of daily priestly sacrifice must be offered. That very night a portion of this latter, the sacrifice of service, was to begin.

With a peace-flooded soul, the youthful Father Moreau retired to his little second-story chamber on the evening of the day of his first Solemn Mass. Tired, yet too happy to sleep at once, before his mind passed the blessed hours of the day; the deep satisfaction reflected on the faces of his dear ones, the joy of his dear old pastor, the reverent faith of the parishioners, the awed wonderment of the young—a hundred scenes passed before his sleepless mind. Suddenly the pleasant reverie was broken, beams of light moved unsteadily upon the rafters above him, muffled voices rose from the street below. In an instant, Basil was on his feet, a second, and he was at the window and could distinguish the voices—

"Cousin, Cousin!" It is the sacristan of the parish church calling as he sways a lantern atop a pole close to the window.

"What is the matter?" Basil replies.

"Cousin, there is a sick person who requests your presence at Boisgar."

"But, my friend, I can do nothing. I have no faculties here."

"Cousin, I give you faculties; the messengers are waiting for us; all is ready."

"But what faculties can you give me, my dear man? Go tell the Curé."

"Cousin, he himself sent me to ask you to take his place at Boisgar, and he has commissioned me to give you all the powers you need."

A few minutes later, Basil Moreau was hurrying through the night to a soul in its hour of need, and as he went was it the angels or was it their Queen, or was it the Lamb of God, Himself, held tightly against the leaping heart of the young priest that whispered of the crying needs of lonely, aged parish priests and lonely parishes where souls were being lost because there was no one to feed them with the Bread of Life, or shrive them in the hour of their passing?

Some time after his memorable first sick-call, Father Moreau stood before the Ordinary of Le Mans, the gentle Bishop de la Myre. It was a tense moment for the young levite—his future, his whole future, we may say, rested in his Bishop's hands, for let us remember above and beyond the solemn promise of obedience to his Ordinary, which all priests entering the service of a diocese must make, Basil Moreau had added the vow of never seeking and of never refusing any appointment. A gleaming sword, his will rested unsheathed, the hilt in his Bishop's hand.

Nevertheless, the young priest felt justified in stating his attraction. He felt drawn to the foreign missions, the ever-glamorous homeland of generous souls. There he felt, more than anywhere else, he could satisfy his ardent desires for mortification and priestly activity. Basil had meditated the words of the gospel. He did not wish to be prophet without honor! How little did the young priest or his Bishop at the moment sense the future. Had they done so perhaps the good bishop would have blessed his spiritual son and whispered— "My son, though one may not be a prophet among one's own, one can at least be a martyr there."

However, Bishop de la Myre had not obtained dispensation for Basil Moreau's ordination at twenty-two, in order to hasten the conversion of the heathen. The good bishop was thinking, and justly so, of the needs of his own large diocese. Basil's piety and zeal, together with the brilliant record he had made at St. Vincent's Seminary, all pointed to the youthful priest as an ideal choice for a future seminary director. To train soldiers is a more important task than to fight their battles. The molding of priestly character is the most important of all works of zeal. Bishop de la Myre wished the young priest to finish his studies and his formation under the Sulpicians at Paris. Father Moreau acquiesced in his Bishop's decision with what was to prove his lifelong spirit of humble faith.

Thus it came to pass that Father Moreau found himself turning his footsteps not to the Foreign Mission Seminary of Paris but to the venerable walls of St. Sulpice. For approximately a year and a half he was to have the advantage of living in daily contact with some of the finest priests born of the Catholicity of France.

The Society of St. Sulpice owed its origin under God, to a remarkable group of earnest priests who gathered about Jean-Jacques Olier in the last decade of the first half of the seventeenth century. The vast parish of St. Sulpice comprising the suburb of Paris lying without the old walls of the city and called the Faubourg St. Germain, became the center of the activity of Father Olier and his associates. Their primary purpose was to provide by means of suitable seminary training worthy priests for the Church. Their generous and at times heroic sacrifices were eventually crowned with success, and from that period the Society of St. Sulpice has not ceased to be a potent factor in formation and maintenance of priestly souls—in the New World as well as in the Old.

When Basil Moreau crossed the threshold of the Sulpician Seminary, at Paris in October, 1822, Abbé Duclaux, whom the young priest soon came to revere as a saint, was the Superior of the Community, while the equally venerable Archbishop de Quelen was engaged in giving to Paris an example of a shepherd going before his flock and leading them in the ways of salvation.

The year Father Moreau passed in these hallowed surroundings left an indelible impression on his character. He was indeed still very young and his letters of this period, while giving us a glimpse of the Paris of that day, also reflect the freshness and simple zeal of their youthful writer. These letters give us an insight into a virgin heart, Salesian, or rather truly Christlike in its tenderness, the genuineness of whose affections would be proven by the detachments of the morrow.

A short time after his arrival at St. Sulpice, Father Basil writes to one of his sisters:

I am happy when I receive a letter, but I am out of myself for joy when I receive two. You know well, my dear sister, that the farther one is from one's country, the more eager one is to receive news of it, and thus, today, I am experiencing the truth of what St. Augustine said: "When we are separated from our friends we feel for them a more vivid sentiment of friendship than when we are actually with them."

While you were playing, your brother Basil was at prayer with the Community, recommending to God his near relatives who are ever in his thoughts, and the dear friends of Le Mans, whose memory he cherishes more and more kindly as the days go by. Which of us was the better occupied? I cannot say whether you were better pleased than I was. Be this as it may, I felicitate you on being admitted to such good company. The time will come, I hope, when I shall be able to share your innocent joy. In the meantime, here is the news I want to give you.

The "Missions" given successively in all the parishes of Paris were as greatly successful as could be expected. At the Law School this visible success was not looked upon with indifference. During class, notes were passed around inviting fellow students to go to the "Missions" and to hiss the preachers. Lately a non-believer was so rash as to say to Abbé Rauzan during his sermon: "You are a liar." In the same church these scoundrels set off fire-crackers, whereupon the missionary remarked: "All this comes from men unable to cause a stir in the world by their talents, who wish, at least, to attract attention to themselves by shooting off fire-crackers in churches during 'Missions.'"

Archbishop de Quelen of Paris is distinguished for his truly apostolic zeal. He reserves for himself a confessional in each parish, where he says he wants the poor to come to him that, insofar as in him lies, he may aid them in their needs both temporal and spiritual. One of the missionaries told us that Monseigneur presided at morning prayers at five o'clock, now in one parish, now in another. The sight of this prelate acting thus must necessarily have had an extraordinary effect on the working people.

I must tell you of a very impressive ceremony that took place on the feast of Our Lady's Presentation. I feel sure that it will edify you. On that feast the Sulpicians renew their clerical promises. Monseigneur de Quelen, a former seminarian at St. Sulpice, celebrated the Mass. The most distinguished of the assistants were the Archbishops of Reims and Arles and Monseigneur Frayssinous, a former director of St. Sulpice, now Grand Almoner to the King. Immediately before the renewal of vows Monseigneur de Quelen gave us an exhortation, short but full of zeal and unction. After this, our Superior, Abbé Duclaux, advanced to the altar to renew his consecration to the Lord. It was indeed an affecting scene. I shall say only that one could not but be moved. Abbé Duclaux told us that night that he had been as if in ecstasy and that he had offered us all, had presented us all to Mary. Literally, he spoke with such unction that we were all moved to tears. I had also the happiness of renewing my clerical promises; and I assure you that a morning thus spent is worth twenty years of wordly pleasures and amusements. I pass over many interesting details and simply tell you that all the dignitaries dined with us in the refectory where we sat down to a well-served dinner, with permission to talk throughout the meal. I do not remember a holier day.

Though Father Moreau did not remember a holier day, he was soon to enter upon what we may well assert as a holier year for him, for the following year, i.e., 1822, will find Father Basil at the famous retreat house of the Sulpicians (at Issy)—called The Solitude—and under the direction of one of the most enlightened and inspiring directors of the century, the Abbé Mollevaut.

VI
ISSY AND MOLLEVAUT—1822-1823

> *It is true I am resolved to devote my time to acquire holiness; it is true that here everything speaks of it: the walks, the stones, and the trees beneath which Bossuet and Fénelon strolled, and the earth in which rest so many illustrious Sulpicians.*
> —FATHER MOREAU.

THE profitable and happy year Father Moreau spent at the Seminary in Paris was but a prelude to the spiritual progress and happiness that awaited him at the retreat house, called the Solitude, and located at Issy.

A year of solitude for the purpose of spiritual formation is a part of the training of the priests of St. Sulpice. Their retreat house at Issy had been restored after the Revolution by the resurgence of Catholic life. In 1819 Father Mollevaut had come to Issy and there his unique talents of administration and direction had quickly made the old Solitude not only the officers' training-school of the sons of St. Sulpice, but had attracted there as well priests destined for the direction of seminaries from all parts of France.

Basil Morcau was the first priest from the diocese of Le Mans to be entered at Issy, and the months spent there were to have a very powerful bearing upon his whole career.

Father Mollevaut, whom Basil found in charge at Issy, was one of the most influential figures in the life of the Church in France in the nineteenth century. A brilliant scholar, a master of the spiritual life, a strong personality, and yet with the balance born of profound humility, Mollevaut entered the Society of St. Sulpice and promptly buried himself in what his keen mind saw to be the great need of the Church—not alone in his day but in every day and land—the formation of holy priests.

In 1819 he was made Superior of the retreat house at Issy, and there his vast zeal found ample play. The inspiration and wisdom of his direction soon carried his name to the far corners of the kingdom, and the spiritual elite of his day wore a path to his door. His daily life combined the asceticism of the early hermits with the labors of a Minister of State.

He rose daily at 4 A.M., and fifteen minutes later awoke the others on his floor, passing from door to door with a candle in his hand. His daily Mass was preceded by the taking of the discipline—like his Master he wished to be not only priest but victim. Cloak as best he could his talents and his virtue, it was in vain. The high, the low, the rich, the poor sought him out for direction and advice. He loved, as all truly interior souls must love, solitude and the hidden life, yet Christ had not lighted His candle that it should be hidden beneath a bushel, but that it might enlighten the world. The world of faith had seen the light and hastened rejoicingly to its source. True sanctity has a mysterious power—it draws to itself the heart of all mankind.

It was under the influence and consequent direction of the saintly Mollevaut that the eager young priest of Le Mans came in the summer of 1822. The result was exactly what we would have expected. Virtue has a fashion of mutual recognition! Mollevaut and Moreau, from the first, read each other's souls; in the clear light cast by God's grace, they looked into each other's eyes and found Christ mirrored there. They became as father and son—and for more than a quarter of a century, Basil Moreau sought and followed faithfully the spiritual direction of his old director of The Solitude, while the elder priest found unselfish paternal delight in watching the fruitful unfolding of his spiritual son's works for God and Holy Church. Nothing, perhaps, reveals more clearly Father Moreau's profound humility than the manner in which he sought and followed the direction of others even to the very end of his life.

Later we shall find Father Moreau inculcating the value of direction to his spiritual children, and like his own beloved director, Abbé Mollevaut, Basil Moreau would lead wherever he called upon others to follow; he would to the end teach by example as well as word.

As we have already indicated, the months Basil Moreau spent under the guidance of Abbé Mollevaut at The Solitude of Issy must be reckoned as the most important in his life from the viewpoint of spiritual formation. From the very beginning this influence began to be marked as a letter of Basil to one of his sisters, dated August 14, 1822, indicates. He writes—

> Frankly, it is grand here, and I am the happiest of mortals. We love one another as brothers. Our family numbers fourteen. Our Superior is a saint and gives us an excellent formation in piety, and so I am at the best possible school. You know how badly I need lessons in piety. Oh, my dear sister, before coming to Issy I did not realize how absolutely necessary meekness is. Be meek, always humble; be gay without being frivolous—here is what I must strive for during the year.

At Issy the intellect and will of Father Moreau were brought to white heat and then carefully forged and tempered to make them the efficient instruments of God's Spirit that they were to be even unto death.

In Abbé Mollevaut, the young priest from Le Mans had before his eyes a striking example of the successful blending of those Christian virtues that must always appear paradoxical to the world. "He"—Basil writes of his model—"is hard on himself, but he spoils us." Has not this been characteristic of

God's greatest saints? After all they have but followed in the footsteps of their Master who stood by Galilee's shore in the gray light of the early morning and called over the waters, "Little ones, have you anything to eat?"

Thus in the best of all schools, that of good example, Basil learned that the servant must be like his Master, that meekness and humility must direct and control the activity of one who would be a true disciple of the Incarnate Son of God. These lessons in humility and meekness were to prove of special value. A brilliant intellect unmindful of its nothingness, a flaming zeal untempered by meekness, these are gifts whose promise quickly comes to naught, whose fruit is bitter, and whose end is only too often destruction.

Everything indicates that Basil Moreau was an exceptional student. The recognition of his abilities is readily attested to by his ordination to the priesthood at the age of twenty-two, and emphasized by his selection by Monseigneur de la Myre for the work of seminary teaching and direction. As to his spirit of piety and zeal, his attraction for the foreign missions together with the vows he had made on the eve of receiving the subdiaconate, bear witness to the enthusiastic consecration of the young levite to the Cause of Christ's kingdom.

Father Moreau had an extraordinary attraction to mortification, interior as well as corporal, as the following quotations from his retreat notes of this period will indicate. God's Holy Spirit was beginning to lead him further into the desert of detachment. Thus at the commencement of the vacation of 1822, which Basil spent at the Solitude, we find him setting down these resolutions:

> I will write to no one except to my parents, and to them only every six weeks, having learned that my correspondence greatly injures my spiritual advancement and harms my exercises of piety. I will never read my letters except during recrea-

tion and I will write to my parents only during the study period following my class in Theology.

Besides this, as the seminarians from Paris came regularly on holidays to the Park at the Solitude of Issy and as Basil liked to mingle with them, he wrote in his "Rule of Life" the following resolution:

> I will not put my foot out of the Solitude even to go to the Park on holidays to seek my acquaintances, or to go to Paris, except by obedience and the desire of my director.

After the two passages just quoted, Basil's "Rule of Life" continues thus:

> Before meditation every morning and in the presence of the Blessed Sacrament, I will recite: 1. the Veni Creator; 2. the Memorare; 3. the ejaculation Jesu mitis et humilis corde, miserere nobis for two intentions: First, to know and to do the Will of God as regards my future; second, to obtain the gift of blind obedience in all that concerns myself, as well as profound humility and charity full of meekness.
>
> In winter and in spring, I will rise at 4:30 A.M., make my bed, and read a chapter of the Old Testament. Then I will recite the Little Hours before the Blessed Sacrament, where I shall greet Our Lord and prepare for meditation.
>
> Immediately following my thanksgiving after Holy Mass (I will devote twenty minutes to this duty), I will go to my room, bless myself with Holy Water, say the Veni Sancte, recall to mind God's presence (this I will do before each study), then I will study the Holy Scripture and Hebrew till breakfast.
>
> During breakfast and between the exercises, I will read the Imitation of Jesus Christ and I will learn some passage by heart.
>
> After breakfast I will make a five-minute visit to the Blessed Sacrament, then, on returning to my room, I will prepare my class in Theology at which I will assist with the intentions Abbé Tronson speaks of in his Treatise of Obedience, which treatise I will read through several times.
>
> Immediately after my class in Theology, I will put in order the notes which I have taken. Then I will read Rodriquez for

twenty minutes, choosing for my reading the treatise on the virtue on which I am making my Particular Examen. Then I will read from the life of a saint until 11:30 A.M. when I will make a visit to the Blessed Sacrament in the chapel of The Solitude.

After vespers I will make a five-minute visit to the Blessed Sacrament, then an examination of the faults committed during recreation, which I will mark down in the following order. . . . Until 3 P.M. I will study the history of France or ecclesiastical history, after which I will write until 4:00 P.M. when I will make a fifteen minute visit to the Chapel of Loretto.

From 4:15 P.M. till time for spiritual reading, I will write something or I will study geography.

Immediately after night prayer when the points for the morrow's meditation are not publicly given, I will make a visit to the Blessed Sacrament, offer my sleep to God, think on death, recite the Memorare and a prayer to Saint Aloysius. On returning to my room I will make an act of contrition while I kiss the floor.

I will go to confession every Friday at least, and to direction every Sunday after the class in Holy Scripture. The same evening I will tell my Superior the faults I have committed against this my rule and that of the house.

We have also in the same copybook the "Resolutions" Basil made during his retreats at Issy. We feel it a duty to give some passages, the better to show the powerful action of grace in this generous soul which God was preparing to become the guide of so many others.

>Resolutions made during my retreat at the Solitude,
>October 22, 1822

I will not fix my eyes on anyone, for "death enters by the windows"; I will walk with my eyes lowered.

I will never take pleasure in the perfume of flowers. I will never seek to get all the latest news. I will speak always in an edifying manner, avoiding loquacity, disrespect for others, and outbursts of passion.

I will never drink undiluted wine, and I will choose whatever least flatters my sense of taste.

I will say neither good nor evil of myself. I will be obedient and submissive to all, and in all things, especially to my superiors, my confessor, and my director. I will not quarrel with anyone. If an argument arises, I will give my reasons and then I will leave the decision to a third party, or I will be silent. I will accept with alacrity the humblest duties and those most repugnant to my pride and vanity.

Far from seeking vengeance, I will not defend myself, even when I could do so. I will bear with great meekness the weaknesses and the oddities of my neighbor, and I will cause no one pain.

I will receive everyone kindly, and I will force myself to wear a pleasant expression during recreation.

I will rise in the morning and will leave my desk at the first sound of the bell.

I will give myself unreservedly to the service of my neighbor, showing most consideration to those who are least agreeable to me. I will ask several of my companions to watch for my defects and tell me of them.

So long as I shall live in a seminary, I will keep the fast I vowed on the Friday of every week, as well as the use of water at the collation of the same day.

So soon as my director will have given me permission, I will rise at 4:00 A.M., and do this in a penitential spirit.

In winter I will light no fire in my room, unless the doctor, or my director, or necessity exacts the contrary.

I will always keep my body straight and unsupported, both in my room and at public exercises.

Finally, when my director permits, I will take the discipline or I will wear a hair shirt on Fridays, determined, however, to do nothing in this matter without my director's permission.

What an apparent impossibility of reconciling the austere program of this ardent young priest with his habitual cheerful countenance and customary lightheartedness! To those who have not the gift of faith, such a life is an impenetrable mystery which defies adequate solution, because they will not use the one light that can clarify such an enigma. But to those who believe in the world of the spirit, in the power of God to elevate and sustain His creatures, to such as these Father Moreau's life becomes an open book wherein the Spirit of God was writing the ever ancient yet ever new romance of Divine Love.

At Paris and Issy Basil came in contact with many of the future ecclesiastical leaders and champions of the Church in the France of his day, including Ravignan, the future Jesuit leader, but none of them held for the young priest from Le Mans the inspiration and charm of his Superior, Abbé Mollevaut. To the closing hours of the latter's life, Father Moreau would turn to him for light and counsel, and his death would leave an unfilled gap. L'Abbé Mollevaut was destined by God to be the real arbiter of Basil Moreau's future. In him Father Moreau recognized the voice of God invoked and humbly obeyed—till death closed the lips of the one and saddened the heart of the other.

In the summer of 1822 a young priest and an older graye-faced cleric might frequently be seen seated side by side on a fallen log in the grove of Meudon close to The Solitude at Issy. The elder of the two would read to his companion from the Life of St. Francis Xavier and ever and anon his gray burning eyes lifted from the printed page and sought through the cathedral arches of the forest the distant outline of the Jesuit Novitiate at Montrouge. The reader was Xavier de Ravignan, the brilliant lawyer who had just turned his back on the legal world of Paris. His younger companion was the future Founder of the Congregation of Holy Cross, Father Moreau. On one such occasion the thoughts of the former flamed into action and breaking off the reading, Ravignan rose and exclaimed—"Will you go? Will you go?" and he pointed toward the distant Montrouge. The vocation of de Ravignan was already clear. Abbé Mollevaut had had little difficulty in confirming the former lawyer's deep attraction for the Company of Jesus, the Marine Corps of Holy Church. The lifework, however, of Father Moreau was still hidden by the impenetrable veils of the future; he could but march forward in eager willingness and humble obedience, confident that God was leading him, also, to higher things.

In the eyes of Abbé Mollevaut, true Sulpician that he was, nothing was so important as the work of molding worthy priests to fill the depleted ranks of the clergy. Constantly in his correspondence with Father Moreau we will find the holy Sulpician returning to this point, and though Basil Moreau's natural gifts and energetic character no less than his supernatural zeal attracted him most strongly to the apostolic mission, his unquestionable spirit of humility made him concur in the views of his director and accept cheerfully the obedience Bishop de la Myre was soon to give him and which would hold his eager soul for twelve long years a prisoner of the classroom, a teacher and director of future priests.

VII
THE TEACHING YEARS—1823-35

> *Religion and religion alone promises that those who have taught justice to their brethren shall shine as stars in the firmament.*
>
> —FATHER MOREAU.

IN the spring of 1823 Father Moreau was called home to Laigné-en-Belin by the last illness of his beloved pastor and benefactor, the Abbé Le Provost. Grateful appreciation and remembrance of benefactions was, as we have already remarked, one of the distinctive traits of Basil Moreau's character. Consequently, the venerable priest who had guided his first steps toward the altar held a special place in his mind and heart, and when the news of the Abbé's illness came to Issy, the young priest was following the dictates of his own heart when he sacrificed the grace-filled solitude and the inspiring companionship of the Sulpician retreat, in order to hasten to the bedside of his dying pastor. The call of death came for Abbé Le Provost on the twenty-third of June. Venerable in years and service the old Curé went home to meet the Master whom he had served so faithfully and so well. The young priest aided him as he slipt quietly into the shadows of the valley.

In the fall of the same year, 1823, Father Basil received his first apostolic assignment; he was sent to teach Philosophy in the preparatory seminary at Tesse.

At Tesse Father Moreau found his former professor, Father Louis Jean Fillion, and from the first their relations were those of a son and a father. Till his death Father Fillion acted as

Father Moreau's confessor and remained one of his closest friends and co-operators. In this congenial atmosphere, Father Basil resumed, as far as was possible, the disciplined life he had learned to love so deeply at the Solitude. He wrote regularly to Abbé Mollevaut for direction, and under the latter's wise counseling devoted himself unstintingly to the teaching of his classes, the upbuilding of seminary spirit and discipline, and the direction of souls. The apostolic zeal of the young priest at this particular period is revealed to us by the letters of his director. On October 13th of this same year, 1823, Abbé Mollevaut writes:

> Dear Friend, I learn with joy that your apostolate has begun and that the good God has placed you, in accordance with your desires, in a seminary. I advise you to be careful of your health. You need exercise, care, and rest. Be moderate in your work. Make your students speak a great deal.

Again on November 23rd the Sulpician writes:

> When the Bishop invites you, accept without reflection. This is a duty and to fulfill it is pleasing to God . . . As to the fast,[1] it is better for you to have your vow commuted; and, as a general rule, in community life, make no vow which can interfere with the common rule.

Adding on March 11th of the following spring:

> They are right in commanding you to take breakfast daily; your health and your work require it.

It is evident from the tone of these letters that the earnest soul of the young seminary professor felt constrained to practice greater mortification. Indeed, as we shall see, the abiding spirit of mortification will prove one of the most striking characteristics of Father Moreau's life. Into the very shadows

---
[1] The reference is to the Friday fast which Basil had vowed.

of eternity, Basil Moreau would seek to follow in the rugged way of the Master, he would be truly a religious worthy of the title "of Holy Cross."

In a letter dated December 8, 1824, Abbé Mollevaut returns to the same subject and emphasizes the greater value of interior mortification, involving as it does the disciplining of the higher faculties of the soul:

> You are right, my friend, we must esteem highly the mortification of Our Lord. More discretion, however, is needed in this matter than in any other. And here above all we must walk in the way of obedience, without ever forgetting that we mortify the body only to arrive at interior mortification. In this matter follow the counsel of your director, but be ready to quit all at the first word.

Basil Moreau had too well-balanced a soul not to realize and put in practice this higher and no less essential form of mortification. The two years he spent at Tesse furnished him several splendid opportunities for its exercise.

The first of these was the question of his preaching. Although Father Moreau had unusual talents for the work of preaching nevertheless he made it a matter of principle to consult his director before accepting invitations to preach. This he did although he knew well the Sulpician's general policy of making this work entirely secondary to that of the Seminary. A less simple and humble soul would soon have sought more pleasing counsel and a director allowing greater liberty in these matters.

The second and more concrete example of Father Moreau's docility and interior mortification is found in his abandonment of the thesis which he had chosen for public exposition and defense by one of his pupils at the close of the academic year of 1825. The thesis Basil had chosen was the famous theory of Common Consent of de Lamennais.

At the moment ecclesiastical France was being agitated by

the struggle between the Gallican and the Roman or Ultramontane schools of thought. Felix Robert de Lamennais, then at the height of his influence, had by reason of his vigorous and brilliant writings become the logical leader of the party who favored the papal prerogatives. About him and du Maistre gathered a remarkable group of Catholic apologists, both clerical and lay. Bonald, Lacordaire, Montalembert, and a host of others, composing the fine flower of the Catholic resurrection, recognized in de Lamennais their spiritual chief. Basil Moreau was blessed with too deep a faith not to favor the papal claims. Instinctively he was on Rome's side. Hence in the choice of the thesis of Common Consent for public defense by one of his pupils, he was but following the attractions of his heart. In the heat of the debate few had penetrated to the unsoundness of this new theory, fewer still could have foreseen de Lamennais' rebellion against the very power of which he had been so ardent a champion.

However, as was his custom, before announcing publicly his choice of subject Basil wrote to his director. Perhaps never more clearly than on this occasion did the enlightened prudence of the latter reveal itself. Father Mollevaut's reply is dated August 24, 1825. He wrote:

> You will get beyond your depth in attempting to solve a question that serious men tremble to approach. I know one who used himself up on the opposite side, and who lost his time and his health in refuting the very arguments that have such a charm for you. It was hard for him to give up the discussion but he did so after he had seen that he had been rash in constituting himself a judge in such matters. The best thing is for you to spend no time on it, and not speak of it, hold yourself neutral, and suspend your judgment for the fifty years necessary to make sure you are not going astray.

The young priest bowed to the prudent counsel of his director and set aside the thesis which he had prepared with much enthusiasm. Events were to prove the wisdom of this course. Lamennais' tragic revolt against the very authority he had defended so vehemently was soon to alienate his friends and sadden many a heart.

Ten years later, in 1835, Father Moreau visited Father John de Lamennais, the saintly brother of the unhappy apostate, at Chesnaie, near Dinan. During the course of the visit Felix Robert, who was staying in the same house, passed by. His haggard face and disorderly dress revealed to the quick intelligence and charitable heart of Basil a soul tormented by its own proud revolt. He would have spoken and pleaded with him on the spot, but the elder de Lamennais stopped him saying sadly, "Even the sight of a priest hurts my brother." One cannot help wishing that Basil had had his way. God's grace is ever God's grace and only God knows how many times the triumph of His mercies has been delayed, if not thwarted altogether, by too great a measure of human prudence and too little a realization of the infinitude of God's mercies. To God all things are possible, yet how few of His children are always mindful of this supernatural and consoling truth!

Although Father Moreau's attraction for the active apostolate continued to be a fixed factor of his inner life yet the young priest found himself being drawn to a teaching career by chains he himself had forged. It will be recalled that before taking the decisive step of the subdiaconate Basil had made, with his director's consent, the three vows of religion. By his vow of obedience he had bound himself never to seek any position, and conversely, never to refuse any assignment given him by his Ordinary. Thus, when in the spring of 1825, Bishop de la Myre called him to the chair of dogmatic theology at the Grand Seminary of St. Vincent at Le Mans, Father Basil had only to obey. Almost at the same time the Bishop named the young priest an Honorary Canon of the Cathedral. Recalling that Father Moreau was at this time only twenty-six years of age, these two appointments are surely indicative of an unusual measure of esteem on the part of his Bishop and the directors of the Seminary.

Father Basil's director greeted with delight the news of the new assignment. A true Sulpician, Gabriel Mollevaut knew that no work of zeal was of such vital importance as the molding of worthy priests. From the beginning his direction of Basil had been guided by this underlying principle. In his correspondence he never ceased to emphasize this truth. On May 3, 1825, he wrote:

> I learn with joy of your call to the Grand Seminary. . . . Reproach yourself for letting your soul doubt for one instant, modicae fides. We are ever the same. How shall we succeed in our teaching, we ask ourselves, instead of thinking seriously, "How shall we be men of prayer?"

A little later, on July 9th of the same year, Basil's director wrote again,

> The good God detaches you little by little from all that would prevent you from loving Him purely and solely, since He detaches you from your thesis and from your philosophical discussions which is no small thing. He finishes by detaching you from yourself by your director's insistence that you are destined to die in a seminary.
>
> You have no reason to refuse the position of honorary canon, but you should consider before God the holiness and the obligations of the office as a means to the practice of humility. It would be a subtle form of pride to say: "I have refused and despised what others seek." It is better to say: "I have accepted the post in order to become a holier and more perfect model and that I may be looked upon as less than nothing."

To "be looked upon as less than nothing" had been the personal program of Abbé Mollevaut since his entrance into God's service. Easily one of the first linguists of the France of his day, master of Italian, Spanish, German, Russian, and

English, a Hellenist of note and a Latin scholar, the doors of the French Academy had been opening before Gabriel Etienne Joseph Mollevaut when on October 31, 1814, at forty-one years of age, he turned his back on the world and entered the Seminary of St. Sulpice. The remaining thirty-nine years of his life were to prove but one continuous act of self-effacement, the rich fruit of which would be a remarkable influence over the souls of others.

The last interview between this master of the spiritual life and Father Moreau took place in Paris, possibly as late as 1849. At this meeting some details of which have come down to us, L'Abbé Mollevaut though bent beneath the weight of his years and labors did not fail to give his faithful son a last lesson in the science of the saints. Approaching the venerable Sulpician, Father Moreau had exclaimed, "Well, Father Mollevaut, you have now only to put in practice the maxim that you have so often taught: 'Love to be unknown and counted as nothing.'" The elder priest replied, "Do not put it that way; make it 'Love to be ignored and to be held as a fool!'" Thus to the very end Gabriel Mollevaut emphasized the importance of humility, a virtue which he had long practiced to a heroic degree. Did the saintly Sulpician have an intimation of his disciple's future? Probably not, yet no better advice could have been bequeathed to one who had still to taste the bitter dregs of misunderstanding and scorn.

In the fall of 1825, Basil Moreau took up his new duties as professor of dogma at St. Vincent's, the Major Seminary at Le Mans. At his first conference he laid down the principles which he had made his own and which, henceforth, he would teach to others. "We ought," he declared, "to study theology in a spirit of zeal, humility and the love of God."

> Firstly, we ought to study with zeal. You sense too well the importance and the necessity of these studies you commence not to give yourself to them with ardor and perseverance.

You know that without a profound study of dogma one cannot administer as one ought the sacraments, nor treat worthily of holy things, nor defend the truth against its enemies; nor last, sanctify oneself in sanctifying others. Consequently to introduce here indolence or laziness would be to injure Our Lord who has chosen us as the defenders of His teaching and of His Church.[2]

A little later in this same initial discourse, Father Moreau picked up the fundamental theme of humility:

Yes, humility ought to accompany us in all that we do, and especially in our researches and theological discussions. I wish you to remember that it is necessary to study both to edify and to be edified, as St. Bernard has said, and not in order to be known, or well thought of by the world and much spoken of. These latter are despicable vanities! We should study for the greater glory of God after the example of St. Ignatius Loyola rather than to secure a place of honor or advantage wherein daily our love of work and study would decrease. We should study in order to exercise more worthily the sacred functions of the priesthood rather than to acquire an empty reputation. Without this spirit of humility we do not study as Christians and far from drawing from our labor solid and lasting fruit we shall see verified in us these words of the Apostle "Knowledge puffeth up." (I Cor. VIII, 1.) Let us, therefore, be humble and, while studying with reverential respect all that we ought to know, let us be on our guard against seeking to scrutinize the Majesty of Him who is veiled from our eyes in light inaccessible. Humility, therefore, in our theological studies; it is thus that anchored in faith we shall abide firm in our belief. But at the same time let us thank God who has deigned to favor us in a special manner with the light of His Gospel.

Finally, the youthful professor set before the seminarians the end to which this zeal and humility should be directed. "Will it be possible," he declared, "to meditate daily on the admirable truths of religion without having our hearts plunged

[2] Sermons.

more completely in the fire of Charity?" In this conference Father Moreau was revealing his own soul. He himself had been nourished on the great truths of faith, and, in consequence of the workings of God's grace, his soul overflowed with energy that seminary walls could not for long contain. To his work in the classroom Basil added the direction of an ever increasing number of souls drawn not only from the seminary but from the larger world that lay beyond its gates. This work soon became so absorbing that the young priest wrote of it to his director who replied in October, 1826, with his characteristic wisdom. "You tell me," he writes, "that you have too many penitents; I would believe you if it was not the will of the Good God. When He demands some work of us, He gives us at the same time the light and the graces necessary, without speaking of the infinite honor He thus bestows upon us and the merit that is attached to all that is done for Him. That which makes things too much for us, is ordinarily the spirit of preoccupation and anxiety and introspective searchings to see if we are capable of accomplishing that which we can do only through Him who holds all hearts in His hand."

Besides the work of teaching and directing, Father Moreau was called upon with ever increasing frequency to preach. This work he undertook, as has already been intimated, only under obedience. He prepared his sermons with great care and this in itself exacted heavily upon his strength. His director felt it wise to warn him against overtaxing his powers. "You will do well to withdraw yourself as much as possible from all outside work. Take fearlessly whatever you are counseled to take, and prefer the mortification of your own judgment to all exterior mortifications incompatible with your health. . . . You have plenty to do in the seminary and besides you must take care of your health."

Father Mollevaut's letters of direction, as well as those of

Father Fillion, Basil's confessor, reflect through this period between 1825 and 1830, a persistent tendency in the ardent yet docile soul of the young priest toward a more active apostolate. Despite the Sulpician's prediction, "You will die in a seminary," and Abbé Fillion's conviction, "God requires you to do all you can for His greater glory in your present position, and nothing more," the young priest had to do violence to himself to suppress his desires for the apostolate of the missions. From this time, too, would seem to date Father Moreau's growing attraction for community life. There is evidence that he considered entering the Sulpicians and also of renewing his offer for the foreign missions.

The summer vacation of 1826 brought Basil the great happiness of a pilgrimage to Annecy as the guest and traveling companion of Father Dubignon, one of the directors of the Seminary, a lifelong and ever-loyal friend of Father Moreau. On the way to Annecy at Chambéry, Father Basil had the pleasure of making the acquaintance of Abbé Fabre, a celebrated missionary of Savoy. At the moment the latter was engaged in publishing his "Letters of Penance" with the purpose of bringing back to the sacraments souls whom the cold fingers of Jansenism had chilled. The missionary recognized at once the enthusiastic zeal of the younger priest, and encouraged naturally enough the idea of the missionary apostolate. Basil, upon his return, communicated these thoughts to his director, and received a reply in Father Mollevaut's usual strain. The Sulpician wrote, "It is only after ten years that you will see the good one does in a diocese when one works always at the same task. . . . You know well I do not blame you for wanting to enter a religious community. I know that there one finds many graces as well as many trials. Nor do I reproach you for taking steps to accomplish what you think is the Holy Will of God in your regard. Avoid, nevertheless, a multitude of desires as well as too much enthusiasm. Rely on faith which is pure, calm, and patient."

In much the same fashion, Abbé Fillion, Basil's confessor, wrote, "Contradictions must not cause you to abandon God's work. They are to be found everywhere: at Issy, Rue du Bac, everywhere and still more at Pekin. To withdraw would be the worst possible way to act. Thank God for having so long inspired you against the thought. I feel to the full the usefulness of an engagement that I would not have recommended to you and on which you ought to congratulate yourself more than ever. Another would do less than you are doing. Do not be too sensitive about the sterility of your efforts and do not be discouraged. . . . Pray and suffer for the intentions of certain souls in whom I am interested." From which counsels we learn that Basil Moreau was human enough to suffer from the temptation to discouragement that the apparent fruitlessness of efforts so frequently induces.

Though Father Basil suffered inwardly, he did not permit these trials to interfere with the zealous performance of his duties. At St. Vincent's, no less than at the little seminary of Tesse, Father Moreau was a conscientious and successful factor for good within and without the classroom. His superior recognized this fact and this very recognition delayed the execution of the young priest's zealous plans.

In 1828, Father Moreau, keenly aware of the need of improving the standards of education among the clergy, had placed before his Ordinary, at that moment Bishop de la Myre, a plan for a society of priests dedicated to teaching in seminaries and colleges. A little later Bishop Carron replaced Monseigneur de la Myre who resigned in 1829. The new Bishop was both enlightened and courageous and to him Basil submitted in turn his plan for a group of auxiliary priests who would assist the diocesan clergy in their various needs, especially by the preaching of missions and retreats. The political conditions of the moment coupled with the objection of Father Bouvier, the Superior of St. Vincent's, who did not wish to lose an efficient assistant, caused Basil's proposal to be defeated.

In 1830, Bishop Carron having selected Abbé Lottin, the Professor of Scripture at St. Vincent's, for his secretary, Father Moreau was assigned to take the latter's place. The new course had a special appeal for the faith-dominated soul of the young priest but its preparation made increased demands upon his time and energy. His success in his new assignment and in that even more vital work of elevating the souls of the seminarians, may be deduced from the following note of his director:

> I have just received the notes you kindly sent me, and I rejoice over all God has done for you. You have the consolation of interesting students in a very important class in which the Word of God is explained and a love for the wonders of our Faith enkindled—just what is needed for the formation of a good priest. What you tell me of your seminary fills me with joy. Once fervor has been introduced into a religious house, we may lead young men as far as we wish.

Some indication of the activity of the young priest at this period can be drawn from a letter written by him to one of his sisters in 1831:

> I acknowledge that it has been a long time since I wrote you. Letters I should long since have answered and two sermons that I was obliged to preach were the cause of my delay. I looked forward to Holy Week that I might send you what you asked for in writing, but I could not do so in spite of my good will; for yesterday I was asked to preach the Passion at St. Benedict's. Consequently it was only this morning I could finish my letter which I had begun eighteen hours before. My first idea was to give you a "Rule of Life" for your guidance; but I am not well enough acquainted with your spiritual needs and daily duties to enter into details. I limit myself, therefore, to tracing the general principles of a truly

Christian life. And now I must be off again to preach at the Sacred Heart, and I have all my Office to read before I go.

Thus between his classes, preaching, and the direction of souls, Basil Moreau found an outlet for the ever increasing zeal that burned within him.

The Moreaus had lost their devoted mother in 1825, their loved father in 1830, and the young priest by reason of his natural character, as well as his calling, had become the spiritual counselor and guide of his brothers and sisters. He kept his relations with his own on a high spiritual level and the result, as must always be the case, was beneficial to all concerned. No priest is so truly loved by his relatives and so truly useful to them as a priest whose own have come to realize that in him their own belongs to God.

VIII

THE GOOD SHEPHERD OF LE MANS

> *You are also united to the Institution of the Good Shepherd, within which the spirit of the Gospel lives in the religious, is preserved in the orphans, and is restored to the penitents.*
> —FATHER MOREAU.

THE accession of Monseigneur Carron in 1830 to the Episcopal See of Le Mans inaugurated for Father Moreau a period of apostolic activity. The new Bishop was a man of enlightened zeal and courage. He was to have need of both. Coming to the administration of a populous diocese at the time when the government of Louis Philippe was receding from the friendly attitude of its predecessor toward the Church, Monseigneur Carron had many problems to face. Among these problems one of the most urgent was that of the support of the Brothers of Christian Doctrine engaged in teaching in the schools of Le Mans and from whom the government now withdrew its subsidy. Bishop Carron called upon Father Bouvier, the Superior of St. Vincent's, for a priest capable of making known the needs of the Brothers to the Catholics of means in the city. The Superior answered, "I see no one able to do that except Father Moreau." The result was the enlisting of the young professor in the more immediate and personal service of the Ordinary.

Father Basil's canvass of the Catholics of Le Mans was successful. Within a short time he was able to place a substantial sum in the hands of Monseigneur Carron. The financial needs of the Brothers were met, and a little later the good

Bishop was enabled to secure for them a home of their own in the center of the city. The zealous Shepherd had thus the opportunity of studying Basil Moreau at close range. He was not slow in recognizing both the ability and the zeal of his youthful assistant.

A second project for the advancement of which the Bishop called upon Father Moreau was that of providing for the aged and infirm priests of the diocese. The Christ-like heart of Monseigneur Carron was anxious to provide for the care of the numerous priests who by reason of age or infirmity could no longer engage in the active apostolate. Once again he enlisted Basil's service and perhaps nothing will reveal more clearly the love of the young professor for his fellow-priests than the offer he then made of a house which had been given him on the outskirts of the city. It is true this property, which was destined to play an important role in the development of Father Moreau's own Congregation, had been willed to Basil for some charitable purpose. Yet Father Moreau was already planning his own foundation, and consequently, could not but think of the property in question as suitable to his own purpose. Nevertheless, when the Bishop proposed the establishment of a home for the infirm and aged members of the clergy, Father Basil promptly offered this property for the needed foundation.

There will be found throughout the whole life of Father Moreau a remarkable readiness to sacrifice personal aims for the advancement of those of others so long as these latter aims should be marked by the characteristic signs of Divine Providence. To the very end of his life, Basil Moreau would be ready uncomplainingly to sacrifice self for the advancement of the interests of Christ. In the darkest hour of the spiritual night of his soul, he would pray, "My God, I consent, provided that the Congregation be saved and that Thou be glorified." The young priest's Gethsemane was at the moment many years distant and circumstances prevented the acceptance of his offer. A difference of opinion had arisen among the clergy of the diocese. Some favored the creation of a fund in preference to a home for their aged members, and in the end, Bishop Carron thought best to combine both features in his plan. The fund was begun at once, the home was not established until 1854. Finally, in 1833, Father Moreau had the happiness of being instrumental in the establishment at Le Mans of a work that was to be an abiding source of good to others and of consolation to its founder. This was the foundation of a Community of the Good Shepherd.

The work of the Good Shepherd for the conversion of fallen women and the protection of innocent children exposed to the danger of perversion owes its origin to St. John Eudes. He laid the foundation of this great work at Caen in 1641, and dedicated it to Our Lady under the title of "Our Lady of Charity of the Refuge." To the three customary vows of religion, the religious were to add a fourth, that of devoting their lives to the salvation of souls. The work spread rapidly and by the time of the French Revolution there were already a dozen foundations in France alone. After the red embers of the Revolt had cooled, the Congregation rapidly regained its lost ground. By 1833, the time of which we are speaking, houses had been founded or re-established at Caen, Rennes, St. Brieuc, La Rochelle, Tours, Paris, Versailles, Lyons, Valence, Toulouse, Nantes, and Angers.

It was from the last named of these foundations, although itself founded as recently as 1829, that the new foundation of Le Mans was made. The sisters arrived toward the end of April, 1833, under the care of Sister Marie de Sainte Euphrasie Pelletier, who was soon after to be the instrument used by God for unifying the work of the Good Shepherd and whose saintly life would be crowned almost a hundred years later by her beatification.

The foundation at Le Mans was made in a small house rented by Father Moreau on Arenes Street. The charity of a few friends supplied the bare necessities of the little Community of seven, and on May 3rd, Feast of the Finding of the Holy Cross, the formal ceremonies of the installation took place in the presence of Bishop Carron. At the request of Mother Pelletier and her Chapter, Father Moreau, who was rightly considered the founder of the house, was named as its ecclesiastical director. Sister Marie Houdin became the first Mother Superior of the Community.

Although handicapped by lack of room the little Community began at once its apostolate. The classes, one of penitents, one for orphans, were formed, and the regular routine of religious observance established. Postulants presented themselves but because of the limited quarters at the disposal of the Community, it was found necessary to send them for their novitiate to Angers, Father Moreau arranging with the administration there to pay for their board during the two years of their training. The Christ-like purpose of the Community made a profound appeal to his priestly heart, and he set himself unstintingly to support its many needs. He prepared a pamphlet explaining its purposes and ideals, organized an association for its financial assistance, and before the end of the year had negotiated the purchase of a larger property near the Beaulieu Abbey, better suited to the needs of the rapidly growing work. Father Basil took upon himself the financial responsibility for this purchase which amounted to 60,000 francs.

The brochure he prepared in order to offset possible misconceptions of the purposes of the new foundation as well as to secure aid reads in part as follows:

> The three classes composing the Community are entirely separated, each one having its own choir, workroom, dormitory, and garden. The orphans are entrusted to Mistresses who give

them special care, remaining with them day and night, forming them to a life which is simple, modest, and useful. They have no communication with the penitents who in turn are separated from the Religious by a wall; so that the penitents have no relations except with one another and with the Religious who govern them and remain with them constantly. Their occupation consists in sewing, embroidering, in attending to the orders for work received from outside, all in accordance with the ability of each one. The penitents are kept from all useless introspection by the succession of their daily exercises. Their varied activities distract them from evil and remind them of good. . . . There is not an hour of the day when the uniformity of their life, apparently so monotonous, is not broken into by prayers and hymns. All necessary religious instruction is generously given to them, and it is certain that there are but few who do not acquire a taste for a virtuous and useful life.

Such are the important services which the Sisters of the Good Shepherd render to the Department of the Sarthe, services which will be appreciated more and more by noble and generous hearts. Thanks to the devotion of these truly heroic souls, when a young woman of weak rather than depraved character comes to shed bitter tears over her faults and her dishonor, she finds sympathetic and charitable hearts to weep with her, to raise her up, and to restore her to her heart-broken family whose joy and edification she becomes. Thanks also to the charity of the faithful of the diocese, to whom alone is due the success of this enterprise, poor dependent children who are without means and who are exposed to the wickedness of the world will find an assured asylum against the attacks of misery and the seductions of vice.

The great joy of the young priest in seeing the rapid development of this foundation, which we may term the first fruits of his zeal for souls, was soon to be turned into sorrow. The good shepherd of Le Mans, Monseigneur Carron, was closer to the call of the Divine Good Shepherd than his flock supposed. From Nevers on the 15th of July, he had written as follows to recommend the new Monastery to his priests:

Gentlemen and dear Co-operators:

By procuring for us the means of founding at Le Mans an establishment which will prove of equal interest both to religion and society, Divine Providence has given us a new subject of encouragement and a consolation. We refer to the House of the Good Shepherd which the Sisters of Our Lady of Charity of Angers have taken under their direction. Before calling this new community to your attention, gentlemen, we wanted to see it at work and to judge from results of its probable success. Now we have reason to hope for most happy results, and we acquaint you with our expectations and beg of you to co-operate efficaciously with so useful a foundation.

This letter of the zealous Bishop was destined to be his last. At the end of August, 1833, Father Moreau was at Evron preaching a Retreat to Sisters. It was there that the news reached him of the sudden death of his Superior. Monseigneur Carron had died of a heart attack on the twenty-seventh of the month. Thus at the beginning of his apostolic ventures, Basil Moreau found himself standing alone. It would be the same at the end of his life, but Father Moreau had the heart of a soldier; and besides he knew that when one fights solely for God, one is never truly alone. The Manual which he prepared soon after for the Associates of the Good Shepherd, whom he had organized to support this work, bears on its first page a picture of the Good Shepherd with a lamb in His arms, beneath which appears the following quotation from St. Theresa:

If I could give a counsel, I would never admit that when God inspires a good work and inspires it several times, we should fail to undertake it through fear of not being able to accomplish it, because if the work be solely for His love, He cannot refuse His assistance. Nothing is impossible to Him.

It is this spirit of absolute confidence in God that has inspired and directed all the great achievements of the Christian centuries. It was the spirit of St. Theresa in the 16th century, of St. John Eudes in the 17th, of St. Vincent de Paul in the 18th, and of Blessed Mother Pelletier and Father Moreau in the 19th. Faith, surpassing faith in God, must always be the bedrock foundation of every truly spiritual achievement.

The names of Blessed Mary of St. Euphrasia and of Father Moreau are placed together designedly, because it is necessary to treat briefly of a controversy involving these two souls, each burning with zeal for God's glory. If the holy ones of God agree that He is to be served, yet even a superficial knowledge of their lives reveals there has never been any universal agreement among them as to the particular methods to be followed in the achievement of their common objective. An example of this diversity of opinion now demands our attention.

The Good Shepherd Community of Le Mans was formally installed on May 3, 1833. The capitulary record reads as follows:

> The third of May, 1833, our Very Reverend Sister Mary of St. Euphrasia Pelletier, Superior of the Monastery of Angers, presided at the installation of the Foundation of Le Mans, the ceremony being performed by the Most Illustrious and Most Reverend Monseigneur Philip-Mary-Theresa-Guy Carron, our worthy Prelate, who at the request of this dear Mother and the Chapter, named for Superior, Monsieur L'Abbé Moreau, Honorary Canon and Director in the Seminary of Le Mans, who is as well the Founder of this House.
>
> Our Very Reverend Mother, Sister Mary of St. Euphrasia, before her departure, left for Superior, our dear Sister Mary of the Seraphine Houdin. This nomination was confirmed the 28th of May of the same year by Monsieur L'Abbé Moreau, our worthy Superior who having come to the choir of the Chapel where the Chapter was assembled, confirmed in the name of Monseigneur, the Bishop of Le Mans, the choice that had been made of this dear Sister for Mother and Superior of this new establishment.[1]

[1] Vie, Basile-Antoine Moreau, Chap. VI, pp. 51-52, Firmin, Didot, Paris, 1898, translation by author.

The Le Mans house was established, therefore, to all outward appearances under the Constitutions given the Congregation of the Refuge by its venerable Founder, St. John Eudes. It is said [2] the Sisters destined for the Le Mans foundation had signed an article with Mother Pelletier and Monseigneur Montault, the Ordinary of Angers. Monseigneur Carron, Bishop of Le Mans, we are assured gave this "his adhesion." If this is true and we shall not question the fact, at least this is also true —Father Moreau, the Founder of this new House was not made cognizant of the new design. Certainly as Founder, he had the right of knowing the essential conditions laid down especially when these conditions represented a unique departure from the established procedure of the Community in question. Moreover whatever the article may have implied it clearly did not imply the actual dependence of the Le Mans religious upon the Community at Angers for it is admitted [3] that it was on the occasion of the establishment of the House at Poitiers, November, 1833, that *for the first time* was it specified—in the act of Nominations—that the Sisters should remain dependent upon Angers.

There can be no doubt, however, as to what Blessed Mother Euphrasia was dreaming of and praying for at the moment. She was dreaming of a conquest for Christ, the Good Shepherd, and Mother Pelletier was a practical dreamer. She had found herself handicapped in the beginning of her work at Angers by the lack of Professed Religious capable of directing the classes. She had appealed in vain to other Refuges for the personnel she needed. More and more her grace-illumined soul became convinced of the need of administrative unity if the apostolate of the Good Shepherd was to go forward keeping pace with the changing conditions of the times. St. John

[2] P. 131, Blessed Mary of St. Euphrasia Pelletier, Burns, Oates, Washbourne, 1933.
[3] Blessed Mary of St. Euphrasia Pelletier, p. 125.

Eudes in founding the work of Our Lady of Charity of the Refuge had been guided by the needs and conditions of his own century. He had thought of his refuges as fortresses of Charity harboring the fallen daughters of Eve beneath the blue mantle of the Holiest yet Tenderest of Mothers. In the plan of St. John Eudes each Refuge constituted an independent fortress under the authority of the Ordinary. That was the plan Christ had sanctioned and blessed by the voice of His Vicar.

Blessed Mother Pelletier grasped clearly the conditions of her own day. She recognized the needs of a hundred cities where there were no fortresses of mercy, no harbors of refuge for the penitent and the fallen. She knew the yearning love of the Divine Shepherd for His straying lambs, and she visioned His arms reaching out vine-like to entwine and protect them. But the vine must have unity, and there Mother Pelletier hesitated for despite her abilities she was a truly humble woman—she knew that the unity demanded a head, and perhaps she knew, too, that God had chosen her for that. She took refuge first in prayer and then in action. Zealous priests approved the project; her Ordinary, Monseigneur Montault, Bishop of Angers, espoused her cause. There should be a Generalate with Angers as its center; the other houses to be founded from this center were to be branches of the vine dependent upon Angers. Quietly with the Bishop's sanction a fifty-second article was added provisionally to the Constitutions given to the Refuges by St. John Eudes, and approval sought at Rome for the new state of affairs.

Now all this was, at least as we look backward from the vantage ground of today, very reasonable and evident fruit of the workings of the Spirit of God. Father Moreau thought so, too, when at Mother Euphrasia's request he went to Angers in September, 1833. The good Mother laid the plan of the Generalate with Angers its center before him. Father Basil recognized the advantages of the plan at once, and gave himself generously to assist in its furtherance. Before his return to Le Mans he presided, at the request of Mother Euphrasia and with the sanction of Monseigneur Montault, at the Chapter meeting of the Community. He left Angers, however, convinced that Rome should be asked for the erection of the Generalate only after the consent of all the houses had been obtained and then in the name of all. Roman to the core, innovation of such a character without the sanction of Rome was to his mind inadvisable. He wished Mother Pelletier to wait.

Upon his return to Le Mans Father Moreau learned that what he had felt should be worked and prayed for, was in the minds of Blessed Mother Euphrasia and Monseigneur Montault already an accomplished fact. Already a fifty-second clause had been added to the Constitutions, provisionally to be sure, but nevertheless in force, and the postulants sent from the Convent at Le Mans, and for whose training Father Basil had agreed to pay, no longer considered themselves as belonging to Le Mans but to Angers and the newly established Generalate. Fearful of delay at Rome [4] Monseigneur Montault and Mother Pelletier had accomplished a spiritual coup d'état which brought upon them God's blessing amid a torrent of opposition.

The older houses of the Refuge, noticeably that of Tours with the Archbishop of Tours taking the lead, opposed actively the new regime. The Eudest Fathers resented what they considered a departure from their saintly founder's plan. What the saint, John Eudes, would have done in the nineteenth century is beside the point. What he did was to make his foundations independent; what Blessed Mother Pelletier did was to make them depend upon a central house. Now, we can be certain, Mother Pelletier's plan was the work of God. Rome spoke and the point was settled, but Rome in speaking gave

[4] Blessed Mary of St. Euphrasia Pelletier, p. 131.

consideration to those who wished to remain under the old Constitution, and thus today fortresses of God's mercy continue the life work of one saint while the ever extending branches of the Shepherd's Vine bear testimony to the wisdom of the vision and unquenchable zeal of another.

Blessed Mother Euphrasia and Monseigneur Montault had moved too swiftly for Father Moreau to follow—his advice had been, "wait." His advice was not followed, nor was he made aware until later of the actual state of affairs. Thus, I believe, Mother Pelletier lost for her holy cause an ardent champion. Father Basil had been treated with the wisdom of the serpent, rather than with the simplicity of the dove. Need we be surprised in the circumstances that he withdrew from Mother Pelletier's party, and adhered, with his Bishop's approval,[5] to the old Constitution, itself the work of a saint and bearing Rome's sanction?

We have gone to considerable length in the treatment of this point because of the unjust assertions as to Father Moreau's motives made elsewhere in this connection. Just as time has made evident the purity of Blessed Mother Euphrasia's intentions in the establishment of a Generalate, so too, we who have looked more deeply into the life of Basil Moreau are certain that no less worthy purposes motivated his actions. Having studied his life we are convinced that sooner or later, by the just decrees of God, his soul will stand revealed to the world as one of highest principles upheld with heroic constancy.

[5] Mgr. Carron died, 1833. Mgr. Bouvier succeeded to the See of Le Mans, 1834.

IX

THE AUXILIARY PRIESTS

> *Would it not, then, be a matter of shame for you and for me not to do as much good for God and for eternity, as the children of the world do for the world and for the short day of this life?*
> —FATHER MOREAU.

IN early October, 1831, Father Moreau received from a Sulpician friend a letter containing the following significant passage:

> I pray the Blessed Virgin to bless the plan with which she has inspired you and to give you grace for all those who are one day to co-operate in it.

The plan of which the Abbé Faillon wrote was one that had long been cherished in the ardent soul of the priest-professor. It was for a company of priests qualified to raise the standards of teaching in the colleges and to assist the parish clergy especially by giving missions and retreats. The idea at least in its primitive form probably did not owe its origin to Father Moreau. He, himself, is our authority that the venerable Abbé Dujarié projected a band of priests who would carry on an active apostolate and had even approached Father Basil as a possible member of this proposed group. In the Annals of Our Lady of Holy Cross, Father Moreau wrote at a later date:

> Father Dujarié also came to make insistences to us, but in spite of his proceedings with the Administration, he had but the merit of his pious project without the consolation of seeing it materialize. However, to reward the good will of this elder

of the sanctuary, the Lord wished that before he die ... he should also see the beginning of the work of the missions, the thought of which he had conceived though vaguely, and that he learn of the first successes of the Auxiliary Priests.

Father Moreau had, as early as 1828, spoken of his plan to Bishop de la Myre, but nothing had come of it at that time. His purpose, it would seem, revolved about the two pressing needs of the day, better instruction in the colleges and the assisting of the parish clergy by the intensive instruction and vivifying impulse of missions and retreats. In 1833, Father Mollevaut had written:

> An association for teaching in your colleges is a good thing, but I entreat you still to consider it long and well, especially because of the circumstances. For several years attempts of this kind have been made but all have failed.

It was not without lengthy and mature reflection that Basil Moreau entered upon the role of a religious founder. It can be said of him as of all apostles of the active life whose works have been blessed by God, he moved forward to this new and arduous undertaking not under the impulse of self, but driven thereto by the charity of Christ. "The charity of Christ presses us," wrote St. Paul long ago and the Holy Spirit has never ceased to drive onward along their appointed courses God's vessels of election.

More than a decade of years of priestly activity had given Father Moreau a clear insight into the needs of his time. The rapid advance that was being made in the field of the natural sciences made it imperative to broaden the scope of ecclesiastical studies if the clergy were to keep abreast of the day. Basil championed this cause and in 1835 had the happiness of seeing a splendid course in physical science added to the curriculum at St. Vincent's. The well-known Thomas Cauvin was its first professor. Side by side with this need of improving the intellectual standards of the clergy was that of combating the growing coldness and even hostility toward religion among the masses resulting from the growth of extreme democratic views and the aberrations of materialistic philosophies. It was this double challenge to the initiative and validity of the Church that Basil Moreau intended his priest-auxiliaries to meet.

The first step had already been taken in 1833. In that year, Father Moreau arranged, with Bishop Carron's approval, to send three ecclesiastics to Paris to attend the lectures at the Sorbonne and to secure their degrees. The sudden death, however, of the zealous Bishop was the cause of further delay in the completion of Father Basil's design.

Father Bouvier, the Superior of St. Vincent's, succeeded to the vacant See of Le Mans, in the spring of 1834. The new Ordinary was a prelate of prudence and deliberation. The unsettled political outlook of the time boded ill in his judgment for the success of Father Moreau's enterprise. Consequently he delayed his approval of the project. Finally, however, after a delay of more than a year, a new memorandum was submitted to the Bishop and the necessary sanction secured. Thus began an apostolate whose extension neither Father Moreau nor Bishop Bouvier could foresee at the moment.

The Abbé Mollevaut answered Father Basil's letter announcing the Bishop's favorable decision in these words:

July 17, 1835:
 The question is ended when authority has spoken; there remains only to build on the unique foundation which is Our Lord. For subjects prefer those who are young, who finish their seminary; prefer before all docility and character.

In order that Jesus Christ might be the one unique foundation of his priests, Father Moreau gathered the six young ecclesiastics who had volunteered for the work at the Trappe de Port-du-Salut, near Laval in August, 1835. There amid the quiet woods and cloistered silence Basil loved so dearly, with the kindly wisdom of the Father Abbot to guide them, and the apostolic zeal of their founder to fire them, the Auxiliary Priests were fashioned and consecrated to the Sacred Heart of the Saviour and the Sorrowful Heart of His Mother.

For the present it was necessary for the little apostolic band to continue their residence at St. Vincent's. Father Moreau's own study became their headquarters, and there they were to meet three times a day: for an hour's meditation in the morning, for particular examen, and for spiritual reading. To these daily exercises were added two weekly conferences, one on the Scriptures, one on Moral Theology. As was inevitable, the difficulty of fashioning a community within a community was in evidence from the beginning. Nevertheless, the group persevered and their fervor reanimated the zeal of their youthful director.

Bishop Bouvier was anxious to have the nascent community receive in its midst priests incapacitated by sickness and other reasons, and with this in mind offered Father Basil for the Auxiliary Priests a portion of the old seminary of philosophy at Tesse. This offer, Father Moreau, after seeking counsel of his director, thought best to decline. It would have involved the presence of an independent group among young aspirants of the Community during their period of formation and besides would have placed the Auxiliary Priests in financial dependence upon the Grand Seminary. On this question Father Mollevaut had written Basil: "If you receive infirm priests, or priests not in the ministry, be sure that they form a separate community; otherwise the observances of the rule will be impossible. . . . In a novitiate all should tend to the constant practice of recollection, meditation, self-denial, humility, obedience, mutual forbearance." Thus it came to pass that like the Divine Master who assembled and trained the first apostolic band while they lived as guests in the homes of His friends,

Father Moreau was destined to train his first group of priestly disciples within gates which friendship and the grateful appreciation of his services opened to him.

The active apostolate of the Auxiliary Priests began in the spring of 1836. Father Moreau and Father Nourry, the youngest of his company, preached the Forty Hours at Teloche, not far from Le Mans. Father Cottereau, another of the priests, went first to Luche and then to Ernée. A mission followed at Mezeray. Then on the eve of Passiontide Father Basil opened a retreat at Chateau-Gontier. Before the year ended successful missions had been given by the Auxiliary Priests at six other places, including Laigné-en-Belin, Father Moreau's birthplace. At the close of these missions the Auxiliary Priests had the consolation of seeing their efforts given a measure of permanence by the erection of the Stations of the Cross in the presence of the clergy and of enthusiastic crowds whose faith and fervor had been restored through their apostolate.

God, however, was preparing for both founder and foundation that sweet though painful seal of His approbation and benediction, the Cross. The youthful Abbé Nourry who had assisted Father Basil in the inauguration of the work at Teloche had returned to St. Vincent's suffering from fever consequent to a chill. His condition grew worse and on the vigil of Corpus Christi this soul which in its innocence and ardor reminds one of the "disciple whom Jesus loved" slipt out of the shadows into the Light. The blow was a heavy one to the little band and especially to Father Moreau. He had long since discerned the qualities of Abbé Nourry and he had counted on their possessor for the development of the work. Thus from the beginning the apostolate of Basil Moreau bore the benediction of trial and the mystical impress of the Master's Holy Cross.

In the founder's letters to his spiritual family of a later date the real tenderness of his heart found expression time and time again in the revelation of his anguish in the deaths of his spiritual children. Beneath the pressure of his zeal he would never cease to ask much of them, but likewise, he would never cease to share their trials nor hesitate to drink with them of the blessed chalice of affliction. Basil Moreau had the indomitable will of a great general but he had as well the heart of a wonderful mother. Twenty years later when his work was firmly established and widely extended, he wrote to his spiritual family as follows:

> Permit me to desire for you the inheritance that Jesus Christ and His saints, whose children we are, have bequeathed us. This inheritance is one of humiliation, of poverty, and of sufferings. It is that of trials and temptations, of labor and of every kind of persecution. In vain shall we seek any other way to heaven than the road of Calvary.

With the foundation of his Auxiliary Priests, Basil Anthony Moreau had entered the road of Calvary, he had begun his own way of the cross.

X

THE BROTHERS OF ST. JOSEPH

> *If, today, I have not the same claims to your confidence as has your generous and indefatigable Founder, at least you will find in me a priest devoted to your interests, which are for the future my own, a priest to whom no sacrifice will seem too great when the welfare or the glory of your Institute is at stake.*
>
> —FATHER MOREAU.

IN the midst of Father Moreau's labors in laying the foundations of the Auxiliary Priests, Divine Providence was preparing for him still another work. This was the direction of a Community of teaching brothers who had been dedicated to St. Joseph by their venerable founder, the Abbé Dujarié, the Curé of Ruillé-sur-Loire. A word concerning this apostolic priest will be in keeping with our subject.

James Francis Dujarié was a native of the village of Sainte-Marie-des-Bois in the department of Mayence where he had been born December 9, 1767. His higher studies had been made at the College of Domfront and the Seminary of Angers. Before the dispersion of the seminarians consequent upon the Revolution he had received his diaconate. During the period of persecution he had been obliged to pass an entire year in hiding in the cellar of a cloth weaver. This retreat he left disguised as a shepherd and a little later we find him reduced to earning his livelihood by selling lemonade on the streets of Paris. Despite these and many other trials young Dujarié persevered in his vocation and was finally ordained in 1795. Henceforth he was of that heroic band of priests who began the work of the Catholic restoration even before the red embers of the Revolution had had time to cool. After ministering to his persecuted brethren in many places of the Sarthe, he became, under the Concordat, the Pastor of Ruillé-sur-Loire in the diocese of Le Mans.

No sooner was Father Dujarié a Pastor than the problem of the instruction of the children of his flock engrossed his attention. Trained by the vicissitudes of the Revolution to resolute action, he began forthwith an energetic and courageous program. The first fruits of his zeal were the Sisters of Providence, a Community of Religious dedicated especially to the apostolate of teaching, and today so well and favorably known by their College and Mother House at St. Mary's of the Woods, Indiana. The Sisters of Providence date their origin from 1806, and their future was assured when God sent the zealous Pastor of Ruillé a noble Breton girl, Josephine Zoe de Rosecoat, who became in due time the first Mother General of the Congregation.

The success of his Sisters encouraged Father Dujarié to attempt a like work in the interests of boys. In 1820 the first candidates for his Community of teaching brothers arrived at the presbytery. The first three applicants were not destined to persevere but in the fall of that year two young men, Andrew Mottais and Stephen Gouffre, presented themselves at Ruillé, and became by God's grace and their own good will, the real foundation stones of the Community of the Brothers of St. Joseph. They persevered to the end, nor are we surprised when we review the austere character and the trials of their novitiate.

The life of these first novices of Father Dujarié was truly heroic. They lived, took their meals, studied and prayed in a single room, some twenty-seven feet square, in the good Abbé's

FATHER DUJARIÉ, FOUNDER AND FIRST SUPERIOR OF THE BROTHERS OF SAINT JOSEPH AND OF THE SISTERS OF PROVIDENCE (SAINT-MARY-OF-THE-WOODS).

rectory. They slept in a garret overhead, the possession of which was contested by a small army of rats. Their diet consisted of dry bread in the morning, with soup and fruit, or soup and a dish of vegetables, at noon and again at night. Their beverage was cheap sour wine. Meat was a feast day luxury. They had for a teacher a young man interested neither in them nor in his class work and who wasted their time seeking to amuse them. As for their spiritual exercises, these were necessarily arranged according to the varying duties of Father Dujarié, and to climax all, the parishioners of Ruillé were as a whole more inclined to mock than to encourage the young men who sought to embrace this novel enterprise.

Despite all these obstacles, God saw fit to bless the supernal faith and superabundant charity of the energetic pastor of Ruillé. The favor of his Ordinary, Monseigneur de la Myre, the good will and co-operation of his fellow-priests and the benefactions of many well-to-do Catholics of Le Mans made possible the stabilization of his foundation. Brothers Andrew and Stephen were enabled to complete their education at Le Mans under the Christian Brothers. Two priests of the cathedral chapter furnished the brothers hospitality and the seminary staff supplied them their studies in mathematics, geography, and plain chant. At the end of a year the two brothers had returned to Ruillé, Brother Andrew as Father Dujarié's assistant novice master, Brother Stephen to take charge of the first school opened by the Community, November 9, 1821, at Saint Denis d'Argues.

From that point the development of the Brothers' Community had been rapid. They filled a real need of the time, and this fact the civil government recognized by an Ordinance of the King, Louis XVIII, dated June 25, 1823, declaring the Community to be of public utility. This civil recognition, besides being a necessary factor for the development of the Brothers' Institute, carried with it the exemption from military service of its members substituting a pledge of ten years' teaching service. Less than a year later, March 8, 1824, Father Dujarié was able to report to the Prefect of the department of the Sarthe the following record of progress:

> We have eighteen brothers in the diocese of Le Mans, one in the diocese of Chartres, one in the diocese of Blois, and four in our novitiate, a total of twenty-four. I have twenty-eight postulants in my presbytery, and I am expecting some more in a few days. The departments of Sarthe, of Mayence, of Indre-and-Loire, of Loire-and-Cher, of Loiret, of Eure-and-Loire, and of Orne are asking for sixty subjects. I intend to establish three secondary and preparatory novitiates in widely distant departments.[1]

Besides the rapid growth in personnel, Abbé Dujarié's untiring zeal and the charity of numerous benefactors including the civil administration, at the moment favorably disposed, made possible the erection of a new house for the Institute at Ruillé at a cost of 18,000 francs. To this new home all the subjects were transferred on the 11th of November, 1824. The years immediately following witnessed a continuation of the Community's rapid growth.

The school year 1825-26 saw fifteen new schools accepted; that of 1826-27, eight more, while before the end of the year 1828 no less than twenty-three foundations were undertaken, including the boarding school at Ruillé.

The easy financial terms that the apostolic heart of Abbé Dujarié had dictated for foundations, coupled with the crying needs of the country parishes for instructors for their youth and which the Brothers of St. Joseph met, on the whole, in a satisfactory manner, furnishes the key to the rapid expansion of their work. The exemption of the members from military service was likewise an important factor in their recruitment.

[1] Vie, P. Moreau, p. 85.

However, this unprecedented growth contained elements of weakness and the seeds of future decay.

Despite the good will of the majority of the subjects, the shortened novitiate, curtailed to meet the urgent demands, could not fail in the end to lessen the spiritual unity of the Community and in many cases the efficiency of the individual brothers. Despite the annual retreat which was a fixed feature of the brothers' life, and the regular visitations of the schools, inaugurated in 1825 with Brother Andrew as Visitor, grave problems soon arose both within and without the ranks. Father Charles Moreau, Father Moreau's nephew, has left us an admirable description of the crisis that then developed in the affairs of Abbé Dujarié's Institution:

> As the year 1830 approached, one felt there was in the air a something which augured evil for the Christian life, and for religious vocations which became rarer and more vacillating. The tide of self-sacrifice which had brought to Ruillé in less than a decade some three hundred young men, went out in 1829. In 1830 only three presented themselves for admission, while defections were numerous. Twenty schools were closed in 1829 and 1830 while only two were opened.

The July Revolution of this latter year temporarily shattered the Brothers' Institute, and was the occasion for many of them abandoning their vocations through fear and other motives engendered by the unsettled state of the times. A number of the more valiant members remained faithful to the Brotherhood, and these assembled for the Annual Retreat at Ruillé in 1831, and confirmed the foundations of their institution by signing a compact with Father Dujarié which Father Moreau had suggested. "The Treaty of Union," as the pact was called, read as follows:

TREATY OF UNION

We, James Francis Dujarié, Priest, Superior and Founder of the Society of the Brothers of St. Joseph, established at Ruillé-sur-Loire, and we, the undersigned members of the above mentioned Society, considering that the evil days on which we have fallen may take away from us, as it were, all hope of expanding and even of keeping our Community together any longer; and seeing that the actual Government would be more inclined to suppress than to encourage and favor Congregations like ours; and yet, convinced as we are that the goodness of God will not permit this state of affairs to become permanent in this truly Christian commonwealth, but will bring back to us days of peace and of true liberty when our Institute will again appear in its former splendor and experience a new growth, reciprocally and unitedly, to assure its continuation and perpetuation for the greater honor and glory of God and the salvation of souls, we bind ourselves by the strictest obligation short of sin:

(1) To remain ever attached to our holy Institute;
(2) To uphold its interests till death;
(3) To remain united as a Congregation and even as a Community, as long as possible, and to follow the same customs and regulations that we have observed up to the present;
(4) In case there is a momentary dissolution of the Institute, to remain united in heart and affection, reciprocally supporting and assisting one another;
(5) To return in a body to the Community as soon as time and place will permit;
(6) We, Brothers of St. Joseph, will continue in obedience to Abbé Dujarié, our Founder and Superior, who, assisted by four Brothers of his Council, when they can assemble, and acting alone when it will be impossible for them to meet, will give his orders according to the circumstances above foreseen;
(7) In accordance with the arrangement in the preceding article, Abbé Dujarié can change and abrogate our regulations as he sees fit, after considering the times and the circumstances;

(8) Our rallying point will always be where our Superior is;

(9) And if we have the misfortune to lose him it will be with the Bishop of Le Mans;

(10) Should one of the members of the Council abandon us, the Superior with the other councilors will elect another.

Made at Ruillé-sur-Loire, Maison Saint Joseph, September first, eighteen hundred and thirty-one.

Only a single brother who signed this compact failed to persevere in its observance. Despite the times, the increase of internal difficulties by reason of the infiltration of a worldly spirit among some of the members of the Institute, and a growing hostility on the part of certain elements among the populace, the Institute opened two new schools in the course of 1831. The following year the Duchess of Montmorency offered the Brothers her château at Saint Symphorien in the diocese of Chartres for a novitiate and a number of brothers went there with Father Hupier, later one of the Auxiliary Priests, as their chaplain. The last foundation of the Brothers made from Ruillé was made at Neaux in the department of Mayence, where a school was taken in April, 1835.

The decline of his flourishing Institute of teaching brothers could not help but prove a heavy trial to the venerable Curé of Ruillé. Yet the end was not come. The Sisters of Providence whose foundation Abbé Dujarié had laid in 1806 were in 1834 a flourishing stabilized Community. Their financial interests, however, had never been separated from those of the Institute of the Brothers of St. Joseph. It would seem that the good Abbé in the simplicity of his heart had counted upon the union of the material resources of the two Communities for the strengthening of the weaker. In 1834, however, the Sisters of Providence thought best to ask for a separation of their financial affairs from those of the languishing Congregation of Brothers. In the circumstances their request was hardly to be considered unreasonable, and was certainly highly prudent from a human point of view.

The Sisters' request, which was granted by the Bishop, proved a severe blow to the aging Founder. The Brothers' Institute was the Benjamin of his apostolic enterprises, and he grieved to see it thus thrown entirely upon its own resources at such a critical moment. God, however, had reserved a special benediction for the last years of this venerable patriarch and confessor. What Abbé Dujarié had built, he had built for God's glory and God did not intend that such building should come to naught. For many years he had prayed earnestly for a worthy collaborator into whose hands he might slip the burdens which the passing years found him ever less able to discharge as he could wish. The Heavenly Father was about to answer this prayer.

In the spring of the year 1835, some of the Brothers of St. Joseph who were more intimately concerned with the future of their Institute and aware of the desires of Father Dujarié visited Le Mans and sought to persuade Father Moreau to consent to undertake the charge their venerable Founder felt no longer able to carry. Bishop Bouvier himself had already broached the subject to Basil, and the latter had given it much thought. The result of his deliberations was a tentative offer to accept the proffered charge but on two conditions which he considered vital for the restoration of the seriously compromised status of the Institute.

The first of these conditions regarded a change in the religious habit worn by the Brothers and which was a source of annoyance to the civil authorities. The second condition was even more vital and involved the transfer of the Brothers' Novitiate and Mother House from Ruillé to Le Mans. Father Moreau considered this latter point essential that he might direct in person the training of the candidates and the government of the Community. He had a multitude of duties to discharge at Le Mans which rendered it impossible to give the time necessary for such direction at a point distant from the city. On June 17, 1835, Father Moreau wrote as follows to Brother Leonard, one of the brothers who had appealed to him:[2]

> No one feels more keenly your sad plight, and no one desires more sincerely than I do to apply a remedy. But for this purpose I persist in demanding the fulfillment of the two conditions which will perhaps be refused. Just now I have at my disposal a house in Le Mans which will suit you admirably and where I shall willingly place you, in preference to another foundation I am about to begin. [The Auxiliary Priests.] I shall, however, wait a while in your interest, and you may tell Brother Andrew what I write. Should you have occasion to speak to the Bishop, tell him that I will take it upon myself to restore and develop your Community, provided I be given a free hand. Before All Saints' Day, your Novitiate will be regularly established.

The sequel of this firm yet sympathetic attitude of Father Moreau was the decision of the Brothers to accept his terms. Once this was decided upon there remained to accomplish only the necessary transfer of authority. Consequently at the close of the Annual Retreat which Father Moreau preached, and in the presence of Bishop Bouvier and Abbé Heurtebize, the Superior of St. Vincent's and the Vicar General of the diocese, a memorable scene took place in the chapel of the Brothers' Novitiate. The beloved Abbé Dujarié advanced leaning on his cane and, resting one hand on the altar, tendered formally to Bishop Bouvier his resignation as Superior of the Brothers of St. Joseph. He then begged the Bishop to appoint Father Moreau in his stead. His words spoken in a voice tremulous with emotion touched the taut heart strings of his hearers and

---

[2] Vie, p. 98.

were soon punctuated by their sobs. When he finished he himself was in tears. Bishop Bouvier replied in these words:

> Reverend Father, I remember well, when you were thinking of founding the Society of Brothers, how you consulted me and how I was the first one to encourage you in your project, because I foresaw the great advantages that would accrue to religion by its means. I consent today to your resignation only through consideration of your failing health and your increasing years which demand this sacrifice. Never would I consent to your resignation if you still enjoyed your health and strength of other days. For the rest, I heartily approve of the choice of Abbé Moreau to take your place among the Brothers, and I know he deserves your full confidence.[3]

One final renunciation remained for this truly venerable priest of God to make; he made it with heroic graciousness. As Bishop Bouvier ceased speaking, turning to Father Moreau, Abbé Dujarié addressed him as follows:

> I beseech you, Abbé Moreau, to accept the direction of my little Congregation, the care of which I have just resigned into the hands of my Bishop because of my many infirmities. I confide it to your paternal care, fully persuaded that you will henceforth be its guide and its father. Yes, it is with a good heart that I confide my dear children to you. Accept them as the greatest treasure I possess, and as a deposit for which you will render an account to Jesus Christ. I desire that they should regard you as their father and that they manifest towards you all the submission, the respect and the devotion that they owe.[4]

We shall not try to penetrate the sentiments that flooded the heart of the ardent seminary professor as he received, in obedience to his Bishop, this precious yet weighty burden from the grasp of the venerable Pastor of Ruillé. Later, Father Moreau would write, "God alone knows what I felt at that moment

---

[3] *Vie*, p. 99.
[4] *Ibid.*

while thinking of the labors that were to be the outcome of my obedience."

In his relations with the aged Founder, following the latter's resignation, Basil Moreau wrote one of the most self-revealing chapters of his life story. With the thoughtful and loving care of a most unselfish son, he sought to surround the closing days of Abbé Dujarié with every mark of consideration and esteem. Instead of striving to replace the Founder in the affections of their spiritual family Father Basil saw to it that the good Abbé should still hold his place of honor in the hearts and minds of all. Before the opening of the first retreat of the Community at Le Mans, he suggested the following letter which the Brothers addressed to their Founder and First Superior:

> Venerable Father and Founder, although separated from you by a distance of thirty miles, at a time when it is not permitted us to surround you with our love and respect, it is pleasant for us to second the inspiration of Abbé Moreau who prompts us to write you our sentiments of respect and love. These have not changed toward you although circumstances caused you to resign as our Superior in favor of Abbé Moreau who esteems and venerates you as a father. Hence, we today lay at your feet the homage of our affection and of our gratitude for all the kindnesses you have ever shown us. Never shall we forget the last tenderly paternal words which you addressed us in the little chapel where our Congregation took its rise, nor the generous sacrifices you are daily making for the uplifting of our wavering work, depriving yourself of your goods and authorizing the sale of what we must sell to establish our Institute at Le Mans on larger and more solid bases, in conformity with the plans you yourself conceived in the beginning when you wished to unite the work of your Brothers with that of the Auxiliary Priests. We like to believe that, aided by your prayers, we shall measure up to your expectations and that these days of retreat will renew us in the spirit of our Institute which cost you so much labor. Such are,

such will ever be, the sentiments, Venerated Father Founder, of your affectionate and very respectful sons.

There is no need of comment on this letter which thirty-six of the Brothers of St. Joseph signed and to which Father Moreau added his signature with this postscript: "Venerated confrere, I hope, once your room is ready here, you will come to pass the spring with us."

In October of the same year, 1836, Abbé Dujarié accepted the invitation extended to him with such genuine graciousness. After resigning his pastoral charge at Ruillé where he had served the needs of the faithful for almost forty years, he came to make his home among his spiritual sons. At a later date Father Moreau described the Abbé's sojourn among them in these words: "He was happy to find himself among his brothers, who up to the last, always showed him due respect and filial affection. We received the good priest with open arms, with deference, veneration and attachment; for the story of his works, and, above all, the story of his trials, had long since filled us with admiration." The best room in the house was placed at his disposal. Brother Antonius, and Marianne, the crippled housekeeper who had served the Curé at Ruillé, and whom he had brought with him to Le Mans, were assigned to take care of his needs. Father Moreau occupied an adjacent room and despite the increasing demands made upon him found time every morning and evening to visit one whom he revered as a confessor of the faith and loved as his spiritual father.

Thus the late autumn of Abbé Dujarié's erstwhile active life was spent in richly deserved honor and repose. His habitually sunny disposition expanded in the spiritual warmth of the atmosphere which a fine sense of the fitness of things had created. The dear old priest was at home once more amid his spiritual children. The friends of former days could visit him, while in pleasant weather he could ride through the peaceful countryside or rest in the soft sunshine of the courtyard. Before long he had become a favorite with the pupils of the boarding school who were quick to discover that the old priest liked to be among them, and that his pockets held sweets for their consumption.

Finally we owe it to record that Father Dujarié's eldest children, the Sisters of Providence, aware that their Founder's charities had left him without material resources, and desiring to manifest their own filial devotion and veneration to their spiritual father, took steps to provide for his material needs.

The winter of the good Abbé's life was now come upon him, his physical and mental powers grew by degrees more feeble, and at the beginning of the new year, 1838, Father Moreau in his letter to the Congregation thought well to write: "I recommend to your prayers Abbé Dujarié, your Founder, who is dangerously ill." An infection appeared in his lower limbs, followed by fever which sapped the strength of his already weakened constitution. The veteran of Christ's priestly legion sank slowly into a coma. Father Moreau administered the Last Sacraments in the presence of the assembled Community and on the 17th of February, 1838, the soul of James Francis Dujarié slept calmly in the arms of the Master he had served so long and so valiantly.

To souls of the caliber of Basil Moreau, even death cannot affect or modify their relationships or attitudes. Father Dujarié received, therefore, in death as in life every possible sign of homage and veneration. His funeral was conducted with all possible solemnity. His remains were laid to rest in the midst of his children, and Masses celebrated in all the houses of the Congregation for the repose of his soul. Besides, Father Moreau inaugurated the custom of having the Brothers go in turn one day of the week to pray at their Founder's grave. To this laudable practice the new Superior gave emphasis by his own invariable practice of continuing to the grave of the good Abbé the daily visit he had been accustomed to make to his room.

Thus did Basil Moreau help to make blessed the last hours of a truly apostolic life; and, if in his turn, he was not to receive like treatment in the evening of his own life, should we not see in this the adorable Will of the Divine Master planning for Father Dujarié a death like that of St. Joseph, while reserving for Basil Moreau one more conformable to His own?

XI

OUR LADY OF HOLY CROSS—THE ASSOCIATION

> *As for myself, my dear Sons, my heart tells me that as long as it beats within me, it will strive to perfect more and more Our Lady of Holy Cross.*
>
> —FATHER MOREAU.

CHRISTIAN charity is a living thing; rose-like it never dies without leaving behind petals of fragrant memories and the seeds for tomorrow's flowers. When in September of 1835 Father Moreau transferred the Brothers from Ruillé to Le Mans, he brought them to an estate dedicated to Our Lady and situated in a suburb of the city, called Holy Cross. Now the suburb of Holy Cross shrined the fragrant memory of the charity of St. Bertrand, sixth-century Bishop of Le Mans, while the estate of Our Lady was the flowering of the seed of fraternal kindness planted by Basil Moreau.

Some years previous, Father Huard, pastor of the parish of Notre Dame de la Couture, had enlisted the services of the young seminary professor for the direction of Father Delile, a venerable old priest, the unfortunate victim of scruples. The affliction had so far dominated this priest of upright but overwrought conscience that for many years he had found it impossible to say Mass or to recite the Office. Charity in all its forms appealed to Basil Moreau but none more so than that of kindness to his fellow priests. He hastened, therefore, to undertake the trying work of assisting Father Delile. Little by little, by patience and tactful kindness, Father Moreau managed to win the confidence of the aged sufferer. He came over from the seminary to recite Office in common with him, and finally succeeded in removing from the timorous conscience of his patient the cruel cilice of scrupulosity. Father Delile even found courage to offer the Holy Sacrifice of the Mass, and thus returned to that service of the altar which had given joy to his early years. The gratitude of the good priest was sincere and profound. He promptly became one of Father Basil's most faithful and reliable friends, and on the vigil of Christmas, 1832, deeded to him as a Christmas gift, the country estate which he possessed in the Holy Cross section of Le Mans.

The Delile property consisted of a mansion with two other smaller houses and sixty-eight acres of land. The gift was intended for the establishment of some work of zeal or piety, and was to be effective only upon the decease of the donor. When, however, it was deemed advisable to bring the Brothers' Institute to Le Mans, Father Basil secured without difficulty the consent of his benefactor for the immediate occupation of the property. At the same time there suggested itself, quite naturally to one who loved the Blessed Mother as did Basil Moreau the title that would be forever associated with his name and his work, a title recalling Mary's share in the Redemption, her grief-filled glory and the glory of her grief, Our Lady of Holy Cross.

Father Basil had need of all his devotion to the Sorrowful Mother for the solution of the grave problems that faced him. Their number and magnitude might well have discouraged a soul less grounded in humility and consequently less reliant upon divine grace. He, however, faced these problems with a confidence born of deep faith and sustained by prayer and the spirit of devotion. He began characteristically by placing his foundations at the feet of Mary, consecrating them to his Sorrowful Queen under the sweet title of Our Lady of Holy Cross. The path he had now entered he would follow resolutely to the end. Because he was human he flinched occasionally, but he never turned back or abandoned his burden till the Master took it gently from him in the hour of his passing. In the longer nights he would seek solace within the silent shadows of the Tabernacle, in the darker hours he would lift his eyes to the gleaming symbol of Salvation and find in the tears of Mary the bright stars of hope newly born.

In addition to his seminary duties and the direction of the Good Shepherd foundation, Father Basil's major problems were five:

1. The spiritual restoration and material development of the Brothers' Institute.
2. The spiritual and material development of the Auxiliary Priests.
3. The uniting of the Brothers of St. Joseph and the Auxiliary Priests into an organic unity.
4. The development of the teaching apostolate of both priests and brothers.
5. The relations of his foundations with the ecclesiastical and civil authorities.

Each of these problems must receive some day a full and exhaustive treatment; to us it will be possible only to indicate both the problems and in broad lines the methods Father Moreau used in their solution.

The graces of faith and confidence were characteristics of the soul of Basil Moreau, as indeed they must be of all who would accomplish great things for God's glory. He wrote his Brothers, "The more trials we have to encounter the better everything will succeed if we seek but God's glory and are ready to sacrifice all for the love of so good a Master. With confidence such as this and with resignation we shall see the Institute of St. Joseph develop and consolidate."[1]

This last thought represented the first major problem confronting Father Moreau upon his acceptance, in obedience to his Bishop, of the superiorship of the Brothers of St. Joseph.

[1] Cir. Letters #5.

That conditions within the Institute were at the moment critical cannot be denied. In the letter Father Basil addressed to the Brothers in July, 1836, inviting them to the Annual Retreat, he does not hesitate to write: "It is certain that if you wish to regain for your Institute the reputation that it has lost with the general public and if you wish to assure your own salvation, there are but two means, piety and science." [2]

"Piety and science" was, indeed, the program for the spiritual restoration of the Institute which Father Moreau adopted. It was as well the goal he proposed at the same time to the little group of priests and ecclesiastical students gathered around him at the Major Seminary under the name of Auxiliary Priests. From the first it represented his idea of a good religious whether priest or teaching brother. In his mind these two elements could never be safely separated or substituted the one for the other. Both piety and science were, he believed, essential elements for the refraction of Divine Goodness and Divine Truth upon earth.

In view of this program Father Moreau began at once to organize and supervise the studies of the Brothers. The transfer of the novitiate to Holy Cross enabled him to utilize the priests and ecclesiastics of his little nascent company to this end. The results were soon tangible and in his very first Circular Letter Father Basil could announce: "We have already admitted many postulants who receive gratis from various professors, lessons in reading, writing, arithmetic, geography, linear drawing, surveying, architecture, singing, sacred and profane history, bookkeeping, Christian Doctrine, and the Religious Life." [3]

From the first Basil Moreau realized the mutual advantages that could be derived from a close alliance between his newly adopted Institute of teaching brothers and his little band of

[2] Cir. Letters #2.
[3] Cir. Letters #1.

priests. Recognizing the crying need of the Church of his day in the field of education in all grades and among all classes, like a wise general he set himself to organize his forces for the greatest possible efficiency in God's service. His priests could furnish him the instructors for the advanced studies of his brothers, the spiritual guides and directors necessary for their spiritual development, the chaplains requisite for the maintenance of their inner life of oblation. Conversely his brothers could supply a hundred complimentary services to the Auxiliary Priests. Truly they could become auxiliaries to the Auxiliaries, and yet do this without losing sight of their own distinctive field. The problems of discipline in colleges—of temporal management and administration, secretarial and a hundred other needs of the teaching and missionary apostolate, Basil Moreau visioned. All these could be met by utilizing the extended mission of the brothers. For the efficient advancement of God's interests, therefore, Father Basil purposed the union of his priests and brothers into an organized society.

Meanwhile as the educational apostolate of his spiritual sons developed, Father Moreau sought to improve constantly the scope and profundity of their education. As early as 1833, with the permission of Bishop Carron, he had sent, at his own expense, three ecclesiastics to Paris to finish their higher studies at the Sorbonne. Despite his own years of study and teaching, Basil Moreau retained that intellectual humility which expresses itself in a willingness to learn from others, and as well, that genius of a true educator which manifests itself not only in the thirst for knowledge, but even more in the ability to convey to other minds the fruitful conclusions of one's own.

It was in this spirit that Father Basil asked his priests and brothers to pool the results of their studies and teaching experience in the preparation of suitable textbooks for the various grades; encouraged research and authorship among their members, and made available as far as lay within his power, the best professors and instructors in every department of knowledge. Basil Moreau was a born educator and many of the accepted methods and practices of modern education will be found adopted or at least foreshadowed in his courageous and farsighted program for improved instruction in his schools.

In 1836, he transferred the languishing boarding school of the Brothers' Institute from Ruillé to Holy Cross, and, as with the novitiate, the change was followed promptly by an upward turn in its affairs. The number of students multiplied and Our Blessed Lady almost visibly protected the foundation. The little seed thus transplanted from Ruillé to Le Mans was destined to grow despite a wealth of opposition into a college of first rank with the hard-won privilege of complete liberty of teaching.

Few things in Father Moreau's career better illustrate his genius and character than his success in opening and developing the College of Our Lady of Holy Cross in the face of the sometimes veiled yet always abiding hostility of the Government to competition in the field of higher education.[4] The sincerity of Father Moreau no less than his courage and tact seems at times to have made friends for him and his work where friends could be least expected. It is true he never hesitated to use the influence of Catholics in high places when such influence was available, but even when such influence was absent, Father Basil succeeded by the grace of God, the charm of his personality and the earnestness of his message. The following paragraph from an appeal he penned in 1837 for the Association of St. Joseph founded in that year for the temporal support of the Brothers' Institute will give us an idea of the vibrant character of that message:[5]

[4] Vide, Thebaud, S. J., "Three Quarters of a Century," Vol. I, U. S. Catholic Historical Society.
[5] Vie, p. 134.

O youth, so bright with hope, you are the future of religion and of society! And if our appeal be heard and understood, we shall open pure fountains where you may drink in truth and life, while learning the way to real happiness. This we know to be likewise your desire, pastors of this diocese, worthy and venerable associates who have approved with solemn and unanimous approbation, the plan of the Association which we proposed to you during your retreat.[6] We are confident that, through you, our voices may reach all religious and political opinions. Who, indeed, will not appreciate the great hopes of our Institute? Who will not admit, today, the superiority of the Christian schools? Far from us be the intention of undermining other schools which promise happy and great results. The professors we offer to the young, behold them, judge them, they are called your Brothers; such they are by the love they bear you, fathers of families, and your children. Rich proprietors, magistrates, statesmen, they are your Brothers by the devotedness with which they sow in the minds of youth, not the search for material interest and cold egoism, but the quest for the great principles of equity and the charity of Jesus Christ, social order and respect for law. They are more especially your Brothers, country people, and you, the poor of every condition. You are frowned down upon by the world and your children are neglected; but you are our brothers and it is in your midst that we take our delight. We shall go then, we shall present ourselves to your children; we shall form them to a Christian and laborious life; we shall make them obedient and faithful; and, we hope, we shall make peace abide in your hearts and in your homes.

It was not alone from the civil authorities Father Moreau had to meet opposition to the wholly providential development of the works of Holy Cross. Almost from the beginning of his superiorship of the Brothers of St. Joseph, undertaken let us remember with reluctance and in obedience to the desires of Bishop Bouvier, the latter began gradually to withdraw from his first announced policy of co-operation. The changed atti-

[6] The Diocesan Retreat of 1837.

tude was the natural result of a number of influences both external and internal.

From the first Father Moreau recognized the necessity of introducing the fundamentals of religious life among his associates if the foundations committed to his care were to have life and fruitfulness in God. From the beginning his concept of the Mission of Holy Cross was both Catholic and Apostolic. Bishop Bouvier thought otherwise. A faithful shepherd and prudent administrator, his vision was unhappily impaired by the unfortunate stigmatism of Gallicanism,[7] and to his mind the mission of both brothers and priests was limited to the needs of the diocese of Le Mans.

Besides to add to the confusion, Father Basil's program for the spiritual renovation of the brothers and the spiritualization of his little band of priests had left plenty of chaff in the wind. There were the malcontents unprepared for the sacrifices of the religious life yet by that very reason ready to raise their voices against the new regime and Father Moreau, its author. Unfortunately for the interests of God in their immediate phases, Bishop Bouvier too often lent hearing and credence to those unworthy of either one or the other. The result was a growing rift, the first and only one in Father Moreau's long life between himself and his Ordinary.

In the face of this growing difficulty Basil Moreau adopted an attitude at once respectful yet firm. He would resign into the hands of his Bishop the offices he had received therefrom, otherwise he must be permitted to develop the foundation according to his prayerful convictions. In the course of Bishop Bouvier's administration Father Basil felt obliged to offer his resignation "time and again."[8]

How mysterious are the workings of Divine Providence! For almost twenty years Bishop Bouvier revealed an ever grow-

---

[7] Vide, Catholic Encyclopedia, Bouvier.
[8] Letter of Father Moreau, Oct. 25, 1853, C. S. C. General Archives.

ing dislike for the developing Institute of Holy Cross yet he never accepted the repeatedly offered resignation of its founder. One act of his will, one stroke of the pen and Holy Cross would have been literally decapitated, yet the Bishop never made that act, never wrote that one word, "accepted," across the letters of his subject. He opposed, but never crushed, the mission he himself had placed in Father Moreau's hands; perhaps he could not do more because deep down beneath the surface movements of human emotions and volitions in the sea of life there is always the undercurrent of God's Most Holy Will. "Man proposes, God disposes." Blessed be the Will of God!

To his program for improving the educational standards of the Brothers' Institute, Father Moreau added a detailed and carefully studied plan for the stabilization of their material interests. Of the varied accusations brought against him at a later date none were so manifestly unjust and unfounded as those relating to his administration of temporals. It was predicted of him after his death, "He will be remembered as long as his debts," yet his debts when subject to examination will be found to be like those of the Divine Master, the debts of his brethren by himself assumed.

From the very beginning [9] the administration of Father Moreau was distinguished by his efforts to promote order, regularity, and economy in the material affairs of his various foundations, and, moreover, he practiced what he preached. "Economy always, love of retirement, fidelity to rule, and modesty everywhere." [10] This was Father Moreau's program and his practice.

Devotion to economy had in the mind of Basil Moreau a higher motive than the desire to balance a financial budget. The servants of God are concerned primarily with naught

[9] Cir. Letters #1.
[10] Cir. Letters #3.

save the extension of Christ's Kingdom. If they practice and inculcate good financial practices and retrenchments, it is because of their fine sense of justice, and as well, their earnest desire that they and their spiritual children should be "poor for Christ's sake." Father Basil loved economy and efficient financial methods as a necessary condition both for the proper development of his works, and for the sanctification of the workers. He loved economy as a practical expression of the spirit of poverty, and he imposed it upon his spiritual children because he desired that they also should be adept in the practice of that virtue which strips souls of earthly possessions that they may the more readily attain to such as are divine. He desired his spiritual sons to be holy, to be worthy of their high vocations, and he knew well material extravagance is a poor setting for the cultivation of the things of the spirit. "In the midst of my labors," he wrote in 1839, "I do not forget that one of my first duties, connected with the office imposed upon me, is to labor for your sanctification and for that purpose, first of all to sanctify myself. For if the spirit which animates the saints did not live in us, the important work of Holy Cross would come to naught and our efforts for the sanctification of youth be vain and useless." [11]

Piety, then, as well as science was the program Father Moreau held as essential to the real progress of the interests of Holy Cross. Direction and the annual retreat were among the means he adopted to protect and advance the spiritual development of the works. There was nothing novel in their use as recommended by Father Basil. Both practices are but the logical development of the example of Christ in the spiritual formation of His first disciples as He walked with them along the dusty roads of Palestine, listening to their questions, reading their hearts, remedying their difficulties and then when they were weary both in mind and heart, calling them

[11] Cir. Letters #8.

apart to rest awhile in the silence of the hills where beneath the starry canopy of the heavens He could speak to them of the paths that led beyond.

Father Basil had a special devotion to the practice of the annual retreat. He never failed to make one himself, he never ceased to insist upon its importance in his intercourse with his spiritual family. The Sulpician Solitude at Issy, and the various Trappist foundations that could be reached from Le Mans were his favorite places for retirement. His soul drank deeply of God's graces in these fortresses of prayer, and his spirit sinking down within itself rested lovingly in God's hands. His letters written at the close of his retreats are filled with sentiments of confidence for the future, gratitude for the past, and courage for the present. It was in these precious moments of respite that Father Moreau renewed his own soul and found strength for the roads of tomorrow.

Direction and retreats, precious means of sanctifying souls though they are, were not, however, in the judgment of Father Basil, sufficient by themselves to lift frail human nature over the long stretches of renunciation that the vocation of his spiritual sons involved. He, himself, had taken privately the three vows of poverty, chastity, and obedience before becoming a subdeacon. Now, as he weighed the times and the lessons of his lengthening experience, came the conviction that only by the introduction of the vows could a measure of stability be given to the Institute of the Brothers, and the finer wheat be separated from the chaff. He felt and judged that only by fastening themselves definitely to the Cross could young men assure themselves and their superiors of a reasonable measure of security in the permanence of their oblation.

Persuaded of this truth himself, Father Moreau proceeded to unfold the vows of religion in all their chaste beauty and crucifying strength to the Brothers of St. Joseph. The retreat of the summer of 1836, which because of lack of facilities at

Our Lady of Holy Cross was conducted at the Major Seminary of St. Vincent's, was closed by a ceremony of momentous import for the future of the rejuvenated Institute. For the first time the vows were taken in perpetuity. To Brother Andrew, first faithful disciple of Abbé Dujarié, went the honor of leading again in the paths of religious renunciation. He was the first of the Brothers to so bind himself to God and the Institute.

The introduction of the vows among the brothers was a source of deep but yet incomplete satisfaction to Father Moreau. He would have wished to have led the way himself. His deep humility and faith made him see in those of his spiritual family who had taken this step, a perfection of sacrifice to which he had not as yet obtained. They were real religious and he felt a holy emulation in reflecting upon this fact. Four years he would have to wait before he, himself, might have the privilege of sharing officially in their oblation. Meanwhile he was to have many opportunities of putting in practice the virtues which the vows consecrate.

The work begun so auspiciously for the Brothers of St. Joseph had as well to be inaugurated in the little band of Auxiliary Priests. Living with the latter group at St. Vincent's Father Moreau was able to gather them daily about him for their various spiritual exercises, but always under the disadvantages involved by the presence of another Community and of the varied duties of his office as assistant superior and professor. He had, as well, the direction of the Brothers' Institute and of the Religious of Le Mans Monastery of the Good Shepherd, works calling him daily to widely separated parts of the city. Father Basil, therefore, welcomed the turn of events that found him replaced in the chair of Sacred Scriptures at St. Vincent's by a young priest whose advance studies as a former member of the Auxiliary Band Father Basil had fostered.

Leaving the Major Seminary in August, 1836, Father Moreau was at last fully launched on his new career. His seminary professorship had constituted a last tie to the life that lay behind him. With that tie broken, he was committed entirely to the uncharted seas and the winds of Divine Providence. He left St. Vincent's without funds and without a place of permanent abode. It was a fitting inauguration of an apostolic mission.

God, however, ever watching over the paths of His servants, soon came to his assistance. A few mornings after his departure from the seminary, Father Basil who had just finished his Mass at the Cathedral was approached by Mr. Barre, a citizen of Le Mans well known for his liberal anti-clerical views. He proposed to Father Moreau the rental of his estate bordering the establishment of the brothers at Holy Cross. The place was admirable in every way. The rental asked was quite nominal. The agreement was quickly made, and Father Moreau found himself most unexpectedly in a position to bring the Auxiliary Priests together under conditions suitable for their spiritual formation and growth.

While the necessary preparations were being made at the Barre property, Father Basil withdrew his little company of ecclesiastics, October 15, 1836, into the solitude of the Grande Trappe of Mortagne on retreat. At its close he had the great happiness of conducting them to their new home, the Barre estate adjoining Our Lady of Holy Cross. There was room for the opening of a boarding school on the property and besides, the priests and ecclesiastics could now give themselves to their Missions and studies under favorable conditions. Before leaving Mortagne all had subscribed to a set of rules which they had discussed and formulated during their retreat and which Monseigneur Bouvier approved for them. Moreover, from this period until 1845 the Auxiliary Priests were compensated for their services to the diocese by an annual grant from the Seminary Corporation of $400.00. Hardly adequate compensation for the services of four priests who were to be always available, but nevertheless most helpful at the moment. The works of Holy Cross were moving forward.

It had been with much reluctancy, and in a spirit of obedience to authority that Father Moreau had added the burdens of superiorship of the Brothers of St. Joseph to the already heavy ones of his seminary duties, the direction of the Good Shepherd Monastery of Le Mans, and the care of his nascent band of Auxiliary Priests. "It required," he wrote the brothers,[12] "the explicit command of my Bishop and the interest I have always taken in your worthy Institute to make me accept the burden which the venerable priest Father Dujarié now lays down because of failing health." But once Father Moreau had prayerfully decided to accept the charge, he set himself to the task of not only perfecting its members and organization, but also of uniting them as well with his own foundation of the Auxiliary Priests. The plan he pursued was the one he conceived when he first called the brothers to Holy Cross.[13]

This plan in its original form, before experience and the will of God as expressed in the authentic decisions of His Church had modified it, Father Basil outlined in his Circular Letter of June 26, 1839, as follows:

> According to this plan, three Societies will be consecrated to the Most Holy Hearts of Jesus, Mary and Joseph; three Societies united among themselves like the Holy Family, but with separate dwellings and with different rules.

The third society, that of the Sisters, we shall speak of in the following chapter. As for the priests and brothers, Father Moreau had already united them in his heart and mind; in his heart by reason of his Christ-like love, and in his mind because, seeking only the glory of God through the apostolate of the spoken word and teaching he realized how mutually

[12] Cir. Letters #1.
[13] Cir. Letters #8.

helpful priests and brothers could be to one another, and how perfectly complementary were their distinctive fields. From the beginning the Auxiliary Priests had guided the advanced studies of the Brothers and served them as chaplains and directors. On the other hand, as we have already remarked, the brothers were able to render varied services to the priests both in the external apostolate of education and the missions, and in the management and upkeep of the individual houses. Not all the candidates for the Institute of the Brothers felt attracted to or were qualified for the work of the classroom, and consequently Father Basil in the first year of his superiorship withdrew those not suitable from the teaching mission and created the coadjutor brothers dedicated to manual labor. It was just the development of this distinct class among the brothers that made it possible for Father Moreau at a later date to answer the appeal from Rome for brothers capable of teaching the manual arts and farming.

The first formal step toward corporate union between the priests and brothers was effected by Father Basil on the first of March, 1837. On that date a Fundamental Act [14] was entered into by the members of both Societies assembled in General Council, and thereafter, the designation, "Association of Holy Cross," was used as a common title of the two Societies. It is true this first Pact dealt primarily with the temporalities of the two groups, but nevertheless by this just and equitable arrangement of their material interests, the surest foundation was laid for that union in things spiritual which in the providential designs of God was being effected daily, and which would constitute in its final and definite form the distinguishing character of the Congregation of Holy Cross. Subsequently there was issued in September, 1839, a supplementary statement announcing that during the previous three

[14] The Act in full may be seen in the Appendix.

years the Auxiliary Priests had "borne one-half the expense of the Brothers' Novitiate without having any share in the receipts; and moreover they provided for their own maintenance and gave their sacred ministration to the Congregation without any remuneration." [15]

Thus step by step Father Moreau labored patiently to bring to pass that union among the workers in the Vineyard which he knew to be so pleasing to the Divine Master, and yet so difficult, at least in practice, for His servants to observe.

In 1840, yet another step toward permanence and unity in the Association of Holy Cross was accomplished, the taking of the vows by Father Moreau and four of the Auxiliary Priests. The date chosen by Father Basil for this event, so ardently desired by him, was the Feast of Our Lady's Assumption, and to commemorate its sacredness, he added on that day the name of Mary to his two baptismal names. Monseigneur Bouvier came in person to celebrate Mass on the Feast, after which Father Moreau ratified formally his oblation long since made, and in the evening, after Vespers, four of his spiritual sons in turn made theirs. Of the four, only Fathers Chappe and Sorin persevered, the latter destined to be the pioneer of the American mission, and the third Superior General of the Congregation. Truly that day Our Lady smiled upon the little band her fervent soldier had assembled for the service of her Son Divine.

It must not be thought, however, that this happy issue was achieved without opposition. From a letter written by Father Basil to Rome in 1853,[16] we learn that the introduction of the vows was responsible for the defection of no less than six members of his little band of Salvatorists, as the priests of the Association from this period began to be called. "At that time, there were," he writes, "three distinct parties in the

---

[15] Vie, p. 156.
[16] General Archives, C. S. C., Letter of October 25, 1853.

Society of Priests: some wanted fixed annual salaries; others merely sharing of goods in common but without vows; and others still, vows and their effects."[17] The events of the 15th of August, 1840, represent, therefore, the triumph of Basil Moreau's own ideals and convictions. In that hour, the Salvatorists were truly born and claimed their heritage of the Holy Cross. Today we can see clearly the providential wisdom of Father Moreau, for without the vows of religion, his work must have perished or at most have lived in the circumscribed limits and uncertainties of changing diocesan administrations.

Finally in the same year, as a presage of fuller and final triumph came the report of Monseigneur Bouvier to the Holy Father, then Gregory XVI, on the Association of Holy Cross.[18]

>Basil Anthony Moreau, Honorary Canon, former professor of Theology and of Holy Scripture in the diocesan Grand Seminary, has with the consent of the present Bishop established a House near the city of Le Mans, and has there assembled certain priests burning with love for souls and led by the love of poverty and obedience, who follow community life under his direction and are always ready to announce the word of God, to hear confessions, and to preach retreats for communities, etc. They are called Auxiliary Priests and are already fifteen in number. They live on voluntary offerings and on the profits accruing from the board and tuition of a hundred pupils.
>
>As the Brothers of the Christian Doctrine do not take charge of schools unless where they can live at least three together and unless they are assured an annual salary of six hundred francs each, they can not teach in the country parishes and in the smaller towns. A pious pastor of Ruillé, named Dujarié, about the year 1820, gathered into his presbytery a number of virtuous young men, kept them at his own expense, taught them and prepared them to become primary teachers for the localities where the Christian Brothers could not establish

---

[17] General Archives, C. S. C., Letter of October 25, 1853.
[18] Dated May 4, 1840; Vie, p. 162.

schools. Thus were founded the Brothers of St. Joseph. Their Society was legally authorized by a decree of Louis XVIII on June 23, 1823.

The present Bishop of Le Mans seeing that the novitiate of these brothers could not be suitably maintained in the country took measures to transfer them to the episcopal city. With the consent of the Founder, Father Dujarié, who was still alive, though weighted down by infirmities, he gave the Congregation as superior the above named Father Moreau. The new superior having nothing in view but the good of religion assumed this heavy burden and united the Brothers of St. Joseph to the Auxiliary Priests. Thus there are now in the same house, yet suitably set apart, the Auxiliary Priests, the pupils, novice brothers, and the teachers who instruct both.

This new Institute of Brothers already numbers eighty-six members, scattered throughout thirty-nine Houses, and forty-five novices. Yesterday three brothers, under the direction of one of the priests, set out to commence a foundation in Algiers, Africa, and soon others will be sent to the diocese of Vincennes, in America.

This Institute has already done great good, and promises still greater. One, two, three, or more of these brothers, according to the need and resources of the locality, direct each house. The Superior visits them every year personally or by his delegate and during the Vacations he gathers them around him for their retreat of eight days, thus renewing their religious fervor.

It was thus under seemingly fair skies that the Association of Holy Cross was launched upon its apostolic mission.

XII
THE MARIANITE SISTERS

> *Where could you prefer to be unless in His Heart? It is there I greet you with the sweet confidence that your visitation will bring light, courage and peace in the renewal of the spirit of your Constitution. It is this I shall beg for you and all your daughters, assuring you I shall remain to my last breath with the sentiments with which you have inspired me these many years.*
>
> —FATHER MOREAU.

AS a consequence of the rapid growth of the boarding school and the associated works at Our Lady of Holy Cross, Father Moreau soon found himself involved in the problem of providing properly for the domestic administration. He turned first to the two Communities of the diocese from whom he might hope to obtain the necessary assistance, the Sisters of Evron and the Sisters of Providence, the latter the spiritual daughters of Father Dujarié. Neither of these Communities felt called, however, to undertake the work. Undaunted by the failure of these efforts, Father Basil enlisted the services of a few country girls and placed them under the supervision of his own sister, Victoria. Father Drouelle, first Procurator General of the Congregation at Rome, gives us a succinct narrative of the resultant development. "After a few years these pious young women decided to renounce all remuneration save what was required for their board and clothing. They wore black dresses of uniform shape and began to live the common [community] life—such they believed it to be. They asked and obtained permission to bind themselves by promises after the form of vows, and the Ordinary, notified of their desires, granted it on condition that they should go under the name of pious girls and that there should be no formal [religious] clothing."[1]

The little group thus assembled by Father Basil had much to suffer in pursuing their chosen work. During the first years they lived at some distance from the College near the Visitation Convent, and in passing back and forth from their work had to bear the not always silent contempt of the unsympathetic elements among the citizenry. Father Moreau was aware of these trials, and strove with his own characteristic fortitude to encourage them. "Have courage," he told them on one such occasion. "It will not rain pitchforks, and if it should, continue just the same!" Before Father Basil's own course would be completed, it would literally "rain pitchforks" upon his own path, and he would "continue just the same."

Besides his sister Victoria in this first group were Mary Gendry, Frances Brehere, Mary Desneux, Anne Desrochers, and Marianne, the poor old crippled housekeeper, who had served Father Dujarié so long and faithfully. They were possessed of a measure of good will but their laborious occupations and lack of education increased greatly the work of their formation to religious life. Consequently until 1841, Father Basil's prayerfully conceived desire for the completion of his foundations by a Community of Sisters dedicated to the Sorrow-Pierced Heart of God's Most Holy Mother, had not materialized.

In the spring of 1841, however, Father Moreau was enabled to make a definite step toward this desired goal. On April 25th in that year, the second Sunday after Easter and the

[1] Letter to Propaganda, Rome, October 15, 1853, Gen. Archives, C. S. C.

MOTHER MARY OF THE SEVEN DOLORS. FIRST MOTHER GENERAL OF THE MARIANITE SISTERS OF HOLY CROSS.

Feast of the Good Shepherd, two young postulants began their training under the maternal direction of Mother Mary of Saint Dositheus at the Good Shepherd Monastery of Le Mans. They were Leonia Chopin and Renée Bouteiller. Some time later these two were joined by Mary Robineau and Leocadia Gascoin. In the vocation of the latter, Father Basil recognized the answer to his prayers for a soul capable of leading others in the paths of religious perfection.

The four candidates had the happiness of being clothed in their new habits on the fourth of August of that same year, receiving names indicative of their founder's desire that his spiritual daughters should be ever mindful of the Sorrows of their Blessed Mother. Leonia Chopin received the title of Sister Mary of Holy Cross, Renée Bouteiller that of Sister Mary of the Compassion, Mary Robineau that of Sister Mary of Calvary, while Leocadia Gascoin became Sister Mary of the Seven Dolors. To emphasize further their special consecration to the Sorrowful Mother, Father Basil gave his daughters the silver image of Our Lady's Pierced Heart and the beads of her Seven Sorrows. Thus with Mary as their breastplate and their sword, they entered into that mystical but very real warfare that all supernatural living involves.

In the fall of the same year the pressing needs at the College forced Father Moreau to call there his first trained Sisters from the peace of their Novitiate and the maternal guidance of Mother Dositheus. Father Basil never ceased to recognize his debt of gratitude to this enlightened religious who during the four years from 1841 to 1845 trained no less than twenty-five novices for his nascent Community.

At Our Lady of Holy Cross, Sister Mary of the Seven Dolors became Father Basil's assistant and directress of the little band. In her handwriting we are privileged to have the summaries of the simple but practical and fervent instructions Father Moreau undertook to give to his spiritual children on Sundays whenever possible. From one of these records only will we quote at this moment. It is from his conference of August 5, 1842: "If you want to be true daughters of Our Lady of the Seven Dolors," he told them, "you will be humble, charitable and silent. The daughters of Our Lady of the Seven Dolors are devoted to penance. This they should do not only for themselves, but for others; they should be mortified, humble and obedient."

In the development of his little Community of Sisters, Father Moreau met again a serious difficulty in the attitude of Monseigneur Bouvier. The Bishop of Le Mans was apparently unwilling to recognize the utility of any Community of Sisters dedicated to teaching other than the two he already possessed in the diocese. In 1841, the Bishop wrote Father Basil as follows: "See that your sisters are pious girls, solely destined to household work and I shall have nothing to find fault with, provided all necessary precautions stated by the rule are kept. But the predetermined end must be clearly stated, and it seems to me preferable that, even in your Constitutions, there should be no mention of these girls, since they are only accessory." [2]

Thus at the very beginning the heart of Father Moreau ever so closely wedded to the apostolate of Christian education found his way blocked in the growth of what he had long conceived of as a third and complementary branch to the Association of Holy Cross. The call of the missions, however, at that moment becoming imperative, furnished him the providential means of fostering the fuller and intellectual mission of his sisters under the jurisdiction of Ordinaries more in need of such service. Meantime he bowed to the will of his superior, and that is why in the Constitutions of the Association published in 1843, the third group of Father Basil's spiritual family

---

[2] Gen. Archives, C. S. C., quoted by Sr. Eleanore, "On the King's Highway."

received but subordinate attention. The Constitution declared: "The Association of Holy Cross is composed of priests, of brothers, and of pious girls devoted to the household work of various establishments directed by the priests in France, but abroad they apply themselves to education, as do the brothers whose rules they are to observe."

In this declaration we have an example of the at once obedient yet firm character of Basil Moreau. In obedience to his Bishop, he limits the apostolate of his spiritual daughters insofar as he is bound to do so, likewise in obedience he declares definitely their "predetermined end" which, where episcopal sanction may be had, is to be that of Christian education.

It is not within our purpose to trace at length the gradual development of the Marianite Sisters as Father Moreau's spiritual daughters came to be called. That work has already been adequately performed by others.[3] Our concern is primarily with Father Moreau's own character and if we treat of his foundations it is only that we may come through them to a fuller recognition of the spiritual stature of their architect. For the present, therefore, let us content ourselves with these few facts. Father Moreau worked unstintingly for the spiritual and material well-being of his spiritual daughters. They held equally with the priests and brothers place within his heart. In 1846, he united their temporal interests with those of the two older groups, i. e., the Salvatorists and the Josephites, and from that date they began to share equally with the priests and brothers in the rights and concurring obligations of the civil society which had been framed to meet the requirements of the civil laws.

Father Basil's first plan, however, was to suffer the modifications which God in His infinite and, at times, inscrutable wisdom dictates. The original concept had been for a trinity of

[3] Notably by Sister Eleanore, C.S.C., "On the King's Highway." D. Appleton and Company, 1931.

Communities reproducing in their mutual helpfulness and united aim the life of the Holy Family, itself, a reflection of the Eternal Trinity in God. "To cement this unity and to perfect this imitation of the Holy Family, Jesus, Mary and Joseph," Father Moreau wrote, in September, 1841, "I have consecrated and I consecrate again, as much as I can, the Auxiliary Priests to the Sacred Heart of Jesus, the Pastor of Souls, the Brothers to the Heart of Joseph, their Patron, and the Sisters to the Heart of Mary pierced with the sword of grief." [4]

Father Basil was to feel himself that mystical sword of grief piercing the Maternal Heart of Mary in the loss of her Beloved Child. Almost fifteen years later, on Palm Sunday, 1856, the Founder would be at the feet of the Father of Christendom, Christ's Vicar on earth, seeking his blessing on the works of Holy Cross, and, observing the Holy Father's preoccupation concerning the prudence of approving the sisters as an integral part of the Congregation, would generously declare his willingness to sacrifice "everything rather than to be an object of worry to His Holiness." [5]

The reply of Pius IX was prophetic of God's ultimate desire, "You will govern them separately; I bless them too, and later on you will submit their rules to the Sacred Congregation." [6] In the course of our narrative we shall see how these things came to pass.

[4] Circular Letters #13.
[5] Vie, Bk. III, Chapter 16, p. 79.
[6] Vie, Bk. III, Chapter 16, p. 79.

XIII
THE CALL OF THE MISSIONS—1840-1850

We cannot be insensible to these sorrows which from time to time pass beneath our eyes, but we must not forget that, in those far-off savage regions, sufferings are as great while there is no help and no solace as in France.
—FATHER MOREAU.

AS early as 1836, Father Moreau had been approached by the prefect of the department of the Sarthe on behalf of the Ministry of Marine and Colonies with regard to a foundation of teaching Brothers in the French possessions of Martinique and Guadeloupe. At that time Father Basil had been able only to acknowledge this sign of the Government's confidence and patronage and to increase the prayerful preparations for the extended apostolate of the Association of Holy Cross.

Again in 1839, bishops from both Africa and America appealed to Father Moreau for teachers for their scattered and oft-times unshepherded flocks. At this later date Father Basil was able to accede, at least partially, to these petitions which struck anew the chords of his own apostolic heart. In his New Year's Letter [1] of 1840, he informed the Association of this fact.

"It remains for me," he wrote, "to tell you that the Council of Administration has decided to send to Africa, sooner or later, three Brothers upon the request of the Bishop of Algiers. His lordship writes the following letter:

[1] Cir. Letters #9.

The Bishop's House, Algiers,
November 17, 1839

Dear Father Superior:

By return mail I reply to your kind letter of October 29, 1839. Here are the conditions of the Foundation which I consider as good as made:

(1) Although it is not absolutely necessary, it would be prudent, in this foreign country, for one of the three Brothers of St. Joseph to have his teacher's certificate.
(2) If I do not obtain free transportation, and you will know this by the next mail, I shall bear the expenses of the journey to Algiers.
(3) We shall look after the expenses of the three brothers once they have arrived in Africa, so that your valuable Congregation will incur no kind of expense for them.

My plan is to entrust to your brothers as soon as possible the primary schools of Algiers as well as those of the chief towns of Algeria. For this purpose it is necessary that your Society should know conditions and be known here. I am now preparing the way for this immense and priceless work of zeal. This I shall have done within a year.

In the meantime, in order to make known your brothers, and in order to acquaint them with conditions as well as to found so interesting a work, a work blessed by God and man, by Christians and by infidels alike, I desire and ask again on my knees for brothers to care for twenty-five orphans, children of poor colonists who died on the plains or fell by the yataghan of the Arabs.

They should be teachers and fathers to these poor children, teaching them the elementary branches suited to their future. They will live near Algiers, in the healthful and agreeable spot not far from the little Seminary of St. Augustine of Mustapha and the Ladies of the Sacred Heart of Tleberali. Probably the children of the neighborhood would attend their school.

All here regard your favorable reply as a most signal favor of Providence. May you and your Society be blessed by God.

The African winter resembles the month of May in France. We hope to have your brothers as a New Year's gift. I myself arrived on Christmas day, under the auspices of Jesus, a Babe and poor.

Good-by, dear Abbé and kind friend. I can not go on. Besides, it is useless. Words would not suffice were I to try to express to you what I have felt and actually feel when thinking of what you have done for us. Pray and get others to pray for me and believe me the most respectful, the most grateful, the most devoted, the most miserable of your friends.

ANT. AD. BISHOP OF ALGIERS.

After quoting the bishop's letter, Father Moreau continued, "Judge for yourselves, my dear Sons in Jesus Christ, if it was possible to refuse such a request!" Already he had himself made that judgment and would soon have to drink the cup of mingled joy and sorrow in the departure of his spiritual sons on that divine adventure of the foreign missions to which he had himself once aspired.

Basil Moreau's interest in the new mission fields opening to the zeal of his children did not prevent him from giving adequate attention to the work of the Association, nearer home, and the supreme work of the sanctification of its members. In the same circular letter of January 1, 1840, we find Father Basil, therefore, making the following recommendations:

(1) Send me a list of the textbooks you need in your classes, and state which ones you prefer;

(2) Teach the metric system and no other in your classes;

(3) Ask Brother Leopold for whatever hymns you need as Our Lady of Holy Cross has a goodly number of Abbé Guyard's on hand at moderate prices;

(4) Tell me your dispositions with regard to our foundations in Africa and America;

(5) Tell me when you will be able to reimburse the Mother House for the money she has advanced so that I may draw upon you by a money-order, and, according to the report of the Secretary General, how much in francs, and centimes, is the sum advanced to you;

(6) Do not ask me for winter coats, nor have them made until

the form has been finally determined according to a religious model;
(7) Make no useless visits, nor journeys in violation of the Rules and Constitutions;
(8) Finally, send me a receipt for the tax on your salaries that I may be reimbursed for it. The Brothers of St. Joseph of the department of Mayence should address their letters, free of charge, to Brother Leopold at St. Berthevin, near Laval.

Thus like the valiant woman whose praises are sung in the Holy Scriptures, Basil Moreau busied himself with apparently inexhaustible zeal in the welfare of his spiritual family in its ever-widening apostolate both abroad and at home.

The first missionaries left Holy Cross on the third of May, 1840, after a touching departure ceremony which has since become a regular part of the rule. The little band was composed of a priest and three brothers. They went first to Lyons where Monseigneur Dupuch, the saintly young Bishop of Algiers had arranged to meet them. The latter, however, found it impossible to keep the appointment, and consequently after a two weeks' delay and with their number augmented by a second priest and two more brothers, this first over-seas contingent of Holy Cross missionaries sailed for Algiers.

Once arrived in their mission field the newly organized works of Monseigneur Dupuch quickly absorbed the energies of both priests and brothers. The priests were given the direction of the little Seminary of St. Augustine which the bishop had opened the previous year at Mustapha-Pacha and where a score of boys of all nationalities were being prepared for the service of the Lord of Nations. The brothers received charge of the Orphanage of St. Cyprian, and aided the priests at the seminary as well. Besides their duties at the seminary and orphanage the two fathers were charged with the spiritual care of some nine hundred sick. The graces of their apostolic vocation were dominant in the little band as is manifested by the following paragraph of a letter written home during the first summer by one of the Brothers:[2]

> Who would not consider himself happy to be called to teach poor orphans abandoned by everyone? My most Reverend Father, that which afflicts me, is that I have done nothing to merit so great a grace. . . . We are here together in community; our worthy fathers preside at our prayers in turn. . . . The health of Father Superior is at this moment quite bad, and we wish he would take as much care of himself as of us. He teaches three classes daily, two to the pupils in philosophy and one to those in the Latin course. . . . Our fathers are ministering to more than nine hundred sick and of this number Father Superior has care of more than half.

Despite other pressing demands, Father Moreau dispatched in September yet a third priest and three more brothers to strengthen the apostolate in Algiers. The priest, Father Haudebourg, shortly after his arrival was made pastor of Belidah where Marshal Valée in charge of the French forces had converted a picturesque Moslem mosque into a church for the Christian population. Just at three o'clock in the afternoon, as Father Haudebourg reported later to Father Moreau, on Friday, the thirteenth of November against the bright sun-washed sky and dominating the towers of the two other mosques of the city, appeared a seven-foot iron cross giving notice of the return of the Faith of the Crusaders to the land of the crescent and sword.

The comment of Father Moreau upon this new venture of the Association found place in his letter[3] of January 8th, of the following year. "As you see," he wrote, "my dear Sons in Christ, the tree of the Cross has been planted in the land where our worthy religious dwell, sometimes tried by lack of sub-

[2] Vie, p. 190.
[3] Cir. Letters #11.

jects, sometimes by lack of funds, sometimes by sickness,[4] sometimes by other trials. But they know how to eat the fruit which grows on the tree of the Cross; and if it please God to keep them in the admirable dispositions which have characterized them thus far, they will never taste death, for the fruits which the Cross produced have the virtue of the fruit of the tree of life planted in the terrestrial paradise. But, oh, how few there are, because of the momentary bitter taste of the Cross, who wish to be nourished by it; and hence how few there are who have real life. I like to believe that all who have so generously put themselves at my disposal for these far-away missions have this life. For to be a foreign missionary one must know the mystery of the Cross and must have drawn strength therefrom, the strength of those apostolic men and generous imitators of Jesus Christ whose life here below was but a continuous martyrdom."

Again, however, before Father Basil finishes this letter the missionary reveals himself as the educator with an eye to practical details. "I remind you to keep your class-rooms neat, to air them regularly, to devote all your spare time to the study of the subjects that Abbé de Marseul assigned you at the retreat, to follow as faithfully as possible the 'Conduite des Ecoles'; and, when you return to the Mother House, not to make useless side trips, but to come straight to your destination."

To the sacrifices exacted by the arid soil of northern Africa others equally great and many times more fruitful were soon to be required of the paternal heart of Basil Moreau. Even before his consecration which had taken place in France in August, 1841, Monseigneur de la Hailandière had requested teaching brothers from Father Moreau for his vast missionary diocese of Vincennes. To Bishop de la Hailandière's repeated

---

[4] During this first year all succumbed to the fever but recovered.

appeals Father Moreau was able to respond favorably in the following year, 1842. There were numerous difficulties connected with this new foundation, the most formidable of which was the great expense involved in the transportation of a number of religious from the Old World to the New and then westward from the Atlantic seaboard to the fertile forest-girdled lands of Indiana. Triumphing in his zeal for the extension of Christ's Kingdom, Father Moreau overcame all obstacles. He obtained the necessary financial aid and equipment from his own friends and the members of the two Associations of St. Joseph and of the Good Shepherd which he had founded for the support of his works, as well as from the Central Committee of the Society for the Propagation of the Faith.

The timeliness of this assistance which the energetic influence of Father Moreau secured for the Indiana missionaries will be made clearer by the following extract from a letter of Monseigneur de la Hailandière who had written:[5] "All the linen, all the vestments which you are able to secure will be useful; these are costly here. . . . One regrets always not having brought sufficient. Take, therefore, everything offered you, chasubles, chalices, candlesticks, lights for church use and for rooms. It will be of great advantage if you have one or two brothers capable of farming. We are surrounded by non-Catholics in the proportion of eighty to three. Do not believe they are all hostile to us; the majority are indifferent. Many love us and favor us, but how often shall we convert them?"

The missionaries for America left Our Lady of Holy Cross on the evening of August 5, 1841. The little band numbered seven, Father Edward Sorin, a young priest whose ardent spirit held great promise for the future, three teaching brothers, and three brothers devoted to the manual services. Returning to his office, after the departure, Father Basil detained the priest

[5] Vie, p. 204.

who accompanied him, revealing the innermost sentiments of his heart in the repeated exclamation, "What a sacrifice!" "What a sacrifice!" The same thought he had previously expressed in a postscript of a letter addressed to Monseigneur de la Hailandière. "Bishop," he had written, "God alone knows what it costs me to permit this worthy confrere of mine to leave me." [6]

Real though the sacrifice was, it was to prove, as so often is the case, the fertile seed which sown in tears and husbanded amid trials would in the end bring to Basil Moreau's life and work the golden harvest of fullest recognition and perpetuation. The little band embarked at Havre on the eighth of August, 1841, and reached New York after a long and trying passage on the thirteenth of September. The next day they celebrated in the New World the feast of the Exaltation of the Holy Cross.

In November of the following year, Father Sorin and his brothers took possession of a tract of land in northern Indiana, originally purchased by Father Badin, the noted missioner and first priest to be ordained in the United States. The latter had given the lands to Monseigneur Brute, first Bishop of the vast diocese of Vincennes. From the beginning the site had been thought of as suitable for the establishment of a college, and in the fall of 1842, Monseigneur de la Hailandière offered it for this purpose to Father Sorin and his brothers. The bishop in a letter to Father Moreau [7] dated the eighteenth of November thus informed him of his gift: "I have the honor to inform you that I have this week given to your Congregation the land of which I spoke to you, and this very day the superior has left with six or seven brothers to take possession."

The spirit in which Father Sorin and the brothers entered into this, their promised land, is well described by the former

[6] Vie, p. 204.
[7] Vie, p. 213.

looking backward over the first decade of years:[8] "Only ten years have elapsed since Providence first brought the sons of Holy Cross to a wild and deserted spot in the north of Indiana. They were six in number—five[9] poor religious brothers and a priest—all equally destitute of those human resources which insure success in this life. An old and miserable log-cabin, well-nigh open to every wind, was the only lodging they found at their disposal to rest themselves after their long journey. The kind offices of two or three good sisters would have been very acceptable. I shall tell you now what I have never told you before. At the moment, one most memorable to me, a special consecration was made to the Blessed Mother of Jesus, not only of the land that was to be called by her very name, but also of the Institution that was to be founded here. With my five brothers and myself, I presented to the Blessed Virgin all the generous souls, whom Heaven should be pleased to call around me on this spot, or who should come after me."

Thus at its very inception the work of Holy Cross in America as in France was placed at the feet of Heaven's Queen, nor is it presumptuous to say, in the light of almost a century of sunshine and tears, that to the white mantle of snow which fell about the first sons of Father Moreau on that late November afternoon was added another, warmer and fairer, the protecting mantle of Our Lady and Our Mother, Notre Dame!

While Father Sorin and his little party of brothers were still out on the mighty bosom of the Atlantic, in their slow passage to the New World, the venerable Monseigneur Bourget of Montreal was knocking at the gates of Holy Cross seeking brothers and sisters for his own vast diocese on the banks of the St. Lawrence. "As soon as you will have made the ac-

---

[8] Quoted by Fr. Trahey, C. S. C., "The Brothers of Holy Cross," pp. 57-58.
[9] Brother Vincent remained at St. Peter's, the original foundation, until later.

quaintance of this saintly bishop," Father Mollevaut had written Father Basil in announcing Monseigneur Bourget's intended visit, "you will rejoice at the opportunity which Divine Providence offers you to spread religion in those distant lands. I know your mind in this matter and am sure that you will grant all that is in your power." [10]

Despite Father Moreau's good will, he could not answer the appeal of the apostolic Bishop of Montreal until 1847. In the spring of that year eight brothers and four of the Marianite Sisters of Holy Cross under the direction of Father Verité reached Montreal. On the twenty-third of May they began in poverty the foundation of their Canadian apostolate in the little parish of St. Laurent on the Island of Montreal. Father Saint Germain, the worthy pastor of the parish, had made what preparations he could for their reception there, and he continued to be the constant benefactor of both the brothers and the sisters.

As in Indiana so in Canada the first years were years of anxiety and hardships. True children of Basil Moreau, they turned readily to him whose duty it had been to care for the needs of the Holy Family of Nazareth, and St. Joseph repaid their filial devotion a thousand fold. As the invisible mantle of God's Holy Mother served to protect Father Moreau's children in the United States, so the staff of St. Joseph well symbolizes the paternal care of the Carpenter of Nazareth for the little Holy Family of Holy Cross that grew and prospered in the Sister Dominion to the North.

Meanwhile back in the homeland the heart and soul of Father Moreau followed with paternal solicitude all the vicissitudes of his scattered flock. As year by year group after group of priests, brothers, and sisters left the Mother House to strengthen the foundations abroad his purse portioned to them

---

[10] Vie, Bk. II, Ch. VI, p. 38.

as generously as possible and his soul sought to pour its wealth of faith and zeal into theirs. Here are his parting words to the second Canadian mission band composed of a priest, five brothers and three sisters that left the Mother House early in 1848.[11]

> What a touching scene you offer to us at this moment, my dear sons and daughters. You have heard and understood these words of Jesus Christ: "If anyone would come after me, let him deny himself, take up his cross and follow me." Since, then, you have understood these words, renew your generous engagement in the presence of the Divine Master, and fear not to be enrolled under His standard. Leave all forever, you who have been judged worthy to work in a far distant vineyard, sublime privilege which His Providence reserved for you from all eternity. On this precious moment, the Master cries out to you from His tabernacle: sacrifice! Answer this glorious invitation, my dear sons and daughters in Jesus Christ, and do not look back. Bid a perpetual farewell to your native land, to your family, to your friends, break all these bonds which are so dear to you and depart for these foreign lands where the Master sends you.
>
> But what heart-rending memories arise to sadden my heart! Where are they now, O my God, those who on like occasions were assembled in this sanctuary. At Your Tribunal? Spare these souls that are so dear to me, and let your judgments of them overflow with mercy. My dear sons and my dear daughters, if it should please Our Lord to be satisfied in a brief time with your good will, present yourselves before Him with confidence—you who have renounced all for Him. But if a long career awaits you let it be one of good works and of sacrifices even to the end. When at times the burden shall seem too heavy, do not forget that you have here a father ready always to share your trials as well as your consolations. But let us not keep Jesus Christ waiting any longer, take up your cross, leave and follow Him!

[11] Vie, p. 333.

This was the spirit of Basil Anthony Moreau, and though he had at the time never left the shores of his native land, yet his apostolic zeal had already burned so brightly therein that its light had passed beyond the frontiers of France and won for him from the Father of Christendom, under the date of August 7, 1844, the coveted title of Apostolic Missionary.

XIV

HOME FIRES—1840-1850

> *He who has visibly called us to cultivate this portion of His vineyard, wishes that we count not on our talents but on our religious spirit, not on pecuniary resources but on the protection promised to him "who seeks first the Kingdom of God" and holiness above all else.*
>
> —FATHER MOREAU.

DURING the decade of years from 1840 to 1850 while the missionary destiny of his foundations was becoming manifest, Father Moreau was not neglectful of the no less vital interests of the Association of Holy Cross at home. We have touched upon these interests before, now we shall treat of them more fully.

In his very first Circular Letter addressed to the Brothers of St. Joseph, Father Moreau outlined a policy at once simple yet adequate for the regulation of the relations of the brothers with both the ecclesiastical and the civil authorities. "Never forget," he wrote, "that the pastor of the parish represents Jesus Christ and that from the moment a group of his children have been confided to you with the charge to instruct them in the paths of virtue you become his co-operator. Consequently you owe him the same respect and obedience as that due your local superior in all that is not contrary to your Rule. If, which God forbid, you experience any difficulty with the pastor or with the civil authorities beware of quarreling. Write me or the Brother Director, that a reconciliation may be effected more surely and more successfully. Be most respectful towards civil authorities and show them as well as the parents of your students all deference compatible with your duties."[1]

In these lines we have a clear statement of the fixed policy of Father Moreau with regard to the relations of the Association of Holy Cross with both ecclesiastical and civil authority. The notable success which followed—with but one outstanding exception—in these vital relations, proved both the wisdom of his program and the constancy of its pursuit. It was just his insistence on this uniform and sane plan of action that enabled the works of Basil Moreau to survive the changing fortunes of the political governments of his day, and win even within his own lifetime, the formal approbation of Rome.

In 1848 when the government of Louis Philippe had fallen amid excitement that served to revive the memory of the excesses of the past in the minds of many, Father Basil addressed his spiritual children in these reassuring words:

> Our Lady of Holy Cross,
> Le Mans,
> March 2, 1848.
>
> My dear Sons and Daughters in Jesus Christ:
> Fearing that you may be anxious as to the state of the Mother House, especially so because of the departure of the boarders, whose return is set for the 9th of March, I hasten to tell you that no untoward accident has befallen us and that all is quiet hereabouts. I hope that the same is true with the other houses of our Association, and I repeat the necessary warning not to be alarmed about the future. Let us put our entire trust in Divine Providence which ever watches over its works. The Postulate and the Novitiate have not been disturbed.
> I advise you not to oppose the new government in any way but sincerely to uphold it. Show yourself full of submission to the authorities who are doing their best to preserve public

[1] Cir. Letters #1.

order. The Christian religion is able to accommodate itself to a wisely organized Republic as well as to a constitutional or absolute monarchy and often better.

I bring my letter to a close by begging you to be more than ever fervent during St. Joseph's month, first for your own needs, then for those of our entire Association, and finally for me in particular, who feels keenly this new trial and who remains always so cordially, my dear Sons and Daughters, all yours in J. M. J.

MOREAU.[2]

The fine intelligence no less than the gentlemanliness and zeal of Basil Moreau had given him a host of friends among the higher classes and the nobility, as the list of the endorsers of his petition for full liberty of instruction at Our Lady of Holy Cross presented to the Ministry of Education in 1845 indicates.[3] But the zeal of Father Basil was too enlightened, too truly Catholic, to be confined within the limits of one class of society. Like so many of God's apostolic servants his contacts with the wealthy and the nobility had been made in the interests of the poor and the salvation of immortal souls. Like his Master, Father Moreau manifested a predilection for the worker, the poor and the afflicted. The material foundations of Our Lady of Holy Cross furnished him a wide opportunity to assist the members of these various groups. The needs of his own ever-increasing spiritual family did not prevent him from succoring this greater spiritual family of God, and this interest in the lower classes stood him in good stead in the trying days of 1848.

In the height of the political unrest of that year, the buildings of Our Lady of Holy Cross were threatened with destruction. Informed by both friend and foe of the impending danger, Father Basil declined to seek safer quarters for himself, although as a measure of prudence he sent the boarding

[2] Cir. Letters #32.
[3] Vie, p. 264.

school pupils home for a brief vacation. To a message from one of the Revolutionary Clubs informing him that his establishment would be blown up soon, Father Moreau replied with so convincing a record of friendliness and benefaction to the workers of the district that his erstwhile foes promptly voted to become his defenders and through their president sent him the following note:[4]

> Citizen Moreau: I am answering your letter which you sent to me, and in the name of the popular and democratic assembly which has done me the honor of choosing me as its president, I hasten to tell you that if in these days of holy insurrection, it should happen that public order should be troubled anywhere in the Commune, we refuse to bear any of the responsibility. We shall, for the sake of others, since we have no reason to fear the just anger of the people; we shall, I repeat, through our patrol and through our discussions in the club, do everything in our power in order that the imposing triumph of the people may not be tarnished. With special care, and at the cost of sacrificing our evenings we shall patrol the places which appear to us most particularly threatened. Le Mans, February 29, 1848.
>
> The Sixth Day of the Republic.

Lying tongues, however, continued to take advantage of the popular unrest to kindle the spirit of hostility and reprisal among the laboring classes. On the evening of March first, violent and continued ringing of the door bell at the College served notice of the presence of a mob. Incited by the fable that at Holy Cross the brothers had installed weaving machinery which eliminated manual labor and thus starved the working classes, a crowd of angry weavers were bent upon investigation and destruction. The brother porter refused to open to them until the timely arrival of Father Basil. Immediately came his order: "Open both doors," and the Founder of Holy Cross was face to face with the mob.

[4] Vie, p. 318.

"Are you a brother?" demanded one of the leaders.

"No, I am a priest and the superior of this establishment. What do you want?"

"They tell us that your brothers here weave cloth, and sell it at scab prices, and thereby ruin the weavers."

"If you believe what they say, come and see for yourselves, but come in the broad daylight and not in the night. Then you will know the truth. I am astonished that men to whom I have given so much work at the Good Shepherd Monastery and at Holy Cross should come here to destroy their own work. Who has done for you and your fellow workers more than I have done?"[5]

Unhappy workers, too often victimized from within as well as from above your ranks, was it not of you the Master was thinking when He declared, "Blessed are they who hunger and thirst after justice, for they shall have their fill!"

A hand fell in ready acknowledgment upon Father Basil's shoulder and a voice broke above the momentary silence of the mob. "He is right: let's get out of here!" A minute more and the crowd was in retreat and the same unknown champion of truth bade good-by to the slim cassocked friend of all men, with the reassurance, "Count on us and be afraid of nothing!" Thus amid the changing tides of political fortune, the genuine charity and courageous activity of Father Moreau preserved his work from destroying hands.

His greatest victory, however, and perhaps his hardest in external relations was the winning of the coveted and at the time rare privilege of full liberty of instruction. The monopolizing control of the University had been maintained by each succeeding government in France. Against this bulwark so well utilized by the enemies of God and His Church for their destructive propaganda, the true friends of liberty had strug-

[5] Recounted by Fr. Charles Moreau, Vie, p. 319.

gled with but little success during the first half of the century.

In September of 1848, Montalembert had led a too sanguine effort to emancipate the entire field of education from these state-forged shackles. He had tried and for the moment failed. The following January found Father Basil in Paris hoping to obtain from the new Minister, M. de Falloux, that full liberty of instruction for Our Lady of Holy Cross which he had been striving for since the month of May, 1842.

An investigation of the College at Holy Cross undertaken by the new Ministry resulted in a report most favorable for the aspirations of Father Basil. The mayor of the commune of Holy Cross together with the prefect of the district and ten of the eleven deputies of the department of the Sarthe endorsed the petition of Father Founder. On the 11th of January, 1849, the latter presented his case before the Minister. The following day to Basil Moreau's unspeakable joy all was concluded favorably, and on the thirteenth, Father Champeau, the legal principal of the College, was sent official notice of the new status of the Institute. The victory had been hard won. Since May of 1842, the litany of the Blessed Mother had been sung in the chapel at Holy Cross by the community and students to solicit the aid of the Queen of Heaven for this specific cause.

The life of a founder of apostolic works will be found in general to have been a succession of labors, trials, joys, successes and sorrows, following each other in rapid if not unvaried order. The life of Basil Moreau proved no exception to the rule. The consolation of seeing the civil recognition of full liberty granted the College of Our Lady of Holy Cross was followed by further trial. Discomfited by the friendly attitude of the Minister of Instruction, M. Falloux, to Father Moreau's institute, some of the extremist elements of the populace launched a campaign of slander. To these attacks, whenever silence would seem to lend credence to their charges, Father Basil made reply, utilizing to this end the columns of the newspapers of Le Mans. But before the summer of 1849 had passed, a more effective means of manifesting the true spirit of the religious of Holy Cross arose. In the wake of all other afflictions, the cholera broke out in France.

At Le Mans the conditions following upon the coming of the plague were particularly distressing in one of the poorer and less healthful quarters of the city. The health officials debated the conversion of the old episcopal palace into a hospital for the stricken, and appealed to Father Moreau for brothers to attend the sick.

The same dauntless courage that had brought Basil Moreau rushing to face the mob at the doors of his College, the same unflagging charity that would find him passing in a small boat through the flooded areas of Le Mans distributing food,[6] now found in the dreaded cholera further opportunity for exercise. Father Moreau replied to the authorities of Le Mans on June 12, 1849:

> Gentlemen, as I had the honor to say to you last evening in reply to your request, I appealed to our brothers and priests to help those infected with cholera. As the majority of the members of the Association of Holy Cross placed themselves at my disposal, I was embarrassed only by the question of selection. You may count on four brother infirmarians and I myself shall go to install them in their work of charity as soon as I receive your orders. I have but one regret, that is to be unable to offer you our own College of Holy Cross as a lodging for the sick but we have boarders here, and their health as well as their education has been confided to our care. I can, nevertheless, offer you our countryhouse of Charbonnière. In short, gentlemen, the brothers and priests of the Association of Holy Cross place all their devotedness at your disposal.
>
> I said "priests," for though you have requested brothers only, if the clergy of the parish, where you open your refuge for the cholera victims, agree, we shall be happy to offer the consola-

---
[6] Floods of the spring of 1856.

tions of faith to those stricken by the dread scourge. You know as well as I do, Gentlemen, that there is not the least cure for our evils, especially when it is a question of a scourge whose causes are unknown, if we do not look to Providence that sends the plague. Allow me to add that, from a supernatural point of view, this plague does not astonish me any more than does the social disturbance, because, when the voice of conscience or that of God's minister is no longer heard by those whose hearts are hardened, He speaks to us by revolt and by the confusion of the elements.[7]

How plainly these sentences reveal to us the soul of Basil Moreau. Here with striking clearness we see his characteristic virtues: charity and fortitude, prudence and faith. Moreover, it is apparent that the spirit of the father has passed into the souls of his spiritual children. They, too, are ready in goodly numbers to face for love of Christ the swift ravages of a deadly plague as well as the slow martyrdom of the classroom or the exile of the missions far afield.

On this occasion the officials of Le Mans found it unnecessary to utilize the good will of the Association, and the heroic charity of its members waited for its baptism of fire till some years later when the fever scourge fell with cruel deadliness on the little colonies of Holy Cross in the New World.

It would, however, create a wrong impression to imply that the trials of Father Moreau at this period came solely from external sources. As long as human nature remains what it is, such an ideal condition will seldom be verified in any grouping thereof. Basil Moreau had grasped this truth early in his apostolic life and had expressed it succinctly in a letter to one of the brothers written in October, 1847. "Nothing important," he then wrote, "can be undertaken without encountering contradictions, but should we be astonished at this when we consider those of Jesus Christ and His saints?"[8] None the less,

[7] Vie, p. 351.
[8] Vie, p. 309.

Father Moreau's soul was sensitive to the wounds inflicted by his own spiritual children which in turn only proves that he loved them.

During the Annual Retreat of the Association in August, 1846, Father Moreau had submitted to the Major Council of the Josephites, duly assembled under Father Chappe, the Particular Superior of the Brothers, a new draft of the Rules and Constitutions of the Association, tending to unite even yet closer the interests of all concerned. The Brothers' Council accepted "with gratitude and without any restriction the proposed Rules and Constitutions, both those that were entirely new, as well as those that represented a remodeling of their own particular Rules, reserving only such modification as time and experience should induce." [9]

The general response of the Association to the newly drafted Constitutions and Rules was favorable and Father Moreau submitted them to Bishop Bouvier for his approbation. The latter, although receiving graciously the report accompanying the draft of the Rules, deferred his approbation, willing to continue the trial he had stipulated in 1841. There were, however, a number of Brothers, who felt their interest would be better served by greater independence in the regime of the Josephites. These discontented religious voiced their opinions and, unfortunately, at least for the peaceful development of the Association, impressed the episcopal authority with their complaints. The result was not helpful to the cordiality of the relations of Bishop Bouvier and the Association of Holy Cross. Thus was yet another thorn woven into the crown Basil Moreau, in common with all superiors and more especially those engaged in apostolic foundations, was called upon to wear.

The response of Father Basil to these and the various other trials was characteristically that of faith. His New Year's

[9] Vie, p. 357.

Letters of 1847 and 1848 contain the following illuminating passages:

1847 [10]—Thanks to Providence, the year just passed found us worthy to suffer some of the tribulations which are the mark of the work of God and which serve to try our faith. I say "us" for ought I not to consider the injuries done to me as done to you? And what can I see aught else than trials in these serious and numerous cases of sickness which have extremely weakened nearly all the members of Our Lady of the Lake, Notre Dame, Indiana? There two brothers, whose names have not reached me yet, have died and for some time past we have been alarmed as to the possible fate of two fathers, one brother, and one sister. Then, too, there are the endless trials which seem to be occasioned by the success of our undertakings and the fear that we shall be too prosperous; the libel which we received but which I did not read lest I be excited to indignation against its authors, a libel which in the judgment of one of its three signers even, is as unjust as it is unworthy of an honest man.

Other crosses are the unforeseen suppression of the annual subsidy of two thousand francs from the Seminary; the arbitrary refusal of a certificate of morality (later granted by a higher authority); the refusal of lay professors to take part in the conference though their decision was condemned by a competent councilor; the perseverance with which the people report that a Minister has found us at fault in this matter though His Excellency has never so much as referred to the matter and has on the contrary honored us with an audience in which he was exceedingly kind. Nor can I forget the false reports spread far and near on our financial condition as well as about my relations with bishops who not only gladly welcomed me but urgently begged me for our fathers, brothers, and sisters. In a thousand ways they have tried to weaken or destroy vocations to our Society. They have worked against the construction of our conventual church and the completion of its stained-glass windows. They have slandered my administration by putting

[10] Cir. Letters #26, 29.

false construction on my acts or by misconstruing my intentions and thus paralyzing their results.

1848—It is quite true that Eternal Wisdom has arranged all things surely and mildly, for if with one hand God offers us a chalice of bitterness, with the other He offers us a delicious drink, like a tender mother who even as she offers her child a bitter medicine, gives it something sweet that it may forget the bitterness. Hence we ought to expect to drink alternately of this twofold and mysterious cup offered us by God. The important matter for us is to receive both with equal conformity to the divine Will of God.

In the General Chapter of August, 1849, Father Moreau was elected Superior General for life. He had been previously elected to the Superiorship in the regular elections of 1843 and 1846, and the Rule, as then formulated, permitted an election for life following upon two previous terms of three years. The choice was inevitable in view of the formative state of the Congregation, and though Father Moreau had requested the Council members not to propose his name for this third and life-term, he bowed prayerfully to their decision, the reasonableness of which was self-evident.

At this same General Council, because of the objections which had been raised by a few of the brothers to the choice of a priest for their Particular Superior, Father Basil arranged, with his usual sense of fairness, for a secret ballot of all the professed brothers on this question. The result served but to confirm his own convictions, all but three of the brothers voting in favor of a Priest Superior.

Finally, the Council sought by a conciliatory message to Bishop Bouvier to relieve the situation created by the circumstances on which we have already touched. The message in part was as follows:

> The General Chapter, after mature deliberation before God, realizes that the Congregation it represents never did anything

reprehensible to change the good opinion which the August Head of the Church entertained for it, and which was shown by the approbation that is today for the members of the Congregation its principal encouragement. In fine, your Lordship, the undersigned, while rendering to God the honor due to Him, do not think they are presuming too much in believing in the efficacy of the work to which they are devoted, for it has all the signs of a work willed and blessed by God. This work met with your approbation in the beginning, and was it not your Lordship who trained almost exclusively all the first members? [11] The undersigned are confident that you will continue to direct them in ways which all desire to work for the glory of God and of His Church, on the same title as so many other institutes of your diocese. They believe they have just as good guarantees as these others for diocesan and Catholic approbation. For this reason, your Lordship, the undersigned humbly lay before you their legitimate desires and their confidence that they will be granted.[12]

To this petition of the General Council Father Basil added his own separate note, and on the seventh of September had the privilege of a long interview with Bishop Bouvier which for the moment seemed to promise clearer skies for the rapidly developing work. The Bishop came to visit the Community and blessed its members, and thus the New Year began with brighter hopes. On January 10th Father Moreau wrote to Mother Mary of the Seven Dolors, then in Canada: "All goes well here; we have some new ecclesiastics and the Bishop paid us a visit." [13] All goes well always—with those whose wills, like that of Basil Moreau, are anchored in the Holy Will of God.

[11] Msgr. Bouvier was from 1819 to 1834 Superior of the Major Seminary at Le Mans.
[12] Vie, p. 371.
[13] Vie, p. 373.

XV
ROME

> *I felt nothing but joy, I wept, and I blessed Divine Providence which has at last brought me to the Eternal City.*
>
> —FATHER MOREAU.

IT was characteristic of Basil Moreau that his own trials and problems could not monopolize his thoughts. Like all who approach the Heart of God, his soul was elevated above the low plain of self and attained in Christ to wider, universal horizons. Thus in the summer of 1849, Father Basil wrote to the Congregation concerning a plan for perpetual adoration of the Blessed Sacrament inspired by both his charity and faith:

> For several months past I have been thinking almost constantly of this devotion as a means of interesting Divine Providence more and more in favor of the Holy See and our Association and also as a means of obtaining help for the numerous victims of the cholera who are being hurled into eternity without the time to put their consciences in order. The desire of my heart became more and more ardent as the needs of society shaken to its foundations became more urgent and as the family of Holy Cross received in the midst of so many calamities more and more striking marks of the protection of Heaven. But I feared to overburden you with new practices of piety unless you yourselves were able to see the necessity which alone could justify what I propose to your faith and your religious devotedness.[1]

Later in the same letter, Father Moreau treated at length the proper attitude of the Association toward the evils then harass-

---
[1] Cir. Letters #37.

ing the country, declaring that "come what may" all members must be prepared to prove that they have in their veins "the same blood which flowed in the martyrs of zeal and Christian charity, and that people accustomed to die daily to the world and to themselves by evangelical renunciation do not fear death, when their lives can be of use to their fellow-men."

After this forceful statement, Father Basil returned to the theme of faith, declaring that by prayer, "the real sanitary zone . . . must be erected about our hearths and our schools," and then promulgated a decree establishing the perpetual adoration throughout the Association, the first article of which reads as follows:

> The Perpetual Adoration of the Blessed Sacrament shall be practiced henceforth in all the Houses of the Association to preserve them from the cholera, to obtain the re-establishment of the Holy See at Rome, for the vocations we need, and to draw more abundant blessings on the work of Holy Cross.[2]

We shall return in a later chapter to the consideration of Father Moreau's lifelong devotion to Our Eucharistic Lord. We have introduced it here because it reveals his real and unselfish devotion to the Holy See. This devotion was soon to be rewarded in a manner we shall now relate.

Perhaps the saddest heritage of war, hate excepted, is the war-orphan—the helpless child who has lost the natural sources of its sustenance by reason of humanity's folly. When the barricades had been cleared from the streets of Rome in the wake of the Revolution of '48, a number of these little ones remained to claim the charity of the faithful. We shall let Father Moreau, himself, describe the genesis of this apostolate:

> The little girls were more fortunate than the boys; in addition to the many institutions devoted in the Eternal City to give them shelter, a holy woman, rightly called "the Providence

[2] Cir. Letters #37.

of the poor and abandoned," the Princess Geneide, the widow of Volkousky, a convert from Greek schism, had opened a special Home for the most helpless of these poor creatures, and she lovingly gathered therein the little homeless girls. This good lady, however, did not give up the hope of helping boys who had no such abode. Immediately the heart of this mother of orphans became larger and larger and she wished to gather in also this second part of her adopted family. She conceived the plan of a work of charity supported by monthly assessments. The Cardinal Vicar Patrizzi gave his approbation to the project; Pope Pius IX blessed it and became its first benefactor. The Dukes Marino, Torlonia and Odelscalchi declared themselves protectors of the new work and faithfully sent in a monthly contribution.

They had no house, so the Cardinal Vicar gave them permission to look for a convent which would be suitable for the purpose, and would not be necessary for the Religious Order owning it. They secured thus Santa Prisca, one of the oldest sanctuaries of Rome, belonging to the Augustinians, to which was attached a small house with a garden.[3]

At Santa Prisca, aided by the alms of Pius IX, a beginning of the work for the boys was made in May of 1849. Their numbers grew rapidly and consequently the problem of their spiritual formation and care. Little by little the promoters of the work became convinced of the advantage of religious to direct these little ones. They needed imperatively the training and guidance that only such as were themselves motivated by the love of God could give or be expected to give. It was the search for religious capable of imparting such training as well as instruction in the various trades and agriculture that directed the attention of the Roman officials to the Brothers of the Association of Holy Cross. The connecting link in the providential chain of circumstances that was to mean so much to Father Basil and his work, was Bishop Luquet, an old missionary from India, at this time living in Rome. It was this good bishop

---

[3] Letter from Rome, Vie, p. 378.

who first wrote to Holy Cross with a view to securing brothers for the care of the orphan boys at Santa Prisca.

In the inquiry and consequent request of Bishop Luquet, Basil Moreau saw opening before him the door to the two things dearest to the heart of every apostolic worker, greater opportunity for service and the approval of Rome. The former means to a founder the expansion of his charity, the latter the confirmation of his faith; for while the zeal of the servants of God drives them onward, their faith craves more and more deeply that visible benediction of their Invisible Master, the sanction of His Vicar upon earth. Perhaps nothing in the life of Father Moreau is more indicative of God's benediction than the graciousness with which from the first he and his spiritual children were received by the Holy Father. The beginning of these favors is at the moment the subject of our study.

Because of the critical attitude of those hostile to his work, Father Moreau thought it best, when the negotiations with Bishop Luquet had been concluded satisfactorily, to slip away quietly to make the Roman foundation. He left for the Eternal City during the night of November 1, 1850, accompanied by the brothers who were to direct the children at Santa Prisca. The little band was composed of Brother Michael, a tailor; Brother Louis Marie, a shoemaker; Brother Simeon, a carpenter; and Brother Pius, a cook, whose name was to furnish the Holy Father the subject for more than one kindly-conceived pleasantry. It was in accord with Father Basil's zeal that, even now, he stopped at Orleans to preach the annual retreat at the Little Seminary of Chappelle-St. Mesmin.

The party sailed from Marseilles on the ninth fortified by letters from Monseigneur Fornari, the Apostolic Nuncio at Paris, and after a pilgrimage to Notre Dame-de-la-Garde, where Father Basil said Mass on the morning of the embarkment.

The little party landed at Civita-Vecchia on the thirteenth and reached Rome the same evening. We shall have Father Moreau's own pen describe their first hours in the Holy City:

> We arrived at Rome at half-past nine in the evening. Then recommenced the unpleasant experiences with the customs officers. At twelve o'clock we were still lugging our traveling bags through the streets, and, like the Holy Family, going from hotel to hotel, seeking, but not finding, a lodging, when a fellow passenger, a Frenchman who lives in Rome, met us, and brought us to the Duke of Torlonia, who made us forget our great fatigue by the warmth of his reception. Next morning, on awakening, we were amazed to see on all sides so many basilicas, ancient temples, arches of triumph, obelisks, colonnades, and statues. In the forenoon we visited St. Peter's. In the evening I was received by the Cardinal Secretary of State, to whom I handed the despatches from the nunciature in Paris. The following day, I had the happiness of celebrating the Holy Sacrifice of the Mass for all our Congregation in the very chapel where M. de Ratisbonne saw the Blessed Virgin. During the same day, I was received by the Cardinal Vicar who told me that Santa Prisca was to remain under the direction of its actual Superior. However, here I am installed, after a thousand difficulties, in one of the rooms of Santa Prisca, where I find eighteen children in the most undisciplined condition.[4]

There then began for Basil Moreau a period of mingled trial and consolation. The trials revolved about the necessarily difficult readjustments of affairs in connection with Santa Prisca. There Father Moreau found himself faced at once with the double task of establishing discipline and order among his wild little charges and at the same time securing from the Commission which directed the house the necessary authority and support. Both problems were complicated by the differences of language and nationality, but Basil Moreau

[4] Vie, p. 383.

was not a soul to be stayed by such barriers and by God's grace assisted by the good will of numerous friends, and above all by the paternal interest of Pius IX, affairs were at last brought to a happy conclusion. An idea of the character of these difficulties may be drawn from a letter of Father Basil's dated November 28th in which he wrote:

> If ever an undertaking was difficult, this one certainly is. Four men, who had been working at Santa Prisca, suddenly disappeared, then two children ran away. When evening came, they asked to be taken in, but I refused, except in the case of one employee and one child. Now we are getting acquainted with each other; peace seems to reign, and I can at last see what I am about in my new position. But everything is very poor here, except the walls and our two gardens. We sleep on straw mattresses, and our furniture is insufficient. Now and then mattresses and pieces of furniture are sent in to us. We have just found and cleaned up a parlor, for which the Duke of Torlonia gave us chairs and a portrait of Pope Pius VII. . . . Our children never have knives for fear of wounding one another; and it is a wonder we have succeeded in making them retire and rise in silence, and file out in a single line. The Pope's Head Chamberlain and Prince Borghese have visited us twice.[5]

But to offset these trials which one by one yielded to his charity and prayerful tact, Rome held for the soul of Basil Moreau a wealth of consolation centered about the person of the Holy Father. Everywhere and in everything Father Basil's faith found fuel for its flame. The ruins of antiquity, the relics of the saints and martyrs, the churches which stood mute witness of their faith, but above all the kindly face and paternal voice of the Successor of Saint Peter, awoke in the soul of Father Basil the song of triumphant faith. Less than a month [6] later he would write, "Pious monuments of Rome, I will hence-

---

[5] Vie, p. 384.
[6] December 9, 1850, Vie, p. 391.

forth carry you in my soul and you will never be effaced. Let others say that not all in the Holy City is edifying for the eyes and for the mind; I forget everything else to see but the stones, and the dead, and one living person. That living person is the Vicar of Jesus Christ, whose benevolence toward me cannot be explained but as a providential dispensation toward the work of Holy Cross."

Father Basil saw the Pope for the first time on the twenty-third of November in St. Peter's. On this occasion the faith that from the earliest childhood had taught him to reverence the Divine Master in His Vicar welled up in his ardent soul. Making his way past the Swiss Guards and Cardinals, Basil Moreau threw himself at the feet of the Holy Father. The heart of Pius IX, witness to so much both of love and hate, of loyalty and disloyalty, read at a glance the motive of this unusual interruption, and Father Basil stepped back into the crowd with the benediction of the Pontiff's smile. In writing of this successfully completed act of homage Father Moreau concluded thus, "This I was enabled to do without receiving a rebuff, to the great surprise, not to say jealousy, of four priests, two of whom, from Paris, had tried to dissuade me."

This first and unexpected meeting with the Holy Father was followed three days later, on the evening of November 26th, by a private audience the impressions of which Father Basil hastened that same evening to share with his spiritual family.[7] He thus describes the occasion:

> At last I have seen this worthy successor of St. Peter face to face and heard him speak. He is just as I had pictured him. He is just as I had dreamed he is, and as kindly as I had foreseen the night previous, when I was still unaware of the fact that an audience was in store for me this evening. Princes and Cardinals were waiting in the ante chambers. Suddenly Bishop de Mérode notified me that the Pope desired to see me and

[7] Vie, p. 391.

came to introduce me with my parcel of crosses, beads, and medals. As he led me toward the reception room my heart beat faster than ever; I entered, made a genuflection, then another, and finally a third that brought me to the feet of the Holy Father. He smiled. "Rise," said he, "my dear Abbé Moreau." All my fears were dispelled and I immediately felt at ease. "Most Holy Father," said I, "allow me, a poor French priest, to remain for an instant prostrate before you the worthy successor of the Prince of the Apostles, and to lay open my soul to you after kissing the feet of Your Holiness." "But you already kissed them at St. Peter's on the day of the Dedication." "Roman in heart," I added, "attached to the Holy See in all my sentiments and through my theological teachings, I have for a long time sighed for the happy moment when I could express to Your Holiness my profound veneration, my filial and boundless devotedness. I am but a poor—." Here the Pope interrupted me to say: "You are not as poor as you say, for you have had a superabundance of temporal blessings and a crown is awaiting you in Heaven."

I felt moved to tears, when His Holiness obliged me to speak, saying to me: "You have a large Institute at Le Mans?" "Three societies in one, three, Holy Father: a society of priests, a society of brothers, and a society of sisters." "Do the sisters take special care of the poor, and give themselves up to humble duties?" "Yes, Your Holiness, that is the principal end of their foundation." "And do your priests teach and preach?" "Yes, Your Holiness." "How many brothers have you?" "Over two hundred, Holy Father, and the four I brought with me are now at Santa Prisca." "How are things going at Santa Prisca?" "The program is being organized, but I thought it advisable to tell the Commission that it would be beneficial to add the teaching of agriculture to that of the trades." "You have done well; I consider this highly important."

"I understand you had nothing when you began your Congregation?" "No, Your Holiness, and up to the present I have spent more than two million francs [$400,000.00], including the expenses of the Monastery of the Good Shepherd at Le Mans. The Mother Superior of that Monastery has requested me to give this modest offering to Your Holiness. Several other persons, too, and our pupils have given me these two hundred francs for you. Will you allow me, Your Holiness, to place these gifts on your table?" "Yes, but I will return it to you for Santa Prisca." "Oh! But I would prefer to be able to say that Your Holiness has kept the gift." "Ah! Well, I shall keep it." After a few minutes, smiling at me, he said, "Now, I give you all this money for Santa Prisca." Just then the Pope rang for the Chamberlain and said to him: "I want to give this Abbé Moreau something for his work in Rome." The Pope then gave me five thousand francs in bank notes [$1,000.00] to be invested in railway companies, relinquishing the capital and dividend in favor of Santa Prisca.

Having expressed my gratitude, I asked for another great favor, that the altar in the Mortuary Chapel of the Community cemetery be made a privileged altar. The Holy Father immediately assented to this request by affixing his signature. I then showed him the plan of Our Lady of Holy Cross. His Holiness examined the road leading to the privileged memorial altar and asked me if there was enough water to supply the property and on learning that a steam pump was used to carry water to every part of the grounds, he said laughingly, "That is all very well but it looks like communism." "That is what I said, Your Holiness, to the workmen of Le Mans, who wanted to rob us in 1848; but when I showed them the whole of Our Lady of Holy Cross they placed a guard around our property to defend us." The Pope laughed and called Bishop de Mérode. I had been with the Pope for half an hour and I felt that I was talking with a kind father. I had all my pious articles blessed, and, as I bent down to kiss the Holy Father's foot, he presented me his ring. I left the audience chamber impressed by the holiness of this great Pope. I then went to give an account of my visit to the Prince Borghese, and to the Duke Torlonia, who appeared delighted with its success.

The impressions of this first visit were but deepened by those that succeeded; in December, the Holy Father received the brothers in an audience which Father Moreau reported to the Congregation [8] thus:

[8] Cir. Letters, p. 195.

December 8th, the Pope received the brothers and seeing them in the distance, cried out, "Here is Abbé Moreau with his priests, or rather, with his brothers, his little brothers. Come, come, my children." The Reverend Father introduced the brothers to His Holiness, who laughingly said to Brother Pius, "Who gave you permission to take my name? Are you a good cook? I have a notion to keep you for myself." The Pope then gave each a silver medal representing the Madonna of Rimini, and on learning that the Commission which had called the brothers had just been dissolved, frightened by financial problems, and that a vineyard had not yet been found for the children, he said, "You have found one, dear Abbé Moreau, for I give you my vineyard in which I had wished to gather abandoned children but God, who plays with the plans of men, has sent Garibaldi, who overturned everything, my property also. Go see it and cultivate it." The Reverend Father presented a petition for the Pope's signature. After five attempts to write with his pen, which did not work, the Pope said, "Assuredly it is not God Who does this, but the enemy of our Work." "Holy Father, your pen is no good." Smiling, the Pope gave Father Moreau his pen which the latter took off with him. His Holiness as well added ten shares to his first donation, each of one hundred ecus, leaving the capital and the interest to the work.

Vigna Pia, which the Pope thus confided to Father Moreau and his sons, was situated on elevated land at little more than a mile outside the Portese Gate and on the road to Ostium. The very next day Father Basil visited the place which the Holy Father had purchased shortly after his elevation to the Papal See, and which from the first he had intended should be developed as an agricultural school for poor and abandoned children. With this in view a large house had been erected on the property, but the Revolution of 1848 had arrested for the moment the hope of the immediate inauguration of the work. The house was still unfurnished when Father Basil took charge and thus the beginning of this new foundation was made in the strictest poverty. A little later he recorded in his simple and direct way this comment: "I was greatly embarrassed about food and beds. I managed somehow to get eight children to bed on two straw pallets. Bishop de Mérode sent me a bed for the Superior, which I now use. The next day, at noon, bread was brought to us; we have now the strict necessities, and everything is being organized little by little." [9]

Little by little is the normal way of growth in life, whether of nature or of grace. Basil Moreau realized this truth, of which the future held for him many illustrations in practice. For the moment, however, his interests at Rome were moving apparently with great swiftness to a greatly desired goal. His third audience with the Holy Father served to emphasize this conclusion. We shall permit Father Basil again to describe the scene: [10]

> I was at dinner in the Vatican with Monseigneur de Mérode, when this kind prelate said laughingly: "The Holy Father wants your rabat and he wants it tonight. Let us go in for an audience." I followed him. I passed through a suite of rich rooms, at the end of which is a plain apartment reserved for His Holiness. There passed before me a number of pilgrims, some Catholic and some Protestant, who had come to kneel at the feet of His Holiness, and I saw some whose eyes were still moist with tears. My turn came, I entered, made my first genuflection, and the Holy Father cried out: "Here is Abbé Moreau! Have you brought your brothers and your orphans?" I hastened to make three genuflections, so as not to keep His Holiness waiting. He advanced, placed his two venerable hands on my shoulders, and said, laughing: "I assured His Lordship, Bishop de Mérode, that I would take your rabat from you. I want to take it away." And at the same time, my rabat disappeared. The Holy Father added that the next day I would receive a little collet like Saint Vincent de Paul's, which I and mine, including the brothers, would wear ever after. What do

---
[9] Vie, p. 397.
[10] Ibid., p. 395.

you think of this scene, my good friends? It was thus, however, that the third audience began.

Then I presented a package of beads and medals to the Pope to be blessed. Afterwards, I asked for a special blessing for M. Pasquier de Coulans, for the wife of the prefect of the department of the Sarthe, and lastly for my family. It was with much affection that the Holy Pontiff granted all my requests and added: "I bless all your priests, all your brothers, and all your sisters, all your large family." Finally, His Holiness handed me a hundred crowns with which to begin our establishment in his vineyard, promising to send blankets for our children and an architect to repair our inclosure, saying: "The Popes thought several times of what I wished to do three years ago, and what Garibaldi prevented me from realizing. Let us pray and hope that the plan will now be accomplished."

I was invited to remain six months in Rome; I answered that it was impossible, but that I would prolong my stay.

In keeping with his word, Father Moreau remained in Rome through the first months of 1851, arranging and strengthening the foundations at Santa Prisca and Vigna Pia, and furthering, as occasion offered, the knowledge and understanding of the Association of Holy Cross in view of its approbation then under consideration at Rome.

By early spring, however, the affairs of Holy Cross urgently demanded his presence at the Mother House, and despite the remonstrances of friends like Monseigneur Barnabo, Father Theiner, a venerable Oratorian who was as well consultor of the cause, and even the Holy Father himself, Father Moreau left for Le Mans on the twenty-seventh of March. He thus described the anguish of his soul on leaving Rome at the very hour when his presence would have meant so much:[11]

> ... God alone knows what it cost me to withdraw myself not only from the entreaties of the brothers associated with me

[11] Cir. Letters #47.

in the foundation in Rome, and from the tears of the children that Providence had confided to us, but also from the honorable importunity of Pius IX, who, placing his sacred hands on my shoulders, said to me with a warmth I shall never forget: "Stay with us, Father, stay; if you leave us at this season, the sea may be rough and you will be exposed to the storms." Then it was that I felt how much attached I was to the august Vicar of Christ, as well as to the Holy City. On leaving the Vatican my regret became more bitter when, on visiting for the last time the worthy priest of the Oratory to whom I owed so much, I heard him say with surprise: "You are going away just when your affairs are about to be settled: now God alone knows when this will take place."

God indeed alone knew when Father Moreau's interests would be brought to their desired conclusion, yet there was only one course open to a soul disciplined to the call of duty as was that of Father Basil. Fresh trials and new burdens awaited him in France, and the kindly words of a saintly Pope were to have an all but prophetic fulfillment. Rough seas and severe storms were in the offing, but the deep faith of Basil Moreau would keep his soul from harm.

XVI

ROUGH SEAS—1851-1855

> *Let us adore, however, the designs of Divine Providence, and, in resigning ourselves to its most severe judgments, let us beware of losing courage.*
> —FATHER MOREAU.

THE period of Father Moreau's life which we are to deal with in this chapter covers the time from his return from Rome at the end of March, 1851, to the summer months of 1855. Within these years the youthful Association and its founder were called upon to sustain, in the mysterious designs of God, a succession of tribulations. During their course Father Moreau could write, "God does not give the Association a moment's respite."[1] While a newly launched craft rides at anchor in the protected waters of the harbor, men may only surmise its seaworthiness. It is the open sea with its sudden storms, head winds, and cross currents that demonstrates the qualities of both vessel and commander. In this chapter we shall study Basil Moreau guiding the destinies of his newly launched Association amid the rough waves of adversity.

The trials of Father Moreau during these months had two specific centers: firstly, the difficulties with Bishop Bouvier; and secondly, the sufferings of the Association, more especially those arising from the heavy toll exacted from its ranks by the Angel of Death. Assuredly these were not the only trials that came to the founder during these months, but they were the severest, and in his reactions to them we shall be

---

[1] Cir. Letters #58, September 12, 1853.

able to discern more clearly the outline of his character. For the moment, however, we must retrace our steps.

As early as October 4, 1843, Cardinal Fornari, then Apostolic Nuncio, at Paris, had written Father Basil in commendation of his Association and expressing his confidence of the favorable reception by the Holy Father of the Rules and Constitutions which he recommended should be submitted to Rome. The letter of the Apostolic Nuncio reads as follows:[2]

> Dear Abbé Moreau:
> I have read your Memoir with intense interest, and with all my heart I join with your Bishop, as well as with His Eminence Cardinal Polidori in congratulating you on your zeal and charity which have deserved so well of the Church. I pray that your pious efforts may be crowned with the greatest success.
> I am confident that the Holy Father who, by his paternal solicitude, takes the liveliest interest in all the good works of the Catholic Church, will be pleased to enrich with his Apostolic favors a work which gives us every reason to hope will edify the faithful and save souls. I believe, then, that you can confidently submit your Rules and your Constitutions to the Holy See, whilst giving at the same time a report of the houses and individuals that make up your Congregation.
> I beg you to make me a sharer in the prayers of your holy Congregation, which hopes for new favors from your charity and wisdom. Accept, then, dear Abbé Moreau, for yourself and for all your brethren, the most tender blessing in Jesus Christ, and believe that I bear you sentiments of the highest esteem.
> Your most humble and most obedient servant,
> F. Archbishop of Nicea,
> Apostolic Nuncio.

In 1846, Monseigneur Fornari had renewed his counsel that Father Moreau submit to Rome the report of his Association with the petition for approbation; and on this advice the latter decided to act. It must have been with a certain anguish of

[2] Cir. Letters #47.

spirit that Father Basil was constrained to affix to his petition in place of a note of praise from his own Ordinary, this letter of Bishop de Montais of Chartres:

> Most Holy Father, I am quite convinced that Father Moreau, a priest of Le Mans, whom I know very well, the Founder of an Association composed of three societies, one of priests, a second of brothers, and a third of sisters, is well fitted to direct and extend the Institute with great profit to souls, to the honor of religion, and to its remarkable extension both in France and abroad. He brings great ardor to this work; he is consumed by his zeal for the house of God and he possesses all the qualities for a leader of such a lofty undertaking. Therefore, I beg of Your Holiness to deign to approve this Institute which he has founded, and prostrate at the feet of Your Holiness, I implore your blessing.
> Your most humble and devoted son and servant,
> CLAUDE, BISHOP OF CHARTRES.

As Father Theiner would presently report to the Congregation of the Propaganda:[3]

> Not only have more than forty bishops of France heartily praised this Institute (the Brothers), but also several of them have fully approved the Association as well as its Constitutions, and also, I who write this report, have in my possession their personal letters of approval.

Yet despite the good will of the French bishops in general, it was not Bishop Bouvier but the venerable Bishop Bourget of Montreal, who undertook to convey Father Moreau's petition to the Holy Father.

The result of the petition was exactly what one acquainted with the prudence of papal procedure would expect. Bishop Bourget received assurance of the Pope's intention to issue the desired Brief of Praise, as the former explicitly declared in approving the Society of Sisters for his diocese, August 24,

---

[3] Father Theiner's report in full will be found in the Appendix.

1849. Yet Rome moves slowly, weighed with the wealth of her centuries of experience and guided by the Wisdom of the Spirit of God, with Whom a thousand years are as a day. The consideration of approval was referred to the Sacred Congregation of the Propaganda, and the Secretary, Monseigneur Barnabo (later Cardinal) appointed Father Theiner, a learned and truly holy priest of the Oratory, to study and draw up the cause. His highly commendatory [4] report was in due time made to the Fathers of the Congregation of the Propaganda, and their own favorable action was momentarily expected, when, in March, 1851, the strong hands of Duty drew the Founder away from Rome.

Seventeen days before Father Basil left the Holy City he received the following note from Monseigneur Barnabo: [5]

To Abbé Moreau, Superior of the Association of Our Lady of Holy Cross, Le Mans.

MY VERY REVEREND FATHER:

In the audience granted me yesterday by the Holy Father, I humbly submitted the request you made to the Sacred Congregation concerning the approbation of your very useful foundation. He consented readily to your proposal, and he will be pleased to read, when the report is presented, the findings of the Committee of Cardinals. I am sure the Sacred Congregation will crown your desires, especially when it considers the letters of approbation granted by so many French bishops, and the laudatory report of your own Ordinary, Monseigneur Bouvier.[6] I feel sure that, if your Reverence had been able to remain in Rome till the discussion of your affairs, your case would have been benefited thereby. Whilst so doing, you could have spent your time very usefully, and with the evident blessing of the Lord at Santa Prisca and at Vigna Pia, among your works of predilection.

Yet I have too much respect for the reasons you offer to op-

---

[4] Given in full in the Appendix.
[5] Cir. Letters #47.
[6] The Report of 1840.

pose your decision to leave us, especially as I am unable to say when the Committee of Cardinals will meet, for they will proceed with their customary prudence. In any case, I would have your Reverence send me by letter any further information I might need, and I beg to assure you of my sincere esteem and respect, whilst recommending myself to your prayers.

>Your devoted servant,
>AL. BARNABO.
>The Propaganda, Rome, March 10, 1851.

It was thus with just reason that Basil Moreau felt his heart torn with conflicting emotions as he hastened resolutely back from the promising warmth of an early spring in Rome. Five trying years would intervene before the promise of that Roman spring would fructify.

"But my presence at the Mother House was constantly being demanded," Father Basil wrote in the following December, adding, "as I found, not without reason." Beneath this last statement was cloaked the story of a wealth of tribulations, for while Rome and the Holy Father had learned in a few short months to revere and esteem the qualities of this ardent yet humble French priest, at Le Mans the case was otherwise. Some thirty years before, as a newly ordained priest, Father Basil had pondered the words of Christ, "no man is a prophet in his own country," and in consequence had turned his eyes to the foreign missions, yet obedience had pointed to the homeland, wherein, if one cannot be a prophet, at least like the Master one can suffer and be crucified.

One of the foremost problems at this time that called for Father Moreau's prudent direction was that of the attitude of the members of the Association to the changing political situation of the day. Before the close of the year, 1851, Louis Napoleon had once again reversed the republican form of government and re-established the Empire. In the wake of the accomplished fact he was asking the sanction of the nation.

The moment was a critical one for the Association and its members. Basil Moreau diagnosed the situation with his usual discernment and courageously annunciated the following definite policy:[7]

> But allow me to tell you first, how we should conduct ourselves with regard to the political events which have been taking place for some days past. One of the greatest follies of our century is to imagine that a state can be set up, or a society formed over night, just as one builds a factory. Societies, however, are not formed thus; nature and time must unite to fashion them under the Invisible Hand, which directs all things with strength and mildness. This is why it is so difficult for them to revive, once the hand of man has destroyed them. This also explains why there is such terrible inconstancy in the institutions which have succeeded one another in these our days in France, governments which take the place of that ancient and long respected power, on which the stability of public order depended, the remains of which have become a sort of rich inheritance over which heirs dispute with arms in their hands. But, my dear Sons and my dear Daughters in Jesus Christ, it will be thus so long as the people are fed on the ideal of their sovereign powers, and refuse to refer to the Supreme Legislator from Whom all authority flows, for it is impossible to exact obedience from wills that consider themselves equal and independent. We are, then, destined for a long time to see the reign of might over right, and who would not prefer it to the ax of the levelers, or to the plunder and murder which threatens us every moment?
>
> In default of all principle, is it not better to accept facts accomplished without our concurrence, and to see in them a new design of Providence rather than to be delivered over to the mercy of those for whom the government means only proscription, confiscation and death? For no one is unaware that if the wicked were allowed to triumph, they would spare neither birth nor riches, neither science nor virtue. If then, you are of age and have the domicile required for voting and for manifesting your sentiments with regard to him who now presides

[7] Cir. Letters #47.

over the destinies of France, you will be acting lawfully and prudently in giving formal adhesion to the government just established.

The wisdom of this policy adopted by Father Moreau is surely apparent in the light of present world conditions. In his own day it reaped abundant fruit for the Association, and besides gave to its author an influence with the civil authorities which with his usual zeal he promptly utilized in the cause of religion and charity.

The College of Holy Cross enjoyed an enviable reputation at this time; and the good will of the citizens of all classes toward the work of Holy Cross was most consoling to the heart of Basil Moreau. A sudden outbreak of fire which razed one of the buildings at Our Lady of Holy Cross early on the morning of December 7, 1851, furnished an unexpected opportunity for the manifestation of the public esteem, the character of which may be deduced from the following letter sent by Father Moreau to one of the local papers:[8]

> DEAR SIR: Kindly allow me to express, through the columns of your paper, my sincere gratitude to the people of Holy Cross and of Le Mans for the speed with which they responded to the call for help on the occasion of the fire which destroyed our building. Thanks to the prompt action of the firemen and the large crowd that gathered, all the other buildings were saved. Among those who came to our rescue I remarked members of the National Guard, police, and citizens, all armed, as they were under the impression that the fire was of an incendiary nature. In the midst of the grave circumstances which now fill the public mind, it is gratifying to note the generous devotedness of all classes who rose as one man at the first call of danger. Honor to the people who are animated by such noble sentiments. Thanks to all who came to our rescue, and especially to the workingmen who came so sympathetically to our aid in our time of trial.

[8] Vie, p. 418.

Under the new government Basil Moreau managed to secure in the course of the next year the civil recognition for his first work of zeal, the Le Mans Monastery of the Good Shepherd. The decree was signed by Louis Napoleon on the 16th of March, 1852, and came as the climax of a struggle which Father Charles Moreau thus describes:[9]

> Seemingly an institution so highly esteemed as the Good Shepherd Monastery would obtain civil recognition without much opposition. However, at this period legal barriers had been devised to block any recourse to the good will of those in authority. During more than two years the prefect, though backed by strong arguments and supported by a memoir of Bishop Bouvier, urged the Ministry for the desired recognition. In the end, it was a providential favor in the form of a decree of the President of the Republic, Louis Napoleon, that swept aside these legal obstacles that had withstood every effort of both the Community and the Provincial Administration.

Thus we glimpse the opposition which greeted even the most reasonable demands of religion in Father Moreau's day. The spirit of evil finds its perennial expression in hatred even as the spirit of goodness instilled by the breath of the Spirit of God finds its characteristic expression in charity and holiness; that is why the Church of God and her children will always be the object of hate.

Taking advantage of the seemingly favorable moment, Basil Moreau enlisted the friendly services of M. Migneret, then prefect of the department of the Sarthe, to secure civil recognition for the Association of Holy Cross. On the advice of the prefect, Father Basil was constrained to make some minor changes in the titles and terms used in the Constitutions of the Association and likewise to omit references to the sisters because they had not been recognized as such by the Bishop of Le Mans. Father Moreau and M. Migneret spent an entire

[9] Vie, p. 430.

night perfecting these changes in terminology with a view to hastening the process of civil recognition. The labor, however, was for the time to be in vain. With a united front all might have gone well, but Father Moreau was not carrying on with a united front. Bishop Bouvier was preparing not only to block the civil recognition of Our Lady of Holy Cross but also to prevent papal approval, something a great deal more vital to the perpetuity of the institution.

Informed of the representations made at Rome by Bishop Bouvier, Basil Moreau at last felt bound in conscience to answer the unfavorable report of his Bishop. Father Moreau's letter dated from Our Lady of Holy Cross May 31, 1853,[10] begins thus:

> MOST ILLUSTRIOUS AND REVEREND LORD:
> With the deepest sorrow I find myself for the first time forced to speak against my Bishop, because of his false report to your Eminence on the actual state of the Association of Holy Cross; but I owe it to God and to the Holy See, as much as to myself and to the work entrusted to me, to tell the truth and nothing but the truth: I do so before God, who will soon mete out to each of us according to his intentions and his works.
> I am blamed (1) for having sent to the French Government Fundamental Statutes which differ from those which I had the honor of submitting lately to the judgment of the Sacred Congregation of the Propaganda; (2) for having lost the best members of our Association one after the other, so that the work was on the verge of dissolution at the very time we were asking for its approbation; (3) finally, if I am correctly informed, for our financial situation which was so unfavorably represented as to make us appear to be on the verge of bankruptcy.
> Surely, if the work of Holy Cross was such as the Bishop's report makes it out to be, we would be, I do not say wretches worthy of universal reprobation, but criminals who wished to

---

[10] General Archives, C. S. C.

play with the Propaganda and even with the Holy See.

But, God be thanked, the work of Providence fails not in the hands of unworthy servants, and each day, on the contrary, is for us a new mark of favor which causes us gratitude and confidence. Your Eminence, I am sure, will come to this same conclusion when you will have the following details.

There follows a lengthy and detailed treatment of the points at issue, ending with these sentiments which carry so well the undertone of sincerity, faith and charity:

> Such is, Illustrious and Reverend Lord, the miracle of Providence in our regard, and if there be a doubt about it, examine the accounts, ask also the French episcopate always excepting my own Bishop, and the civil authorities governing us.
>
> If I be permitted to call upon other testimonies I do not fear to say that all the members of our Congregation (I speak of the professed only) are ready to subscribe to this declaration, although I have never opened my mouth about my embarrassments and difficulties so as not to scandalize weak souls; and never did there leave my mouth a word which wounded the respect I owed my Bishop who, as everybody knows, opposed the work—yet I do not ask this testimony unless the Sacred Congregation imposes it upon me as a duty. Finally, I bless God for having thus revealed once more the strength of His arm and beg Him to finish this work by the Decree of Praise from the Holy See, and I hope, etc.—
> (Signed)
> B. Moreau, C. S. C.

Despite the fact that the issue was now joined at Rome, Father Basil strove to preserve the attitude dictated by his faith toward Bishop Bouvier. The latter presided at the closing exercises of the College in 1853, and on the twenty-ninth of June, Father Moreau in a Circular Letter [11] reiterated under the heading of Relations with the Bishops, his lifelong convictions from which nothing could make him depart:

[11] Cir. letters #54.

Hence, if we are happy to testify to the Supreme Pontiff our filial obedience and limitless devotion, we should also show our bishops submission and gratitude; for if it is necessary to remain in absolute dependence on the common Father of the faithful because he is the Vicar of Christ, the visible Head of the whole Church and the center of Catholic Unity, it is equally important that we gather about our venerable prelates with a devotion full of obedience, since they have been established to govern particular churches and should therefore be, each one in his diocese, a center of unity for all the faithful submitted to their pastoral crozier. You have always understood this, my dear Sons and my dear Daughters. Hence you will share my happiness in learning of the good understanding which exists between the Mother House and the venerated pontiff who presided over our foundation. But that my joy may be complete you must continue to live in great union with the pastors of souls who have called you to aid them in their ministry, whether by administering the Sacraments, by preaching, or by teaching their spiritual children. Show them all respect, and deserve, by your regularity, that they take an ever increasing interest in your work even though they show it only by visiting your schools.

In these last words I see a pathetic eagerness on the part of Father Basil to make the most of the least signs of good will on the part of Monseigneur Bouvier. Father Basil speaks "of the good understanding which exists between the Mother House and the venerated pontiff who presided over our foundation." Puzzled as to how he could feel justified to make such an assertion, I find the answer in his closing words, "even though they show it only by visiting your schools." Monseigneur Bouvier has just deigned to visit Our Lady of Holy Cross and to preside at the Commencement exercises, and Father Moreau in the meekness and simplicity of his soul had hastened to interpret the visit of his Bishop as the dawn of peace. As a storm-tossed sailor interprets the least abatement of wind or sea as a sign of fairer weather, so did Basil Moreau translate the visit of Monseigneur Bouvier as the overture of better understanding. If Father Basil had any misgivings, like a courageous captain he kept them to himself.

The storm, however, was not over. What Basil had hoped was its completion, had been instead only a passing lull. On September 20th, of this same year, 1853, Monseigneur Bouvier addressed to the Sacred Congregation of the Propaganda, a long letter stating at length his opposition to the approval of the Association of Holy Cross. The writer has had the opportunity to study this document in the copy [12] made by Father Drouelle, at the time Procurator of the Association at Rome and who had been entrusted by Father Moreau with the handling of the interests of the Congregation there. The charges, therein enumerated, Father Basil promptly answered in a letter addressed to Monseigneur Barnabo, Secretary of the Propaganda, and dated from Le Mans, October 25, 1853.[13] In his reply, one by one, Father Moreau takes up Monseigneur Bouvier's charges and breaks them on the anvil of truth with the hammer of fact. The orderly way in which Father Moreau went about this disagreeable duty will be seen by the following paragraph with which he prefaced his refutation:

> In the present case, however, the triple exposition of the facts, bolstered up by the authoritative accompanying documents, will easily demonstrate to your Eminence and to the Sacred Congregation that all these new objections are either false or of no account. To prove my assertion, I shall first take the objection and then give the replies (I) as to the Priests or Salvatorists; (II) as to the Brothers or Josephites; (III) as to the Sisters or Marianites; and lastly as to the entire Association.

As the purpose of this biography is exclusively the study of the life and the character of Father Moreau, not the discom-

---

[12] General Archives, C. S. C.
[13] Idem.

fiture or disparagement of those who saw fit to oppose him, we feel justified in leaving thus the story of this controversy. Rome rarely approves formally in the face of open opposition of the local Ordinary, and so Father Basil and the Association had to wait for justification. In the end that vindication came to Basil Moreau as to all other true servants of the Master.

On the other hand, we should credit Bishop Bouvier with acting according to his lights, without forgetting that an opponent who feels his course justified makes a situation only more difficult and exasperating. Rome understands well the value of time in the settlement of human affairs. Bishop Bouvier was to die at Rome, December 28, 1854, and his successor, Bishop Nanquette, would lose no time in lifting the heavy cross which Father Moreau had carried so bravely and so patiently for the greater part of twenty years.[14]

We must beware, however, of painting in too dark colors this period of Father Basil's life. The fundamental optimism of his faith was constantly asserting its influence. In his letter of June 29, 1853,[15] he declares:

> Never has God so lightened my burden since He united us by the bonds of religion in spite of the objections of some against the religious vows which are the basis and foundation of the religious life. I see in the Mother House, as never before, the frequentation of the Sacraments, fidelity to the vows of poverty, chastity and obedience, respect and love for the Rules, and among our students, conduct which is truly Christian, and a spirit of hard work.
>
> As to the other houses, if I except one single house, I know by correspondence and by the reports of the Visitor that at home and abroad there is more regularity, more fidelity to the prescriptions of obedience, more stability in vocations, and more zeal for the development of the work. I have been especially consoled by the many requests for profession, by greater regu-

---

[14] Fr. Moreau worked under six Ordinaries of Le Mans, Bishop Bouvier alone being opposed.

[15] Cir. Letters #54.

larity in the recitation of the Little Office of the Blessed Virgin and St. Joseph, by the sentiments of faith and of piety shown by those who have written me during the past year, as well as by the fidelity in attending the conferences established by rule.

Moreover, despite the fact that the Association of Holy Cross had not yet received formal approbation or even the preliminary Brief of Praise, the Sacred Congregation of the Propaganda had already entrusted it with a mission field in eastern Bengal, India, and this manifestation of confidence on the part of Rome no less than the precious opportunity to labor for the extension of Christ's Kingdom, was a deep and abiding consolation to the Founder.

In replying to the first letter from Cardinal Fransoni, Prefect of the Sacred Congregation of the Propaganda, requesting information as to the disposition of the Association of Holy Cross as regards the apostolate of the foreign missions, Father Moreau had written [16] words that might well be held as the proudest heritage and ideal of the Congregation:

YOUR EMINENCE:
 The letter you did me the honor to send me, November 15th last, filled me with joy. For many years past, I, all the priests of our Congregation, the brothers and the sisters, have been prompted by the charity of the Master to attempt everything for the salvation of souls that are still in the shadow of death and in the darkness of paganism.

The result of this declaration of the mission-mindedness of the Congregation of Holy Cross, was the little band of eight,[17] priests, brothers, and sisters, under the direction of Father

---

[16] December 8, 1851.

[17] The original band had numbered nine leaving the Mother House, November 5, 1852, but storms and sickness delayed the passage, three of the members being forced to return and two replacements joining the band at Plymouth, England.

Verité, who sailed from Plymouth, England, January 17, 1853, for Bengal.

The joy of Father Moreau in seeing his spiritual sons and daughters carrying the light of the Gospel into the far places of the world was soon to be stifled in the cloud of sorrow that settled over his spirit when, as to the Job of old, messages of calamities were brought in.

In his letter of June, 1853, Father Basil had announced the deaths of three Brothers, one of them, Brother Victor, a teacher in the little Holy Cross colony of New Orleans. It was the beginning of sorrows. The hand of the Lord was lifted to consecrate the youthful Congregation; He marked it even as He had His Only-begotten with the sign of the Holy Cross. For the time being, the children of Holy Cross in New Orleans were in the vortex of the storm. Letter after letter brought to the truly paternal heart of Basil Moreau its message of swift death. New Orleans was in the grip of yellow fever. Father Gouesse, one of the Salvatorists there, thus graphically describes the scene: [18]

> Farewell to business, farewell to the noise and gaiety of other days. On the streets we now hear only the doleful noise of hearses bearing dead bodies to the cemeteries; everywhere our eye sees naught but mournful processions. New Orleans is a Necropolis where death reigns supreme.

The spirit of Basil Moreau was still, however, equal to the demand, as his comment on this letter demonstrates:

> This shows, my dear Sons and Daughters, the need these unfortunates have of our prayers and of new apostles not only for our houses, but for the entire city of New Orleans. Pray both for the living and for the dead; pray too for those whom obedience is sending to that dangerous post, and more than ever let us prove ourselves worthy of our vocation.

[18] Cir. Letters #56.

The ravages of the fever continuing, on September 10th,[19] Father Basil was obliged again to notify the Congregation of the duty of their suffrages for both the living and the dead. He did so in a letter recording these brave sentiments:

> This letter is to tell you that we have incurred a new loss, and that we must increase our fervor to appease the wrath of Heaven, for God alone can save the remnant of our little colony, by bidding the epidemic cease in reply to our prayers and penance. Surely the designs of Providence on this foundation are truly mysterious; and a host of circumstances, more or less painful, make its ways incomprehensible. We are obliged none the less to submit and to adore God's Holy Will. Although we cannot understand the reasons for the sudden deaths of workers so necessary to the vineyard we are cultivating in this deadly climate, we must not for that reason abandon this foundation so long as there are other members of the Association willing to consecrate their lives to it. What I am most anxious about now is to know who still survive those we mourn. Great indeed would be my joy if I learned soon that the good brother of whose death I am to tell you, were the last victim, and that the local superior, despite his excessive fatigues, has escaped death!

Two days later, on the Feast of the Holy Name of Mary, Father Basil was forced to announce yet another death, this time nearer home, but the faith-fortified soul of the Founder is still successfully breasting the waves of adversity. He writes:[20]

> The losses afflict us, it is true, but at the same time they increase our confidence in God, for they indicate that whether to try us, or to punish us, or to warn us to be ready to appear before His Tribunal, Divine Providence watches over us.

Before closing this letter, like a captain rallying his troops in the midst of battle, Father Moreau cries out for the closing of the ranks:

[19] Cir. Letters #57.
[20] Cir. Letters #58.

In the name of God, of His work, and of your souls, give me the consolation of knowing that your rising is according to Rule, that you keep the silence which it exacts, that you frequent the sacraments, that the directors see that their assistants work, that the spiritual exercises be made in common and that the conferences are held regularly.

The storm of tribulation, however, still continued to rage. Before September had closed Father Moreau was forced to add another entry to the logbook of his journey. On the twenty-eighth of the month, he wrote:[21]

Besides the five sisters dead in New Orleans, where good Father Gouesse has but one brother in good health, the typhoid fever makes havoc with our Community at St. Laurent. This house, some days previous, had the happiness of receiving His Excellency, the Apostolic Nuncio, accompanied by several bishops, and behold it is now plunged in mourning. Add to all this the lot of the two sisters, one of them the Superior who started for New Orleans seven weeks ago, and who have not been heard from since. Increase your prayers, then, for those whom Heaven thus afflicts, that God may be glorified and souls saved.

In October there came a temporary lull in the storm and Father Basil was able to announce to the Congregation the opening of two new foundations in Italy, a house of studies at Rome for the Salvatorists, and a reform school at St. Balbina, undertaken at the request of Pius IX. The succeeding months the sorely tried founder devoted to the task of improving the teaching methods and curriculum of the schools, regulating the material administration of various houses, and strengthening the spiritual foundations of the Association.

Father Moreau was further consoled at this moment by the visit to Our Lady of Holy Cross of Father Sorin, the Superior from Notre Dame du Lac, a visit which was utilized to regu-

[21] Cir. Letters #60.

late the relations of the eldest of the American foundations with the central administration, a subject which, owing to distance and other reasons, had given the Founder considerable concern.

The New Year of 1854 found Father Basil promoting with all the ardor of his soul the definition of the dogma of the Immaculate Conception. He encouraged the members of the Association in their efforts to this end and approved their joining and forming the groups, the so-called "Crowns," which were being established for this purpose; each crown being composed of thirty priests or lay persons who pledged themselves to a monthly Mass or Communion to this end. In February [22] he wrote the Congregation:

> With pleasure I permit you, or rather urgently invite all the members of our Association to form as many Crowns of Associates as possible, and to send me the list so that I may have the names inscribed in the general register at Rome, and make them known to the Sovereign Pontiff;

adding a little after in the same letter:

> Let us unite then, and pray with fervor to obtain of Jesus Christ through Mary, that He deign to shorten the time of trial on which we are now entering, and to grant at last to His Church a grace to which are attached so many and such precious favors. Whatever be the outcome, it will be for us, as further on St. Leonard writes, a great consolation at death, to be able to say to the Blessed Virgin that "we have spoken for her" during our life and prayed for the increase of her glory. Finally, in acting thus, we shall but imitate our venerable Bishop, since His Lordship has become a member of the Union of Masses to obtain the dogmatic definition of the Immaculate Conception.

This last sentence we have quoted as an example of the constancy with which Father Basil carried through his oft-

[22] Cir. Letters #64.

reiterated policy of homage and respect for his Bishop.

The joy Father Moreau found in promoting among men, and especially among his own spiritual children, the honor of the Queen of the Angels, was at this time like a glimpse of the stars through the storm-rack. The winds of adversity were rising again. In June,[23] 1854, Father Moreau writes:

> You know what joy would be mine if in reply to your greeting on my feast I could announce the conclusion of our affairs at Rome and at Paris. But if we are always in a hurry, because we must die soon, God, Who never hurries in anything, conducting all things to their appointed end with as much mildness as strength, has not as yet deemed it fit to grant us this consolation, and we must be resigned until the time appointed by Providence arrives. It will come, be sure, because human passion cannot prevent the designs of God from being accomplished. But it is for us to make ourselves worthy, more and more worthy, and to shorten by our fervent prayers as much as by our regularity, the time of trials through which our Association must pass; for every year brings us new crosses along with blessings more copious, for both are inseparable from any work inspired by Faith.

Then, after recounting the continual sufferings of the colony at New Orleans and making a touching appeal for the spirit of fraternal charity and union, the Founder thus announces to the Congregation a new trial, the withdrawal of his spiritual sons from the Little Seminary at Orleans; characteristically he views the brighter side of the picture:[24]

> It was a great pleasure for me to see all the members from Our Lady of Holy Cross who were employed at Orleans, ask to leave if their Superior were taken away; and I believe we established the principle . . . that we must never place any of ours in houses where they would be under superiors other than a priest of our Association.

[23] Cir. Letters #65.
[24] Cir. Letters #65.

There was plenty of occasion for Father Basil's courageous faith and optimism, for the letter continues with a long list of trials both in France and in the missions abroad, which the Founder acknowledges with simplicity, and then promptly balances with the victories of faith and graces the passing months had brought. "Never, in fact," he declares, "have I noticed such a fine spirit in the members of our Association. Even those who allowed themselves to be seduced by the illusions of the enemy of all good, have returned to those sentiments I have desired from them from the very beginning."

September,[25] the month dedicated to the Sorrows of God's Mother, brought fittingly new sorrows to her faithful servant. On the nineteenth Father Basil was constrained to write:

> For some weeks past I had premonition of new trials that would befall our Congregation. Today I learned that God has been pleased to call to Himself four of ours: Brother Alexis who was drowned at Notre Dame du Lac, the 19th of August last; Sister Mary of St. Aloysius, who died a saintly death in the same house on the Feast of the Assumption of Our Lady; Sister Mary of St. Dominic, who died in the same place in her fortieth year, after receiving the Last Sacraments; and Brother Leontien, a Novice, who has just died at the Mother House. . . .
>
> Remember in your most fervent prayers the sick who were still an anxious care to the Superior at Notre Dame du Lac, when he last wrote me, and those of our Community at New Orleans, so constantly tried, in spite of all I have done the past year to aid them in their many needs.

The needs of Father Moreau's spiritual children, however, increased rather than decreased as the wings of death continued to hover over the houses of the Congregation in many lands and the letters of the poor Founder became like a litany of woe. Here are the deaths recorded in his very next Circular Letter: [26]

---

[25] 1854.
[26] Cir. Letters #67. Undated but written in September, 1854.

Father Salmon whom I sent to New Orleans as Visitor and afterwards as Steward died there on September 6th.—Just at the time the yellow fever epidemic broke out and took off 223 victims.

Father Curley died the 4th of September at Notre Dame du Lac, of dysentery, after a four weeks' sickness during which he edified the whole community.

Sister Mary of St. Anastasius died on September 5th, the following day, at the same house.

October came, but the Queen of the Holy Rosary was asking for the Sorrowful Mysteries, and Father Moreau continued in faith-sustained fortitude to tell his beads. His letter of October 13th [27] requires no commentary:

Dear Sons and Daughters in Jesus Christ:
May the Grace of Our Lord, the blessing of His Mother conceived without sin, and the protection of St. Joseph, be always with you.

I am informing you to offer up the suffrages for Sister Mary of St. Anthony who died at Notre Dame du Lac on August 28th last. It was only the other day Father Rezé informed me of the above fact, and I waited a little to get word from Father Sorin on the condition of his Community. The latter has finally written me, but what sad news his letter brings. The angel of death has passed over Notre Dame du Lac and his arm seems to become heavier, judging from the number of victims who succumbed. In the first place Brother Dominic, professed, who had come back from New Orleans but a few months previous, died September 16th, after receiving the Sacraments of Penance and Extreme Unction.

For two months Father Cointet had expected the little colony from France destined for New Orleans. Ordinarily it ought to have arrived at Notre Dame on July 16th, instead of, as it did, on the 10th of September. Were it not for the extraordinary delay, Father Cointet would have been at his new obedience on August 15th. He remained at Notre Dame, however, awaiting the brothers who left Holy Cross, until Heaven

[27] Cir. Letters #68.

called him to a better life. For this zealous missionary this is a gain, but for the work of Father Sorin, it is an irreparable loss. The latter feels most keenly Father Cointet's death, and this blow which has struck him so hard goes straight to my heart. The memory of so many virtues, of so much devotedness, and of so many crosses; the need I had of him to aid our subjects in New Orleans, so frightfully tried—is not all this enough to cast down the Superior of Notre Dame and myself? Let us adore, however, the designs of Divine Providence, and, in resigning ourselves to its most severe judgment, let us beware of losing courage. Let us increase our fervor, and if we hear the voice which calls us to the Foreign Missions, let us be docile in life and in death.

I was just about to finish this letter when a second letter from Notre Dame brought me news of two more deaths in the Community there; two Novices, Brother Cesaire and Brother Joseph. Father Sorin regarded the latter as a veritable treasure. Poor Father Sorin! How my heart goes out to him!

"We are obliged," he writes, "to bury our dead secretly. Each day for the past week we have been going in silence to the cemetery."

How anxious I am going to be till the next mail, for Sister Mary of the Immaculate Conception, Brother Ambrose, and three postulants were in great danger when the last news was sent.

May God pity us! I would have all the members recite the Psalm "Deus Misereatur nostri" during nine days, offer up a Communion or a Mass, and make the Stations of the Cross once; also to offer up the usual suffrages for our dead, and thereby merit God's mercy for our work!

In the midst of these painful trials I have the great consolation of being able to reassure you with regard to the sanitary condition of the Mother House. All here are in perfect health, although around us dysentery has been raging. Just now, however, this scourge seems about to disappear.

I forgot to state in my last Circular Letter that all whom I recommend to your prayers had made their profession.

And the present Circular Letter shall be read in Chapter, or in Spiritual Reading and then preserved in the archives of each house.

Given at Our Lady of Holy Cross under our signature and the seal of the Association on the day, month and year as above.

B. MOREAU
Rector, Apostolic Missionary.

In November the heaviest of the storm of tribulation was over, though deaths continued to be reported intermittently from the various houses of the Association. By this time the toll of death at Notre Dame du Lac alone totaled eighteen, this number including some postulants and students, and the paternal spirit of Basil Moreau poured itself out not only in suffrages for the dead but in spiritual and material aid for the living. Above the troubled waters his voice, even as the Master's, spoke the words of peace. His New Year's Greetings of 1855, conveyed this brave message to the tried family of Holy Cross:[28]

> May these cruel trials be useful to us, by weaning us away from this life which is so brief and so full of bitterness. May these be as so many warnings of the coming of the Celestial Spouse, so that at our death He will find us ready to receive Him, carrying in our hands the lamp filled with the oil of good works. In the meantime let us bravely use the talents confided to us; let us heap up in the granaries of Heaven those treasures of which the worm and the moth cannot despoil us; let us fight with the shield of faith and the sword of prayer our three mortal enemies: . . .

Father Basil would soon have need of both his faith and his spirit of prayer, for his own Gethsemane was approaching.

[28] General Archives, C. S. C.

XVII
OUT OF THE DEPTHS—1855

> *I never see the return of the month of October without a sense of profound emotion, because it recalls that terrible trial which God permitted, either in the interests of the Congregation, or to render me more compassionate toward the spiritual trials of others.*
>
> —FATHER MOREAU.

THE first lesson in the school of sanctity is the knowledge of one's own nothingness. God in His Infinite Justice and Truth requires this recognition on the part of all His rational creatures. In the case of His chosen servants, however, this recognition is the more urgent for it furnishes the necessary foundation in faith both for their apostolic works and for the unspeakable graces of the fullness of the Divine Adoption. In the latter case the Divine Teacher ordinarily exacts that the lesson of finiteness be not only learned in the classroom of theory, but receive demonstration as well in the laboratory of experience. Thus almost without exception we shall find those destined to do great things for God, plunged, at some moment of their careers, into an abyss of self where they remain, for a greater or less time, suspended by the invisible thread of faith and the fingertips of prayer. Such is the purifying process by which the Heavenly Father ordinarily prepares His children for the final graces of the spiritual life. We have now to witness this trial in the life of Basil Moreau.

In October, month of the Holy Rosary, 1855, Father Basil

commenced to tell again the mystical beads of sorrow. God was designating the meditation subject for His faithful priest; this time it was the Agony in the Garden. October 2nd the Founder announced to the Association the deaths of four members: Brother John of the Cross of Notre Dame, Indiana; Brother Clement of New Orleans; Brother Benedict of Bengal; and Brother Prosper of Vigna Pia, Rome. Seemingly the wings of Death were hovering everywhere. The sorrowing Superior thus ends his letter:[1]

> I do not know what sad presentiment made me fear to have soon to add a new name to these which precede, and this name—I have scarcely the courage to write it, such grief it causes me—is that of the Superior of the Bengal Mission, the excellent Father Voisin, who died August 14th, worn out by the climate and the fatigue connected with his ministry. Grant the aid of your suffrages to these souls so worthy of our sorrow, and pray that I may not give way under the weight of the crosses that crush me.

These closing words furnish the clue to the interior trial which had now gripped the soul of Father Basil. All souls who attempt notable achievements for Christ have need of walking with their eyes fixed on the Master. Like Peter they are walking on the waters, and no matter how the waves may lift themselves, the soul must not permit itself to turn even for an instant from the face of Christ to the contemplation of the raging elements. As in the case of Peter, so now in that of Father Moreau, Christ permitted the ardent soul of His apostle, habitually overflowing with the graces of trust and confidence, to be in this hour flooded with consternation and alarmed by the waves of tribulation. Immediately, like the chief of Apostles, Basil Moreau saw himself and his work being engulfed. Like Peter, he cried out to his Master, but the Master in the inscrutable designs of His loving wisdom, saw

[1] Cir. Letters #74.

fit for several weeks to withhold the sensible consolations of His support.

A trial such as this will be with difficulty appreciated in its fullness by those who have not experienced the sweetness of living intimately with God. "Taste and see that the Lord is sweet," cried out the Psalmist of old, and those, who like Father Basil, have tasted of the beginnings in time of the delights of the Eternal Union, can know no trial comparable with that of the deprivation of the consciousness of God's sustaining love. For the rest we are fortunate to have preserved for us Father Moreau's own description of these hours which he himself has termed "the most painful trial of my life." [2] Because of the intimate nature of such soul-crises, the party who has passed through such an experience must ever be, though not always its best critic, certainly its best narrator. To the clerical novices of the Congregation at a later date, Father Moreau thus described his darkest hours: [3]

> "I never see the return of the month of October," said Father Moreau, "without a sense of profound emotion because it recalls that terrible trial which God permitted either in the interests of the Congregation or to render me more compassionate towards the spiritual trials of others. I had lost my director, Father Mollevaut, several years before. My confessor was absent. It was first of all the fear of political revolutions and the high cost of living which obsessed me. I clearly foresaw, so it seemed to me, the imminent and complete ruin of the Congregation at home and abroad. On this subject a strange light, without doubt the operation of the devil, took possession of my understanding. That ruin I saw so clearly that there was not the shadow of a doubt. The thought pursued me everywhere. I saw no means of escaping the catastrophe and I begrudged myself even the bread I ate. In vain did my devoted friends try to console me, saying, 'How is it that you who trusted so

---

[2] Cir. Letters #77.
[3] Cir. Letters #9, Very Rev. James W. Donahue, C.S.C. From the notes of Father Sequin.

much in Divine Providence now permit yourself to be overwhelmed?' I could make no reply but only say that there are moments when those who undertake God's works must be broken and confounded, moments when all must crumble into ruin. In tears my relatives surrounded me with their vain consolations. Sadness was all about me. I suffered greatly seeing the pain I caused the many friends who would not forsake me and I continually recommended myself and the entire work to the prayers of the disconsolate community. It was this which saved me.

"This was only the beginning of my agony. I had discharged our help, suspended all building, stopped all payments and persuaded certain members of the community to obtain the money we would need when the catastrophe occurred. I dismissed our postulants regretting that I had burdened the house with them. I denounced my own administration, telling the religious who offered me help and even a stranger who brought me 1,500 francs not to entrust this money to me as all was over. Each stone as it was hoisted to its place in the choir was a frightful torment to me. I dared not look at the building and I kept repeating 'Great fool, what a scandal you have caused in God's Church.' I insisted that we could not in conscience admit students for the opening of school nor accept their parents' money, being convinced that this would be an injustice. Only the brother econome could get me to sign any document. He would take the pen and force me to use it. It is a remarkable fact that during this time no one asked us for any money.

"We did not abandon prayer, however, and you know how sadly we went each evening to ask Jesus, Father of the poor, for our daily bread. Then when the community had retired I remained long hours in the chapel. And what did I there? I went from station to station seeking for a ray of light, for a single thought—and I found—nothing, absolutely nothing. I returned to the sanctuary. I mounted the steps of the altar. I knocked at the door of the tabernacle. I waited but I received no response; not the least encouragement. I understood, then, something of the abandonment of Christ, Our Lord, in His agony as He went from His Father to His disciples without finding any relief. I understood then perfectly the suicide of Judas and I would have considered it a real service had someone taken away two objects which I kept on my desk. One was my passport which I had obtained from the Minister of Foreign Affairs, the other was five hundred francs destined to pay my passage overseas.

I certainly would have yielded to the temptation to run away had I not kept my eyes constantly fixed on my crucifix. For entire days I never took my eyes from it. At night, alone, I suffered even more during my continual sleeplessness; and yet I found the nights so short. 'My God,' I said to myself, 'how quickly the time flies. The sun is soon to rise again. Oh, why is not this night eternal?' At last convinced that all was tottering about me I came to believe that I must go begging from door to door. I saw myself mocked, driven away, and I said, 'My God, I accept all provided that the Congregation be saved or that You be glorified.' And I added as if such an event were only a dream, impossible of realization, 'Oh, if I were permitted once more to see the Congregation re-united in a general retreat.' It was a happiness I hoped for no more. . . .

"At that time the rumor circulated that I was crazy. Nothing could be more erroneous. I was as calm as I am today enjoying all my faculties, but I saw no way out of the catastrophe. I believed the end had come.

"For almost two months this continued, without, however, our ceasing to pray, when I received a letter from one over a hundred miles away and who could not, so I supposed, have known of my condition. He wrote: 'I see you in the same plight as Peter sinking in the waves.' In the twinkling of an eye my soul was flooded with light; all my confidence returned; the trial was over. . . ."

The one Circular Letter [4] addressed during these weeks of anguish by the Founder to his spiritual family throws further light on the immediate causes. On October 25th, he had written:

[4] Cir. Letters #76.

Trials continue to rain down on our Congregation, and never has my heart been so sad. Scarcely had I announced the death of Father Voisin, Superior of Bengal, when I received news from Bishop Oliffe of a frightful wreck which precipitated three of our Fathers and one of our Sisters into the river near Noakhali. Two of the Fathers were saved, but Father Montigny and Sister Mary of Victories were swallowed up in the waves. The impression of this sad news was still fresh when letters from New Orleans came, announcing the death of Father Guesdon and of Brother Martial, carried off by the yellow fever, the one on September 18th, and the other on September 26th.

Confronted by such heavy casualties among the personnel of his little army, should we be surprised that the captain of Holy Cross flinched. In his anguish, unconsciously to Father Basil's lips came the question that once crossed the lips of a grieving Mother as she found the Object of her search, "Son, why has Thou done so to us?" In his anguish, Basil Moreau also cried out: "Why has God deprived these two missions of their Superiors and of such necessary subjects?"

In vain had the Afflicted Mother sought to fathom the response of her Divine Son. She who had experienced naught save the most perfect, love-filled thoughtfulness from her Boy, could not then realize that He Who had chosen her to be His Mother, had destined her as well to be the new Mother of Humanity, and, hence, Comforter of the Afflicted, and that as a consequence her Heart must sheathe—in common with a million other hearts—a sorrow which she could not understand. Like his Sorrowful Queen, Basil Moreau bowed beneath his grief submissively: "Impenetrable are the designs of Providence," he then wrote, "and we must bow our heads with resignation under the most painful blows."

Thus in the depths of its own insufficiency the soul of Father Moreau remained during the latter part of September, October, and the first weeks of November, 1855. In the unfathomable yet ever wise and merciful designs of God, "gold must be tried by fire" and the gold of Basil Moreau's soul came forth bright and fair from this purifying process. Throughout its course he had held the helm of his will to the course of God's Holy Will in a spirit of faith and abandonment, and having learned how completely the creature is dependent upon his Creator, he was now prepared to see his life work, the Association of Holy Cross, recognized as a vessel of election by Christ's Vicar and thus brought to safe anchorage in the port of Father Basil's deepest desires.

XVIII
SAFE ANCHORAGE—1856-1857

> *It was the month of May, the month of Our Lady of Holy Cross. Soon dawned the day which was to see the definite conclusion of such long negotiations, a day forever to be remembered with gratitude, a day which the Lord really made for us.*
> —FATHER MOREAU.

THE storm clouds had hardly lifted from the horizon of Father Basil's soul when across the waters gleamed the harbor lights his eyes had so long sought. Monseigneur Bouvier died in Rome in December, 1854, and the following June, the Sacred Congregation of the Propaganda passed a favorable vote on the approval of the Institute in its session of the 18th of June, 1855. The wording of the approval, however, involved an obscurity that made it unacceptable to Father Basil.

The affirmative vote of the Cardinals had been phrased as follows:[1]

> The answer to the first doubt, whether it is expedient for the Holy See to approve without further trial the Institute of Holy Cross, is affirmative and is drawn up thus: "THERE IS REASON TO APPROVE THE INSTITUTE ACCORDING TO ITS PRIMITIVE FORM AND LIMITS."

An approbation thus worded involved the problem as to what constituted the "primitive form" of the Institute of Holy Cross, and, again, what were its "limits"? It was of paramount importance for the future of the Congregation that

---
[1] Cir. Letters #77.

these fundamental issues be made clear. Nor will this seem surprising when we reflect upon the unique feature of the Association of Holy Cross in which the two Societies of Salvatorists and Josephites have been made one without the absorption of their individual character and aims. "We were all the more unenlightened," wrote Father Moreau,[2] "as to the meaning of the vote since the Sovereign Pontiff had deigned to make known to me his personal opinion, which was to approve both the priests and the brothers just as they existed and as His Holiness saw them functioning at Vigna Pia. I, therefore, resolved to beg for a decision more in conformity with the Holy Father's intention, which was unknown to the Congregation of the Propaganda."

Bishop Nanquette, Bishop Bouvier's successor, following upon his accession to the see of Le Mans, visited Our Lady of Holy Cross, examined the material and spiritual status of the Association, and promptly prepared the following favorable report:[3]

> Most Eminent and Most Reverend Seigneur:
> As the Reverend Father Moreau, Founder and Superior of the Institute of Holy Cross, is now on his way to Rome in the interests of his Congregation I take this occasion to recommend this foundation to Your Eminence. This Congregation has come into being and developed in the midst of innumerable obstacles. In spite of these it has succeeded, nevertheless, from the financial point of view in establishing itself solidly and its situation today is prosperous and flourishing.
> The Congregation, moreover, is animated by a truly religious spirit and by filial devotion to the Holy See. It has already rendered educational and missionary service and could render still more if the approval of the Holy See were to favor its development and draw to it a greater number of subjects remarkable for learning and virtue.

[2] Cir. Letters #77.
[3] Original in the Archives of the Propaganda. Certified copy, General Archives, C.S.C., dated from Rome, 1856.

Deign to accept the homage of the profound respect with which I remain the most humble and most obedient servant of Your Eminence.

James,
Bishop of Le Mans.

Thus it was with a peace-flooded soul that Basil Moreau was enabled to leave for Rome in March, 1856, after what he describes as [4] "a personal affliction whose remembrance still frightens me, and deliverance from which will cause me to be forever grateful."

This second visit of the Founder to the Eternal City was undertaken on the advice of Father Drouelle, the Procurator General at Rome, who deemed the moment auspicious for concluding the business of the Association then pending before the Sacred Congregation of the Propaganda. Father Basil desired also to visit the Italian houses of the Association, tried as well as the foundations elsewhere, by sickness.

The Founder reached Rome in time to participate in the closing ceremonies of Lent. On Palm Sunday he had the happiness of receiving the blessed palm from the hands of the Holy Father, and, in the audience which followed, Pius IX continued that manifestation of paternal graciousness which had so deeply impressed Father Moreau during his first sojourn in the Eternal City. Noticing the Holy Father's preoccupation with the question of the inclusion of the Marianite Sisters in the Institute of Holy Cross, Father Basil, with the docility born of faith, hastened to sacrifice this cherished part of his plan. In the thought of Basil Moreau, the three Societies, Priests, Brothers and Sisters, distinct yet united, were to constitute a fair image of that earthly yet heavenly reflection of the Eternal Trinity, the Holy Family. Yet before the evident hesitancy of Christ's Vicar to sanction the prudence of the plan, the Founder bowed, eager to spare the Common Father

---

[4] Cir. Letters #77.

of Christendom the least of cares. This ready docility did not pass unrewarded, for Father Moreau heard from the lips of the Pontiff these reassuring words: [5]

> You will govern them separately; I bless them too, and later you will submit their Rules to the Sacred Congregation.

Learning from Monseigneur Barnabo that the members of the Sacred Congregation had need of clearer ideas concerning the genesis and scope of his works, Father Moreau hastened to prepare a fresh exposition of the facts of the Association's origin and development. In its pages the Founder briefly but clearly and adequately treated of these points and as well answered the objections which had been raised against the unique constitution of the Association.[6]

MONSEIGNEUR:
Led here by Providence the very eve of the reunion of the Most Eminent Cardinals who deign to concern themselves with our approbation and not yet aware of the result of the Sacred Congregation's deliberations on this important matter I beg Your Excellency to permit me to submit to him the following observations:

It is probable after the interviews with which Your Excellency honored me that the opposition of Monseigneur Bouvier to our Institute, the manner in which my procurator explained things and perhaps what I may have written have combined to delay the fulfillment of our desires despite the zeal which for the last five years you have displayed for our most sacred interests; for what is more precious in our eyes than the favorable vote of the Most Eminent Cardinals to whom the cause of our approbation has been so happily entrusted?

Monseigneur, I have thought that the best way to scatter the clouds with which the enemy of all good may have enveloped this question which so greatly interests us would be to recall briefly the history of the Congregation of Holy Cross, and this I now proceed to do in as few words as possible.

[5] Cir. Letters #77.
[6] General Archives, C.S.C. Dated from St. Bridget's, Rome, April 3, 1856.

A former pastor of my diocese, priest in a country parish, a confessor of the faith and an old man grown gray in the practice of charity, named Father Dujarié, undertook to found a society of brothers who would teach and act as sacristans and organists. He was aided in this pious enterprise by a young priest who became his vicar. A third priest, moreover, who is today a member of our institute, co-operated with the venerable founder.

The brothers, although few in number, were already instructing children in the country districts and acting as organists and sacristans in several parishes when the revolution of July occurred almost annihilating the institute of Father Dujarié. The zealous founder having neither the health nor the money to continue as director of the brothers begged Bishop Bouvier to entrust the burden to me. Upon the repeated insistences of my Bishop I consented on condition that I would be left free to develop the Institute as God would inspire me.

As a result, Monseigneur, I opened a novitiate at Holy Cross of Mans for at that time there were no novices. One of the three priests, used by Providence as instruments to first found the brothers generously helped me, giving me thirty thousand francs with which to begin anew. I myself consecrated to the foundation a magnificent estate which had been given me for a pious purpose and thus the new Institute was founded on the ruins of the first.

In place, however, of the organists and sacristans I substituted brothers destined for farming for I knew there was a general need of these latter. As a result of this move I was happily in a position to respond to the desire of His Holiness Pius IX who deigned to entrust to me the foundation of Vigna Pia which I could not have accepted with the primitive organization of the brothers. Let me say, nevertheless, that in our Congregation the brothers engaged in farming and the co-adjutors in general, are much less numerous than the brothers employed as teachers, numbering only fifty out of three hundred and eighty.

I have had also the good fortune to develop the society of priests that my predecessor had vainly endeavored to found. Thanks to the assistance of generous confreres we are able at present to exercise our zeal not only in the apostolic ministry but also among youth in our colleges and in the houses of formation of our brothers who could not support their houses financially without our aid. This is due to the fact that the brothers are recruited for the most part from the families of very limited means and their schools do not contribute enough to pay the expenses of their novices.

If Monseigneur, Your Excellency were to again ask me how to establish the bond of union between the priests and brothers without absorbing the latter I would have the honor to reply that despite the diversity of employments and although there is equality between the Salvatorists and Josephites in almost all their relations (for among us there is the same end, the same means of sanctification, the same kind of clothing and lodging, food and furniture) there is nevertheless but one and the same Superior General elected by an equal number of brothers and priests, and, it is the Superior who unites one and the other authorities by the one same central authority.

I had realized another part of the project of my predecessor by founding at the same time a society of sisters but His Holiness having manifested to my procurator his repugnance to this I did not hesitate an instant to separate this branch from the tree of Holy Cross. If Father Drouelle has taken up this matter again, I am happy, Monseigneur, to have this opportunity of declaring that this has been done without my orders and that desiring above all to satisfy the least desire of our Most Holy Father I do not wish this question to be raised again by the Most Eminent Cardinals; unless I may humbly beg Their Eminences to occupy themselves with it later on and then to consider the sisters as constituting a distinct society which will have its proper rules and its own government.

Therefore, I have the honor of begging you, Monseigneur, to present to the most eminent members of the Sacred Congregation this faithful summary of facts. I have all the more confidence in the success of this new appeal to Your Eminences because it is recommended by the very favorable letter which the new Bishop of Le Mans has written on our Congregation at your request, a letter written by the good Bishop only after he had made his regular visit to our Mother House of Holy Cross.

While awaiting the definite decision of the Sacred Congregation I entrust my cause to Jesus, Mary and Joseph as well as to your zeal.

Father Moreau had terminated his report by entrusting his cause to the Holy Family and to the zeal of his constant friend, Monseigneur Barnabo,[7] Secretary of the Congregation of the Propaganda. The Holy Family, however, had not quite finished the lesson in patience intended for its ardent lover. The death of Cardinal Fransoni—the Prefect of the Propaganda and a friend of long standing to Father Moreau and his Institute—intervened; and as a result the deliberations of the Sacred Congregation were delayed for a month. The Founder took advantage of the time thus placed at his disposal to go on pilgrimage to Loretto where the Countess of Jurien desired to make a Good Shepherd foundation with religious from the Monastery of Le Mans.

As at Rome, so at the Holy House of Loretto, and afterwards at the shrines of St. Francis and St. Clare at Assisi, the warm faith of Basil Moreau flamed at contact with these scenes so redolent with sacred memories of the past. On his return to the Holy City, he wrote:[8]

> I shall not try to describe what I felt in this venerable sanctuary; but I do not wish you to be ignorant of the fact that I prayed for you all there, as well as at Assisi, before the tomb of St. Clare, on the very spot where Our Lord spoke to her from the Ostensorium, and put to flight the Saracens who were attacking the convent.

Back in Rome, fresh favors awaited the Founder of Holy Cross, presaging the one that was nearest his heart. Toward the end of April, the Holy Father doubled the property at

---

[7] Msgr. Barnabo was not elevated to the Cardinalate until June, 1856.
[8] Cir. Letters #77.

Vigna Pia, the added land including the historic chapel dedicated to St. Praxedes. This grant was followed early in May with the more important one of the spiritual administration of the Vicariate of Dacca, whose Ordinary, Bishop Oliffe, had just been promoted to the Archbishopric of Calcutta. Of this honor, which carried with it weighty obligations, Father Moreau wrote the Association:

> In spite of the terrible responsibility which was thereby laid upon us, especially upon those who devote themselves to it so courageously, I took it upon myself, being unable to consult my counselors, to present the Very Reverend Father Verité for the Mission, first as Pro-Vicar only.[9]

Moreover the hour so ardently desired had arrived at last. The information furnished the Sacred Congregation by the Founder of Holy Cross coupled with the ready approbation of Monseigneur Nanquette, the new Bishop of Le Mans, made possible the speedy and happy termination of the cause of the Association pending before the Sacred Congregation. On the nineteenth of May the last difficulties were arranged, and the Cardinals passed a laudatory vote on the Institute, the wording of the Brief emphasizing the unique feature of the twofold character of the Association and the express will of the Eminent Cardinals that this feature should be inviolably preserved. The vital clause of the Brief reads: [10]

> The most Eminent Cardinals declare worthy of praise the institute composed of priests and laics who, however, must be so united among themselves in a friendly union that while the nature of each Society is preserved, neither prevails over the other but both concur in the best possible manner to attain their proposed respective ends.

Six days later, May 25, 1856, the Vicar of Christ added his signature to the findings of the Sacred Congregation, and

[9] Cir. Letters #77.
[10] Brief given in full in the Appendix.

Father Moreau's soul entoned its Magnificat. On the twenty-sixth, he wrote from Vigna Pia: [11]

> Thanks to the God of all consolations for having brought to an end the anxieties and tribulations which plunged us so long in sadness. For, I understand, my dear Sons and Daughters in Jesus Christ, that you have had to bear a part in this painful burden, and that the uncertainty of the present as well as of the future has more than once disturbed your souls. I am aware, too, of the contradictory reports spread even outside the Congregation. Doubtless this new trial was reserved for the work of Holy Cross that it might emerge therefrom with greater strength and vigor. Let us bless, then, Divine Providence which strikes but to heal, which chastises but to purify! Blessed be the august hand, which, not satisfied with resting on my head several times and with giving me Communion Holy Thursday along with many Prelates eager to enjoy this happiness, has heaped to overflowing His favors by signing the Brief you will read. Blessed be the Princes of the Church who, by their kind votes, gave the Congregation a canonical existence, and have placed it on a solid footing. Blessed be the Bishop placed over the diocese who hastened, by his own most favorable approbation, the decision of the Sacred Congregation.

Before leaving Rome for Le Mans where a wealth of work awaited him, the happy Founder of Holy Cross hastened to assure the Cardinal Prefect of Propaganda of the actual conformity of the Institute to the insistent will of the Sacred Congregation relative to the maintenance of the distinctive character and equality of the two societies of priests and brothers. Father Basil wrote: [12]

> Besides, you do not need to fear that we will ever wish to make working brothers out of the teaching brothers, for these latter who are sufficiently instructed to teach would never consent to any such change as our experience of the past twenty years proves beyond a doubt. Finally, Your Excellency does

[11] Cir. Letters #77.
[12] Gen. Archives, C.S.C.

not need to fear at all that the priests wish to absorb the teaching brothers by opening to them the gates of the Sanctuary and by augmenting their number to the disadvantage of the Josephites, . . . our Rules and Constitutions are opposed thereto, . . . during the past twenty years, but one brother became a priest.

Now as to the bond of union between the priests and the brothers—without which the Salvatorists might be able to have the upper hand over the brothers, it appears also, Your Eminence, that what exists in the last manuscript edition of our Rules and Constitutions can actually continue to exist without fear of this eventuality.

Yet again, Your Eminence, if the bond of union does not appear to be sufficiently strong in the eyes of the Sacred Congregation, I consent to this that the Superior General have as assistants two priests and two brothers whilst preserving in accordance with the holy canons precedence to the priests in our assemblies (meetings of any kind soever) as the articles of our Rules and Constitutions demand, and as has been practiced from the beginning of the work and that without any complaint. And the above said four assistants will each defend his or their respective interests with authority in the eyes of the Superior General as has been already practiced by common agreement by the priest delegates and brother delegates in our General Chapter. In this way the two brothers and the two priests assistants will be the chief (principal) branches of a tree on which has been grafted two species of fruits and which bind all the branches to the trunk representing the Superior General.

The roots of the youthful tree of Holy Cross had been nourished by the waters of tribulation; its trunk and branches now felt the friendly warmth of the sunshine of grace which invariably accompanies the benediction of Christ's Vicar upon an apostolic work.

In 1843, Father Moreau had written:[13]

It is true that each passing year reveals to us new designs of the very special providence watching over Our Lady of Holy

[13] Cir. Letters #17.

Cross. We now see the words of the Prophet accomplished: "After the storm, O my God, Thou givest calm; after the groaning and tears, joy."

Thirteen years later experience had added many further proofs of God's providential love both for Basil Moreau and for his Institute, but to the Founder of Holy Cross no heavenly benediction could rival the approval of God's Holy Church. In the remembrance of that benediction the soul of Basil Moreau would find safe anchorage through the storms that awaited below the horizons of the future.

XIX

THE FINISHED TEMPLE—1857

> *But what purpose will the blessing of these stones, cut and arranged at such expense, serve, if we who are the living and spiritual temples dwelling therein, are not found pure and holy in the eyes of the Sovereign Majesty?*
>
> —FATHER MOREAU.

DRAB indeed must be the life that has not had its moment of power, its hour of exaltation, its own Palm Sunday. Though the Heavenly Father deems it best for the most part, to guide His children's feet along the winding valley roads where they may find their path revealed to them hour by hour beside the deep flowing waters of His Providence and His grace, at other times He directs their way—even as once that of His Only Begotten—into the desert of temptation, and again at still other times, but rarely because of the frailty of their spirits, He leads the sons of of His adoption up into the mountains and there transfigures them with joy in the fuller realization of His supernatural love. In this chapter we are to witness in Father Moreau's life, this hour of triumph, the happiest day of his life.

Arriving back safely at the Mother House early in June, 1856, Father Moreau devoted himself to the perfecting of the work which the Master had placed within his hands. His first task was to complete the Circular Letter begun at Vigna Pia.[1] No other letter of the Founder which the writer has been

[1] Cir. Letters #77, Gen. Archives, C.S.C.

privileged to read manifests as clearly as this the remarkable blending in Basil Moreau's character of intellect and heart, of nature and grace. Herein we see the man of faith, the loving father, the careful administrator, the grateful friend, and the educator fully abreast—we might well say, ahead—of his times.

From this same source [2] we know that having learned from a study of the reports he had asked from the various schools of the Congregation, "the want of anything like uniformity and plan so essential in this important matter," and despite the pressing character of the business that awaited him at Rome, Father Basil before leaving for the Holy City had found time to prepare "a treatise on Christian Pedagogy for the use of the primary grades." "But uniformity in the method of teaching is not all," he goes on to declare; "it must be found in the works placed in the hands of the children." Hence he calls for the adoption of uniform policies: in the first place "only works of authors known and sanctioned by long experience are to be adopted"; secondly, he desires "that the Josephites should edit books." The Founder of Holy Cross was not only using his own talents in fullest measure in the cause of the Master; he purposed that his spiritual sons should do likewise.

From the needs of the little ones the comprehensive vision of Father Basil turned next with discernment to the needs of the higher classes. His ideas of post graduate studies seem strangely modern for a pronouncement made in 1857, when he writes:

> But there is something lacking in our system of education which would have most pernicious effects on our teaching and which must be remedied at once. I refer to the formation of well-trained graduate professors who can give not only the ordinary instruction required in our colleges, but who can direct higher studies as well. Years ago I conceived this plan,

[2] Cir. Letters #77.

and shortly before the death of Monseigneur Carron,[3] attempted to carry it out. . . .

It was in accordance with this plan that the establishment of the House of Studies at St. Bridget's in Rome was announced by Father Basil to the Congregation at this time.

From the problems of education, the Founder turned to console his spiritual daughters for their separation from the Congregation. "You will form," he wrote, "a regular society, vowed to the education of youth, as are the brothers and priests. Continue in peace, then, the work to which you devoted yourselves with so much zeal and courage Be ever assured that your spiritual and material interests will always be dear to me."

Then, permitting his thoughts to follow the affections of his heart, to his spiritual children in foreign lands, Father Moreau pleaded for that unity in charity which was so habitual a disposition of his own soul elevated above the pettinesses of personalities:[4]

> All of you, then, my dear Sons and Daughters in Jesus Christ, whom all-consuming zeal for souls has separated from France, carefully preserve union, peace, and charity as the most precious of all gifts and the indispensable condition of all happiness in the religious life. In case of need, pardon one another and recall with the Royal Prophet: how sweet it is for brothers to live together, forming one heart and one soul. To this unity of purpose and of interests, to this concentration of efforts and of labor, are intimately joined the prosperity and the extension of our Association. Among children of the same family, what other rivalry ought to exist save that of welldoing and of order? With this confidence I call the attention of the members of the Congregation in America to the fine college at Notre Dame du Lac. I urge them to seize every opportunity of sending subjects there. By thus procuring for

[3] Mgr. Carron died August 1833.
[4] Cir. Letters #77.

them the advantage of a Catholic education they will acquire a new right to my gratitude. For there, also, the hand of God has been felt and trials have been multiplied. The blows of the angel of death have deeply pained both me and Father Sorin, the Superior of the House. With profound grief I recall the long list of those who died within the past few months in this colony. Our annals contain no such cruel calamity.

From the tribulations of the foundations overseas, the Founder turned next to those nearer home. He asked for careful economy that there might be greater means to assist the needy. Floods had devastated several departments in France in that spring, 1856, and Father Basil was preparing to extend to the sufferers the resources of the Congregation.

> Just now I most earnestly urge you to administer each of our houses with great economy, so as to tide over the new crisis caused by the floods in many departments, for the unfortunate must be aided by our alms.[5]

From the needs of the flood sufferers, the Founder turns again to the trials of his own immediate family of Holy Cross. He is happy to be back at the Mother House in the midst of his spiritual children where the absence of some of the members alone limits the completeness of his joy. "Nothing is wanting at this moment," he declares, "but the presence of those, my dear Sons and Daughters in Jesus Christ, whom devotedness and obedience keep so far from me in foreign lands. I console myself, however, with the thought that I shall soon see you again, for if God spares me another year, I shall cross the sea which separates us."

Intent as he was in the service of others, Father Moreau was too deeply grounded in the spiritual life to be unmindful of the needs of his own soul. Humbly he asked for the alms of prayer: "Obtain for me the grace of walking in the footsteps

---

[5] Cir. Letters #77.

of my holy Patron. In return, I shall remember you at God's altar and at the foot of the crucifix."

The passage of this Circular Letter which follows is especially revealing of the closeness of the soul of its author to the Heart of that Divine Master, where nothing but forgiveness awaits those who have given pain. The resentment so natural in upright hearts who have met with injury, is lost, in the case of Father Moreau, in the ocean of Divine Love wherein his heart has been unconsciously immersed. That is why he can write:[6]

> I shall call down on you God's choicest blessings. I shall pray particularly for those whose souls are most tried, for those who, after putting their hand to the plow are tempted to look backwards and to retrace their steps; for those who yielded to temptation and preferred the vain joys of the world to the sweet and holy peace of the religious life; for, in spite of their separation from us, they were our children, and perhaps faithful to the voice of the Shepherd, some of these poor sheep may return one day to the fold. I recall, not without great sorrow, the astonishing number who were full of good will when they entered the Congregation, but whose courage failed before they completed the sacrifice so well begun. May their defection be not to their eternal loss!
>
> Oh, if there be any among you whose hearts are about to give way to the temptation to abandon their vocations, let them enter into themselves and spare my eyes new tears and my heart new sadness. Let them remember the happy days when the voice of the Saviour was heard in their hearts, and when, docile to the inspirations of grace, each one answered, as did Samuel of old, "Speak, Lord, for thy servant heareth." With what courage you then broke the bonds with which the world and passion sought to retain you! With what joy you made the offering of your heart to the Divine Master! You experienced then how sweet the Lord is, and how light His yoke to those who love Him. Why, then, be troubled and discouraged, now that temptation is upon you? Why be aston-

[6] Cir. Letters #77.

ished at the inner trials you have to undergo? The love of Jesus is recognized above all in the crosses He sends His servants. He lavished His favors on you to draw you to Himself and to prepare you for the combat. His consolations were but an encouragement to more generous efforts: 'You have not yet resisted unto blood.' And should a disciple of a Master crowned with thorns fear and fly from sufferings? If you are faithful and courageous, grace will not be lacking and consolation will come in its own good time.

Before terminating this letter which is so precious a testament of his spirit Father Moreau wrote: "I reserve to myself the right to convene the General Chapter when our church will be consecrated." To appreciate the full significance of these words, it will be necessary for us to retrace our steps for a few moments to the earlier stages of Father Moreau's story.

Is it not characteristic of true love to desire to build a dwelling for the object of its affection? When the Object of the affections is God, and the lover blessed with faith in the living Presence of the Incarnate Word in the Eucharist, then the dwelling built, at least in desire, will be a church worthy of its sacred purpose. Basil Moreau had too deep a faith and was, as well, too true a lover of Our Eucharistic Lord, to escape this almost inevitable desire. Besides in his case, there had arisen the actual need for more ample accommodations for the liturgical services of the growing Community of Holy Cross. Long before he broke his silence on the subject Father Basil meditated the design. In May of 1840, during a recreation period he had voiced his sentiments, "If I had only five thousand francs I would begin."[7] The next day at dinner Father Moreau found a check for the five thousand francs neatly folded under his napkin. Father Hupier, one of the Auxiliary Priests who shared wholeheartedly the sentiments of his Superior, was the immediate source of this benefaction, yet with

[7] Vie, Bk. II, p. 250.

NOTRE DAME DE SAINTE-CROIX, LE MANS. MOTHER-CHURCH OF THE CONGREGATION OF HOLY CROSS, SOLEMNLY CONSECRATED IN 1857, SOLEMNLY RE-CONSECRATED ON NOVEMBER 9, 1937.

his usual faith and devotion Father Basil hastened to look beyond to Heaven's Gracious Queen.

At the closing exercise of the Month of Mary in the overcrowded chapel of the Delile estate, first sanctuary of Our Lord among the children of Holy Cross, Father Moreau announced publicly his intention of beginning the erection of a Church to be consecrated to Our Blessed Mother and adequate for the needs of the Community. The very next day the work of excavating the foundations was begun.

The plans of the Founder were in keeping with the fuller purposes of his heart. With neither God nor his fellow men was it possible for Basil Moreau to deal niggardly. The architectural designs for the new Our Lady of Holy Cross were furnished by Father Tournesac of Notre Dame de la Couture and were too generous and too imposing not to arouse the ready criticism of little minds. From the moment when the rich fragrance of Magdalene's costly spikenard filled the banquet chamber, the world has never lacked both souls happy to lay their wealth at the feet of Jesus, and others unhappily ready to decry a course of action whose motive must ever remain unintelligible to souls whose vision has no focus beyond self. This latter class were not slow in raising the dust clouds of insinuation and calumny in proportion as they saw rising the imposing walls of the new conventual church.

In the little publication, called "Etrennes Spiritualles," issued yearly for the edification and information of the friends and benefactors of his works, the Founder in 1844 gave the following comment on the situation thus created:[8]

> Since that time we have been able to appreciate the consequences that straightway attend the erection of a church in which, at certain times of the year and in perfect recollection of a conventual solitude, spiritual exercises will be held, like those practiced so fruitfully in Brittany, and in which, at every

[8] Vie, Bk. II, p. 244.

moment of the day, the sacred tribunal of reconciliation will open to all our brothers! How many souls secretly wish for a circumstance so favorable, to yield finally to the voice of a conscience enslaved by fear or human respect! What guarantees will they not find for that holy and so precious perseverance! We do not fear to say that our vital desire of attaining this end has been one of the most powerful motives which made us conceive, under such large proportions, the plan of the church which is going up under the skillful and active direction of Father Tournesac, to whom we have very great obligations. We have not deceived ourselves that this gigantic enterprise is beyond our forces, although our first impulse was one of fear coming from the knowledge of our weakness. However, in reflecting on the proposal before God, we asked ourselves: Is it well for you to forget that Providence can never fail prayer? We recalled then the promise of Our Lord, we considered that the work we undertook was less difficult than the removing of mountains, we put our hand to the work and we hope indeed never to repent of it, in spite of the difficulties that we have already undergone, and that we yet expect, being well convinced that if our work is of God, it will pass through the ordinary trials of divine works, that is, it will never arrive at its termination except by traversing obstacles of every kind and it will be the target of every species of contradiction, in order to reveal on a great day the thoughts of many.

Indeed, insinuations, the meanest, most unchristian and false have been occasioned by this enterprise. Persons who by their position and by charity have towards us a duty of respect and love, have not feared to advance, without any proof, that we have despoiled families, etc., etc.

Thus through the lengthening years paralleling the spiritual growth and material development of the Association there arose in the suburb of Le Mans where a kindly Providence had laid the foundations of Father Moreau's Work, the stately conventual Church of Our Lady of Holy Cross, symbolizing in enduring stone the purposes of its Founder. In his New Year's

Letter of 1857[9] to the Congregation, Father Moreau, looking forward to the happy day of the solemn consecration of the almost completed edifice, dwelt on the even more sacred consecration of the members of the Congregation whose souls were by baptism and religious profession chosen temples of the Holy Ghost. The Founder wrote:

> Let us all remember that it is written that we are the temples of God, that His Spirit dwells in us, that this temple is sacred, much more sacred than the material temple where we assemble to pray. This is true not only because we have been exorcised, anointed, washed and purified by the sacramental waters of baptism but especially because of Holy Communion. This has many times made us more sacred than the sacred vessels themselves, His Flesh and His Blood not only being contained in us, but being incorporated with our body. That is why St. Paul says that God will exterminate whosoever violates His Holy Temple (I Cor., Ch. III). What a horrible misfortune if, when the Saviour of the world will come to solemnly dedicate His church, whilst uniting in His glory all the elect of heaven, of purgatory and of the earth, one single member of the family of Holy Cross were then rejected as a worthless stone that could not be used in the edifice for which it had been destined. To escape this horrible condemnation it is necessary that we all strive to become more and more temples of the Holy Ghost purifying ourselves in the bath of penance and frequenting the Eucharistic table where God Himself is the food of our souls. Would to heaven, especially on the day of the dedication, which I announced to you, that there might not be one among you, my dear Sons and my dear Daughters in Jesus Christ, who fails to respond to this appeal, so that while the conventual church of the Mother House is being consecrated, the whole congregation will consecrate itself to the Lord.

Concisely, yet with humble joy, the Founder proceeded to reveal the detailed motivation of his labors and expenditures in the erection of the Mother Church:

[9] Gen. Archives, C.S.C.

May I be permitted here, my dear Brothers and my dear Sisters in Jesus Christ, to answer those who wish to know why I have spent so much money in the construction of this church? It is because I wished to leave to the family of Holy Cross a temple where all its members might sometimes pray together, a sanctuary which would excite the respect and nourish the piety of the students of the college, annexed to the Mother House, and which would be useful also to the surrounding population. I wished to erect a monument of our love and of our gratitude to Jesus Christ, the sole Founder of our Congregation, which for this motive has made His Sacred Heart the object of our titular feast. I wished to express my gratitude to Mary whose protection over our work has been felt always; as well as to St. Joseph who has so often shown us his powerful intercession. Besides, I have thought from the beginning that if I could build a dwelling place for God as fitting as our future resources would allow, His Providence would never leave us without shelter in the different places to which He will call us, and above all, that He will deign to admit us into the abode of His glory. Finally I do not believe we could better employ the money which I have received through the generosity of one of my Auxiliary Priests and the legacy which the Reverend Father Dubignon has given me.

Would it be possible for one who walked so wholeheartedly in the ways of trust and gratitude before God, as these lines show Father Moreau to have walked, to be left without the reward the Divine Master has promised to such pilgrims? The answer came in overflowing measure to the Founder of Holy Cross in the spring and early summer of 1857.

While Father Basil gave himself to the upbuilding of the spiritual walls of the Congregation and directed the finishing of the conventual Church, at Rome the affairs of the Congregation were being brought to a speedy and a happy termination. On April 28th, Father Drouelle, the Procurator General wired the glad tidings of the approbation of the Constitutions of the Congregation.[10] The Founder received this final benediction upon his Institute with a fervent "Quid retribuam."[11] On the twenty-ninth he hastened to thank the Vicar of Christ in a letter of jubilant gratitude which reads in part as follows:

> Words fail me, Most Holy Father, wherewith to express the feelings of my heart overflowing with gratitude. . . . How then shall I show my gratitude to the Most High God, the Only Giver of priceless gifts, as well as to Your Holiness for the many and great favors I have received, except by offering you my homage and that of the whole Congregation of the Blessed Virgin, commonly called, of Holy Cross.

Though Father Moreau at once notified the Congregation of the granting of the long-awaited decree of approbation which would be henceforth their most precious heritage, he resolved to wait for the approaching moment of the solemn consecration of the conventual Church for formal promulgation of the decree. He would thus associate forever the consecrating benediction of Almighty God upon these two works of which one was intended to symbolize in enduring stone what the other would be in the invisible—though no less real—realm of the spirit.

The seventeenth of June of this same year, 1857, witnessed the fulfillment of Father Moreau's deepest desires. Every detail of the lengthy ceremonies had been carefully prepared for in advance and God added even the natural benediction of a fair warm day. The consecrating prelate was Cardinal Donnet, Archbishop of Bordeaux, assisted by no less than nine bishops, itself an adequate vindication of Father Moreau's standing with the hierarchy of France. The Canons of the Le Mans Cathedral, priests of the diocese, members of the religious orders and a numerous host of other dignitaries both of Church and

[10] The decree was not given officially until May 13, 1857. See Appendix.
[11] His letter of acknowledgment written in Latin begins with these words.

State,[12] likewise took advantage of this occasion to manifest their esteem and cordial relations with Father Moreau and his Congregation.

The famous Dominican preacher, Father Souillard, at that time Superior of the Convent of his Order at Bordeaux, had preached an eight-day retreat in the new church as a spiritual preparation of the religious and people of Le Mans for the event. There had been a splendid response.

The ceremonies of the day commenced with the procession from the Convent of the Visitation to the church bearing the relics that were to be enshrined therein. Then followed the solemn rite of consecration both for the church and for the eight altars whereon the Holy Sacrifice was to be offered morning by morning by the priests of the Community. Cardinal Donnet performed the ceremonies at the main altar, and at the same moment, seven of the assisting bishops proceeded to the consecration of the side altars and the altar of the crypt.

The main altar was very fittingly dedicated to Our Lady of the Seven Dolors, the altar in the north transept to the Sacred Heart, that in the south transept to St. Joseph, and the remaining four, to St. Michael and the Holy Angels, St. Basil, St. Charles Borromeo, and St. Pius V, respectively. The altar in the crypt where the Founder had so lately sounded the depths of spiritual anguish, was consecrated to the Holy Cross. The officiating prelates were besides His Eminence Cardinal Donnet, Monseigneur Guibert, Archbishop of Tours; Monscigneur Nanquette of Le Mans, Monseigneur Dufetre of Nevers, Monseigneur Angebault of Angers, Monseigneur Pelerin, Vicar Apostolic of Northern Cochin-China; Monseigneur de Parc of

[12] Among the guests were Mgr. de la Halandière, former Bishop of Vincennes; Mgr. Charbonnel, Bishop of Toronto; Very Rev. Dom. Coquereau, Head Chaplain of the Navy; the Very Rev. Dom. Gueranger, Abbot of Solesmes; Baron Pron, Prefect of La Sarthe; General Pointe de Gevigny, Commandant of the Department.

Blois and Monseigneur Bara, Coadjutor Bishop of Chalons. The prelates not engaged in the consecrating of the altars, carried out the rites of blessing the crosses set within the walls, while the Community rendered the accompanying liturgical chant in its entirety.

Following the rite of consecration came the solemn Mass sung by Monseigneur Nanquette, who from the beginning of his accession to the See of Le Mans had proved a loyal friend to Father Basil and his Institute. At the Gospel, Cardinal Donnet delivered a masterful discourse. The extract given by Father Charles Moreau in his life of the Founder [13] we reproduce in part because it will furnish an insight both of the spirit of the whole discourse as well as of the character of this truly great ecclesiastic whose life so enriched the Church and France in the last century.

> Even at the present time we meet men who are full of respectful admiration for the very essence of Christianity but who condemn all that exceeds, according to their views, the strict necessity of dogma, of morals, or of cult. Why all this expense, they say, when they see monumental structures built at such sacrifices in the cities and country places? But hearts truly animated with faith feel the value of a house of God among men. The life communicated to them by the Divine Word could not remain inactive; it interprets itself by sublime conceptions. Art places itself at the service of the Church and identifies itself with it. Such were the prodigies brought forth in the olden days by the faith of our forefathers; such, my dear brethren, is what is taking place in your beautiful city.
>
> Honor, then, to you, Reverend Father, and to the skillful architect to whom are due the plans and the direction of the remarkable edifice on which we are to call down the blessings of Heaven. Hail, august consecrated altar, on which flows the Blood of the Pacifying Victim; may the Father of Mercies open the treasures of His grace to all those who enter thy sanctuary! May all the members of the Society to which thou

[13] Vie, Bk. III, Chap. XVIII, p. 92.

art more particularly destined, renew in themselves the spirit of the Institute. May they never cease to comprehend in the language of St. Caesarius, that, like the grains which have served to make the Eucharistic Bread, they can never more be distinguished, and like that drop of water which, in the same mystery, being mixed with the species of the wine, can never more be separated from it; so too the members of one Congregation according to the Heart of God should be so inseparable by the practice of their holy Rules, that neither the inconstancy of their will, nor human interest, nor death itself can ever disunite them. You will follow these counsels, prompted by our most tender affection, indefatigable missionaries, zealous and pious brothers, and good little sisters; you will live in God's House, having the same wishes and permitting no other emulation among you than that of virtue and of science. . . .

The impressive exercises of the morning were followed by a luncheon for the officiating dignitaries and invited guests, and then at 4 o'clock came the crowning events of this, Father Basil's day of days. Following the chanting of vespers, Father Souillard preached the final sermon of his eight-day course and prepared the hearts of his hearers for the dramatic moment which was to follow. As the famous Dominican finished, Father Moreau advanced to the steps of the altar and in a voice taut with emotion read the decree of approbation which placed forever the seal of Christ's Church on his labors.[14]

A brief pause succeeded and then above the bowed heads of the multitude a golden monstrance was uplifted in the hands of the Cardinal Archbishop. The Source of all true zeal, the Foundation of all spiritual building, the Founder of all truly apostolic works, was giving His own Benediction to Basil Moreau and the Congregation of Holy Cross.

Who but the Divine Master could fathom the sentiments of the Founder's soul in this moment of victory? Of this, we may rest assured, no heart thrilled with deeper gratitude or

---

[14] For text of the decree see Appendix.

bowed with profounder humility in that happy hour than the heart of Basil Moreau. Like the soul of her whom Father Basil venerated as his Mother and his Queen, God's Consecration of His Temple prompted only a Magnificat of grateful, adoring praise.

So absorbed had Father Basil been with the details of the ceremonies and the care of his illustrious guests, as well as with the tremendous significance of the day, that he had failed even to eat. The Annals of the Marianite Sisters are our authority for this naive statement:[15] "One could almost picture him as a disembodied spirit—he took no refreshment until 7 o'clock in the evening, saying even then that he was not hungry, but that if there were anything left he would take it."

Late into the evening the portals of the newly consecrated church remained open to receive the faithful of Le Mans, and when at last they had departed, and night treading softly through the June twilight had encircled the brightly illumined walls, and the great bells overhead that had waited so patiently[16] to herald this blessed day slept amid their own reverberating echoes, Father Moreau knelt alone with God. Who can doubt that in that hour the mantle of One fairer than the night encircled the soul of the humble priest while he listened to the joyous chiming of his heart?

[15] Vie, Bk. III, p. 97.
[16] These bells were three in number and had been blessed in 1842 and dedicated to the Sacred Heart, to the Immaculate Heart of Mary and to St. Joseph, respectively.

XX

AMERICA—1857

> *God, however, gave me the grace to fear nothing; and although at the moment I write these lines our steamer is rolling in a fashion that threatens to bury us in the abyss, my confidence remains unshaken.*
> —FATHER MOREAU.

THE happy conclusion of the memorable events of the spring and early summer of 1857 furnished Father Moreau the long-desired opportunity to visit his spiritual children in America. A sense of duty as well as the affection of his heart caused the Founder to undertake this arduous journey at this time. The Rule of the Congregation called for this visitation and the houses in America had been, besides, severely tried by sickness and other difficulties consequent upon new foundations so far distant from the central authority of their Institute.

After presiding at the departure ceremonies of three Salvatorists[1] who were leaving for the Bengal Mission, Father Moreau bade farewell to the Community of the Mother House on the twenty-sixth of July and hastened on his way. Two days later he embarked at Havre, on the packet-boat "Fulton" which made a passage of fourteen days to New York. From the latter city where he landed on the eleventh of August, the Founder sent the community at the Mother House an interesting record of his journey.[2] His deeply affectionate nature recalls with pleasure the evident signs of their devotion mani-

---
[1] Fathers Rinkes, Rondet and Cambows.
[2] Letter August 11, General Archives, C.S.C.

fested at his departure, their final assembly in the beautiful sanctuary of Our Lady of Holy Cross, and his last visit to the crypt where he had bowed in prayer before the image of the Holy Face, and where he trusts they will not fail to keep a light burning until his safe return. When rough weather is encountered, Father Basil with his usual self-forgetfulness thinks of the Salvatorists on their longer way to Bengal in a small sailing vessel.

As the Canadian houses were his first objective, Father Moreau left New York without delay for Montreal by train. Arriving on the evening of the twelfth, he was received with gracious hospitality by his old masters, the Sulpicians, at the Grand Seminary. The next day found him at St. Laurent among his own.

The message wired from New York had not been delivered, and, as a consequence, the joy of his reception had the added note of surprise, the brother who announced Father Moreau's presence to the sisters receiving for his charitable service the assurance he had lost his mind. With his spiritual children gathered around him in the parish church, Father Basil tasted briefly of the consolations of reunion, someday to be renewed before the heavenly throne of God.

The gladsome welcome was followed quickly by the official business of his visitation. The presence of the Founder radiated confidence, courage and fresh zeal. On the succeeding days the formal installation of superiors and officers was carried out. All the members of both communities were received in direction, daily conferences on the Rules and Constitutions given, and the special needs of the houses settled. The Founder had also at this time the happiness of presiding at the profession of three of the Marianite Sisters and at the clothing of three postulants, two of the latter, Sister Mary of St. Chantal and Sister Mary of St. Basil, being a widowed mother and her daughter.

The separation of the temporal interests of the sisters from those of the priests and brothers, which the decision of Rome rendered imperative, Father Basil was able to inaugurate among his Canadian children, without difficulty, a marked docility to his desires which were, moreover, those of Christ's Vicar, being evidenced on all sides. Leaving St. Laurent on the evening of the twenty-second of August, the Founder started for his second objective, the original American foundation, Notre Dame du Lac. He spent the next day, Sunday, with the Sulpicians at Montreal, visited several of the religious communities of this truly Catholic city, and had the privilege of a long interview with Bishop Bourget who had so valiantly espoused the cause of Holy Cross in darker hours.

The morning of the twenty-sixth found Father Moreau at Notre Dame. Father Sorin was absent at the moment, not having returned from the sisters' retreat he had conducted at Chicago.[3] The presence of the Superior General was, however, soon broadcasted, and he found himself at once the object of a demonstration of affectionate welcome similar to that accorded him in Canada. While the bells[4] overhead joined their voices to the welcome, Father Basil entered the church, entoned the Te Deum, and offered a Mass of Thanksgiving. What deep emotions must have stirred the Founder's soul on that August morning, as he lifted the White Host for the first time amid the beauties in which Nature had enshrined the first enduring sanctuary of Holy Cross in the New World! Surely the Founder's sentiments were those of profoundest gratitude; and from the Chalice-lips came, too, I am sure, to the humble French priest, strength and courage for the labors and the burdens of the day.

The next morning witnessed a scene equally impressive.

[3] Father Sorin had sent Father Granger to meet Father Moreau at Detroit, where the latter's arrival was expected only on the following day.
[4] A carillon of twenty-five bells cast by Bolle of Le Mans.

NOTRE DAME DU LAC, INDIANA. FIRST SHRINE OF HOLY CROSS IN THE NEW WORLD. HOME OF NOTRE DAME UNIVERSITY AND ADMINISTRATIVE CENTER OF THE CONGREGATION.

Father Sorin had now arrived and attended his Superior at St. Mary's, where the sisters were waiting with their pupils. Always responsive to the touch of affection, tears glistened in Basil Moreau's eyes as the reception terminated with the chanting of the Magnificat.

The formalities of his reception over, Father Moreau threw himself into the serious work of his visitation. During an entire week he gave three conferences a day to the religious at Notre Dame, besides arranging the affairs of administration, the installation of the provincial officers, and caring for the spiritual direction of the members of the Community.

In his Letter to the Congregation written during the return voyage to France,[5] the Superior General wrote:

> There again, how often I had occasion to thank Our Lord for the spirit of faith, the child-like simplicity and the admirable docility with which all opened their hearts to me and listened to my counsels.

The truth, however, is only partly told in these lines, Father Moreau was forced to add:

> However the enemy of good was not sleeping, and I felt an invisible force which resisted me. . . .

The visitation of the sisters which followed served to deepen this latter impression on the part of Father Moreau. The grace of God, however, was dominating souls under the inspiration of the Founder's presence. With the rare ability of recognizing the difficulties under which others have labored and the ready tact born of his selflessness and humility, Father Moreau was able to accomplish a world of good. Mother Elizabeth of St. Mary's [6] recorded in her diary that the visitation inaugurated "days of deep reformation in which the community life had

[5] Dated from Havre, October 3, 1857. Gen. Archives, C.S.C.
[6] Quoted by Sister Eleanore, On the King's Highway, p. 216.

a new beginning," and Father Moreau, himself, has left us a pertinent description of these days.[7]

> There [at St. Mary's] as at Notre Dame, and in the other houses of the Vicariate, what cruel trials, what sufferings physical and spiritual! Nor did this astonish me, when I considered the astounding work accomplished by the zeal and the devotion of our religious in the midst of these ancient woods.

Each morning the indefatigable Father Basil crossed over through the groves to St. Mary's, gave the Sisters' meditation, celebrated his Mass, and spent the rest of the day hearing directions and organizing the provincial offices. Returning in the evening to Notre Dame, the Founder would give a conference to the community or to the pupils, who were now beginning to return from their vacations, and then late into the night adjust with the Provincial Council the various problems of administration.

From New Orleans he had summoned Father Shiel and Mother Mary of the Passion, the Superiors, and with them Father Moreau arranged as best he could the business of their sorely tried houses. Much as he would have loved to carry to his spiritual children in the South the message of faith and zeal his very presence imparted, the Founder could not delay. Already affairs in France were demanding his return.

Accompanied by Father Sorin, on September 12th, the Superior General made a hurried but for him consoling visitation of the Chicago communities, returning after midnight of the following day, a Sunday. The fourteenth was devoted to the problems of the novitiates, and early Tuesday morning, the fifteenth, Feast of Our Lady's Dolors, having celebrated Mass and blessed the assembled religious of both communities, the Founder of Holy Cross bade farewell to his spiritual children, many of whom he would not see again till they should meet beyond the skies.

[7] Cir. Letter, dated from Havre, October 1857.

Father Sorin accompanied the Superior General on his eastward journey. Thursday evening the travelers reached their destination, the Convent of the Sisters of Holy Cross in Philadelphia. The time at his disposal was all too short for rest. Here is the program Father Moreau faced and carried through. He began by giving an opening conference on Religious Obedience [8] before partaking of supper. After supper he heard the religious in directions until 2 A.M.[9] He followed this by giving the Meditation at 5 A.M., received the remaining religious in direction and then gave another conference at eleven. In the afternoon he presided at the ceremony of clothing and at the profession of six novices and preached again. There followed a visit to Monseigneur Neuman, C.Ss.R., the venerable Bishop of the city. After supper he delivered a last sermon to the Religious, in which he dwelt on the trials and the consoling fruits of his visitation. At 1 o'clock the next morning, Father Moreau bade farewell to Father Sorin at the Philadelphia station, the latter being unable by reason of extreme fatigue to complete the gracious courtesy of accompanying his Superior to New York for the embarkment.

The next morning at five, Father Basil and a brother who was to return with him were back in New York. Six hours later they were on board the packet-boat, "Arago," homeward bound for France.

Out on the stormy Atlantic the soul of Basil Moreau was at peace. Always ready of appreciation, he forgets no kindness that he has received. The proprietor of the Hotel Astoria though not a Catholic had insisted on giving hospitality without remuneration. Father Basil prays his reward may be the grace of faith. The recollection of the eager, friendly faces he will never see again stirs him with paternal emotion, but what

---

[8] Father Sorin acted as interpreter at these discourses.
[9] The Sisters who could not speak French received direction through an interpreter of their own choosing.

costs him most, he tells us, is to part from Father Sorin, my "dear confrere who had not ceased to surround me with the fullest attentions of charity, although his exhaustion prevented his accompanying me on the return trip to New York."[10] The Superior General and his spiritual son, the patriarchal pioneer of Holy Cross in America, had embraced as they parted in Philadelphia "with a devotion," Father Moreau declared, "like that of Jonathan and David."

Rough weather awaited the valiant little "Arago" off the Grand Banks, but the Superior General of Holy Cross, traveling in the poorest of accommodations by reason of his poverty, was yet rich in confidence and faith. The wild seas but roused the deeper emotions of his heart while he sang:

> Toward thee, I sail, O everlasting city!
> Whilst advancing I redouble my effort;
> But for my heart my bark is too slow;
> May a stronger wind finally waft me to port.[11]

Stronger winds were indeed awaiting the courageous bark of Basil Moreau's soul.

[10] Cir. Letter, October, 1857.
[11] Cir. Letter, October 1857.

XXI
FATHER MOREAU'S TESTAMENT—1858

> *I have nought to do now, my dear Confreres and my dear Brothers, but to raise my eyes and hands to the Sovereign Legislator, to beg Him to accept these Rules, and to bless these Constitutions edited for His glory, and to conjure you to practice them in letter and in spirit with ardent zeal.*
>
> —FATHER MOREAU.

THE immediate task of greatest import that awaited Father Moreau upon his return from America was the publishing of the Constitutions approved by Rome,[1] together with the revision of the Rule, the first draft of which he had drawn up in 1838. This work the Founder recognized to be of utmost importance for the present and future stability of his Congregation and consequently to its accomplishment he gave the fullest measure of his time and energies. By mid-April, 1858, the work was completed and he was able to announce the new edition to the priests and brothers in the following Circular Letter:[2]

Our Lady of Holy Cross
April 13, 1858.

MY DEAR CONFRERES AND MY DEAR BROTHERS:

May the grace of Our Lord and the blessing of His Mother conceived without sin, with the protection of St. Joseph be ever with you.

---
[1] May 13, 1857, vide Appendix.
[2] Cir. Letter, April 13, 1858, Gen. Archives, C.S.C.

Finally, I put into your hands the Constitutions so long anticipated, but which circumstances not depending on my will have prevented me from sending you sooner. I have added an index together with the Rules which are but a development and an application of the Constitutions. It is sufficient to say that I have been obliged to make a new edition of the Rules, not only because the last was exhausted, but also because the Constitutions which the Holy See deigned to approve at the same time that it approved our Congregation, exacted this revision. Setting to work immediately after my return from America, I have never ceased to consecrate my every moment to this task.

You would have had the results of my labors in your hands sooner, had I not feared to compromise its success by a too great precipitation, and had I not wished, before I finished the work, to gather from the experience of the past the lights and teachings it furnished me. Here I feel the need to justify all the modifications and diverse changes made in the Rules from the first draft of 1838, even to this last revision, for I am well aware that you were often astonished and murmured; however, what was more simple and more natural? If I could have foreseen the development of our Institute from its origin, I would then have been able to regulate and to co-ordinate everything in advance; but were that so, Holy Cross would have been a human work and not that of Divine Providence; whereas it began and developed in a manner so mysterious that I take to myself neither the glory of its inception nor of its merit. In this is the certain proof that God alone is the Author of this work, since, according to St. Augustine, "When we cannot find the cause of a good work, we must recognize the Lord as its beginning and author."

Taking this for granted, I had either to take the providential plan of modifying our Rules as light came, or await, as St. Vincent de Paul did, to give them to you in the decline of my days. But by adopting this latter plan I would leave without Rules and without direction all the scattered members of the family of Holy Cross. I would refuse to establish uniformity in the administration of all the houses of the Congregation; and I would have to fear being surprised by death before having put the finishing touches to this most important part of my work. I would add further that whilst editing these Rules as the need was felt, and whilst thus putting them into your hands, you were already quite prepared to receive them and to practice the new changes the future would necessitate, because principles never change.

In sending you these Rules, my dear Confreres and my dear Brothers, I regret my inability to give them a stronger mark of authority—their sanction by the General Chapter—but I am convinced that the General Chapter will accept them with gratitude, whilst, at the same time, reserving to itself the power of making such changes and additions as the Spirit of God will inspire. To secure the approbation of the General Chapter, moreover, I would be obliged to defer the publication of these Rules to its next sitting, a time too remote, since the Chapter will not be held until 1860. Then too I fear I may not then have the free use of my sight which is very weak. I am convinced that it was necessary to complete this revision, not only because the last edition was exhausted, but also because on the occasion of my visit to Canada and the United States the request was repeatedly made that the Rules be translated into English and German for the postulants and novices who speak only these languages. Finally, how could I defer longer this undertaking without delaying receptions of the Habit and Professions, and having done so, must I not put this new edition in accord with the Constitutions? These reasons especially caused me to re-edit the Rules with the changes necessitated by the canonical approbation of our Congregation. To make this edition more exact, I believed I should submit it to the approval of M. l'Abbé Lottin and afterward ask for the imprimatur of our Bishop, always so devoted and so well-disposed toward us. This imprimatur, besides, is exacted by Canon Law.

Notwithstanding the care I have taken in this revision, I am far from presenting it to you as perfect. Our Rules will always remain liable to new changes as experience will show this to be useful. I have reserved to myself, then, the right to give at our annual retreats, and especially at the General Chapter, my interpretation, and I shall willingly accept any changes which are recognized as useful or necessary; but such as it is, my dear Confreres and my dear Brothers, I offer it to you from the heart of a father and a friend with the confidence that you will receive it with your usual docility, and that it will be the source of the blessing of God on each member in his work.

I have nought to do now, my dear Confreres and my dear Brothers, but to raise my eyes and hands to the Sovereign Legislator, to beg Him to accept these Rules, and to bless these Constitutions edited for His glory, and to conjure you to practice them in letter and in spirit with ardent zeal, with the fervor of a lively faith and tender piety. The Constitutions will appear worthy of your entire veneration if you but consider their holy source and the august authority which has sanctioned them; the Rules, although their author is but a simple priest, will also be the object of your fidelity and respect if you will but consider that they are the result of long experience, of the substance of the evangelical counsels, of the writings of the great masters of the spiritual life, and of principles of conduct handed down by the holiest Founders to their disciples. You will respect, then, both the Constitutions and the Rules, but in different degrees: you will look upon them as the sole rule of your duties; you will speak of them with the honor and reverence that is their due. You will take this book of the Constitutions and Rules, and read and reread it unceasingly; you will be spiritually nourished by studying and meditating on it; you will devour it as the Angel of the Apocalypse recommended the Beloved Disciple to do when there was question of another book; and if at first you feel some bitterness, afterward you will find in it a taste like unto that of honey.

We have given this letter of Father Moreau at some length because of the light it throws upon his own character, at once ardent yet ready to take counsel, decisive yet eager to profit by the lessions of experience, and withal a man "subject to authority" because a man who lived continuously in the atmosphere of faith. It must be ever so with God's true servants, and more especially so with those whom He has chosen for the inauguration of apostolic works. In them we find an abiding sense of the necessity of authority, ever a sensitive docility to the guidance of Divine Providence, ever a consciousness of that seeming paradox of their own littleness and yet the greatness of the work committed to their care.

The Rules Father Moreau now furnished in revised form to his spiritual children were the fruit of more than twenty years of prayer and apostolic labor. They constituted his most authentic gift to his sons, for in their pages his spirit still lives and has power to breathe into the hearts of successive spiritual generations that flame of divine charity that burned so warmly within their author's breast—"His last will and testament" as they have been aptly termed.[3] In them we find the spirit of the Gospel translated without fear or diminution and made specifically operative under the conditions of modern religious life.

To emphasize this spirit of the Gospel, which he wished before all else to be the very soul of his foundations, Father Moreau headed in his final revision[4] each of the forty-six chapters of the Common Rules with a quotation from the New Testament, and then proceeded to the solution of some particular point of religious life in the light of the Gospel teaching. To be appreciated in their full beauty of apostolic terseness and simplicity, the Rules Basil Moreau bequeathed his spiritual children must be read in full. Since, however, this is beside the scope of the present work we must content ourselves with a few quotations which will serve to illustrate, in some degree, the character of all.

Rule I—The End of the Congregation.

(5) Since the end of the Congregation is the perfection of its members and the sanctification of others by the

[3] Letter of Very Reverend Father General, Rules Edition of 1934.
[4] Edition of 1864: These four headings are from the Old Testament, vide Rules C.S.C.

ecclesiastical ministry and the education of youth, the members should endeavor above all things to acquire the virtues of their vocation, and then to secure the salvation of souls, after the example of Jesus Christ, who began by practicing what He taught others. Both clerics and brothers shall, therefore, labor to become living copies of the Divine Model and so render their work more efficacious.

Rule VII—Mass, Communion, and Devotion to the Blessed Sacrament.

(70) Night and day Jesus Christ dwells in the tabernacle to receive and hearken to those who visit Him, to listen to their petitions and to pour down on them all kinds of graces. It shall, therefore, be for the religious a duty as well as a pleasure to respond to His love. The members shall make a visit to Him each day, usually after the noon recreation, and preferably in common, at the time designated by the Superior. No one is to miss the hour of weekly adoration, assigned to each member in every house of the Congregation.

Rule IX—Humility.

(81) The members of the Congregation are not to envy other religious institutes which have greater resources, more subjects, and greater reputation, credit, and success than Holy Cross but shall bless God for it, since He is glorified by it—regarding themselves unworthy to be compared to them.

Rule X—The Spirit of Faith.

(85) The religious who has the spirit of faith acts in all things according to the maxims and example of our Saviour, so that the remembrance of God animates all his thoughts, affections, words, and actions. This is what is meant by the expression "to live by faith."

Rule XI—Charity.

(90) Even more, as Our Lord has recommended to His disciples, we should return good for evil. If the Congre-

gation, or any of its houses, or any of its members become the object of calumny or persecution, we should, instead of taking revenge or even complaining, pray for the wrongdoers and seize every occasion to oblige them.

Rule XII—Meekness.

(92) Meekness, the flower of charity and the fruit of humility, fills the soul with tenderness, indulgence, and pity, and gives to the whole exterior a simple natural grace, accompanied by a cordiality which inspires affection and confidence.

Rule XIII—The Spirit of Union and Community Spirit.

(97) The spirit of the Congregation should be the spirit of Jesus Christ Himself, and all of its members should be united as were the disciples of Christ, for whom He so earnestly asked of the Father that union when He sent them to preach two by two, that they might preserve unity of thought, sentiment, and action.

Rule XIV—Zeal.

(107) If we really live by faith, we cannot think of the outrage done to the Divine Majesty by mortal sin and of the misfortune of those who are guilty of it, without mourning, praying, and doing penance. We shall be ready to undertake everything to teach the eternal truths to others, to form their hearts to virtue, to do our part towards maintaining order and the Rules or repressing disorders. We shall be disposed to suffer all things and to go wherever obedience sends us, to save souls that are perishing and to spread the reign of Christ upon earth.

Rule XV—Mortification.

(111) Beside Christian abnegation, which consists in avoiding everything forbidden by God or by the Church, there is another kind, which consists in the practice of the evangelical counsels, and this, above all, constitutes religious mortification.

(112) Accordingly, the members of the Congregation shall endeavor to deny themselves in everything they can do without, to deprive themselves of permitted pleasures not authorized by the Rules, and to restrain their natural inclinations by bringing under subjection all their senses and propensities, repressing even the least outbursts of their natural disposition.

Rule XVI—Modesty.

(115) There is no doubt that the modesty of our Lord Jesus Christ charmed those who had the happiness to see Him. The thousands who hastened even to desert places to enjoy His presence were drawn not only by His words but also by the sight of His countenance and His whole demeanor.

Rule XVII—Recreation and Conversation.

(140) Jesus Christ has willed to give Himself as a model in all the circumstances of life, and so in conversing as well as in keeping silence, the members of the Congregation are to imitate Him in their recreations and conversations.

Father Moreau was dominated in the framing of these Rules by the underlying motives that had directed the course of his own life and to which we made reference at the beginning of this work. To his faith-guided mind the purpose of the Rule was before all else to fashion the souls of his spiritual children in the unique mold of Christ. In that mold of Christ he himself had been formed first in its profound effectiveness in the bosom of a Christian Mother, then by its subtle action in a truly Christian home, later by the precious years of Catholic education in college and seminary; always from the cradle of the baptismal font to the cradle of the Last Sacraments by the mysterious yet not less real influence of God's most holy grace.[5]

[5] The author has been able to find no evidence of deliberate moral aberration in the entire life of Basil Moreau.

Thus in his Rule, illustrated so perfectly in his own life, Basil Moreau has left to his spiritual family in successive generations a testament of abiding validity and inspiration. Therein may be measured the true height of his spirituality and the true depth of his character.[6]

[6] The Rule, as presented by Father Moreau to the Congregation in 1858, was approved with but minor changes at the General Chapter in 1863. The Revisions of 1872 and 1932 have likewise effected but few changes and none in matters affecting its spirit which remains that which Father Moreau imparted to it. Vide Introductory Letter of Very Reverend Father General, Rules Edition of 1934.

XXII

RAIN AND SUNSHINE—1858-1861

> *But I fondly hope that grace will make up for the bitterness of so many sacrifices and that you will end by rejoicing with me that the Divine Master has found us worthy to drink of the chalice of His humiliation and of His suffering.*
>
> —FATHER MOREAU.

FRUITION upon earth is, by the mysterious designs of God, the result neither of endless sunshine nor of unceasing rain but of that succession of these elements in that dictation of the Divine Wisdom which we are accustomed to term the ordinary course of Nature. If this be true in the material fruitfulness of the earth, it is no less verified in the harvestings of the spirit; in the order of grace, no less than in that of nature, abundant fruition demands plentiful rains as well as sunshine, and the fields of the soul must be not only seeded by grace but furrowed by crosses and well watered with tears if the harvest is to be golden.

The years that followed the return of Father Moreau from America were well supplied with both these essential elements. The hidden designs of God called for the perfecting of the Congregation of Holy Cross and of the soul of its Founder. During these months, then, we shall see the Master busy about His Father's business, assuring the future harvest He desired to reap from the life and labor of His servant.

The closing days of 1858 brought to Father Moreau the consolation of seeing the little Breton Community of Our Lady of Hope seeking affiliation with that of Holy Cross. The former Community had been organized in 1843 by Father Le Pailleur, the Founder of the Little Sisters of the Poor, for the work of diocesan missions in Brittany. Father Le Pailleur's work for his spiritual daughters having required his presence at Rennes, his priest-missioners whom he had established in the diocese of Meaux were thus necessarily deprived of the inspiration of their Founder, and had struggled on precariously until the date of their union with the stronger and already approved Congregation of Holy Cross. In this uniting of a Community dedicated to Our Lady of Hope with one consecrated to the Holy Cross, may we not see a symbolism of a fundamental Christian truth which fitly finds expression in the motto of the latter Congregation—Ave Crux, Spes Unica!

Among the trials of this period two in particular are worthy of detailed study because of the insight they offer of the character of Father Moreau. The first of these trials is the Dubignon will case; the second, the financial debacle arising out of the unfortunate administration of temporalities at the College of Ternes. We shall study the latter first.

On the eve of sailing for America, July 28, 1857, Father Moreau had been at Paris visiting the community of Ternes. Before he left he was persuaded to sanction the ambitious designs of some of his spiritual sons for the upbuilding of the College. Always anxious to yield except where principle was at stake,[1] the Founder of Holy Cross thus consented to the undertaking of a program that would—even with careful management—tax heavily the financial resources of the central administration. To the initial investment of 80,000 francs, Father Moreau now added to satisfy the importunities of his spiritual sons, a further investment of 100,000 francs for the purchase of land and buildings.

[1] "They knew," wrote Father Charles Moreau, "that the good Superior General apart from his Council, could refuse nothing except when his conscience obliged him strictly to do so." Vie, Bk. IV, p. 114.

The sacrifices thus generously underwritten by Basil Moreau failed to awaken a like spirit in the administration of the Paris house, and in September, 1859, the Founder sought to safeguard the material interest of the Congregation by sending to Ternes as Assistant Superior and Procurator, a trusted brother who was as well one of the Assistant Generals of the Congregation. At Le Mans, this religious had functioned in a similar capacity with marked ability and religious exactitude. His selection, therefore, as procurator for Ternes was logical but proved unfortunate in the extreme.

The Superior of the Ternes Community granted his new assistant unwarranted liberties both in the administration of the temporalities and as to personal conduct. The spirit of evil was not slow in taking advantage of the novel situation.

In this new environment the religious who had functioned so successfully under the regular discipline and prudent supervision of the Mother House, soon found himself launched upon a most compromising career. A swindler posing as a Count with a government contract, in the profits of which the community of Holy Cross was to share, induced the hapless econome to sign for him or others note after note heavily obligating the College. The process of mulcting the house went on apace with the poor brother becoming each day more hopelessly involved. Possibly the culminating point in the whole fabrication was the establishment of a fictitious "Bank of the Good Samaritan" for the relief of supposedly impoverished individuals with the multiplying notes of the tricked econome as the source of the funds. Though the nature of this latter deception bears witness to the natural good intentions of the Brother the result was inevitable.

Studying in retrospect the details of the case it is not difficult to trace the probable course of this compromising development in the material affairs of the Congregation. Caught in the mesh of his own folly, cleverly manipulated by his victimizers, the Ternes econome stumbled on. Deprived of the protection which the supervision of his superior would and should have given him, his final ruin was assured. One finishes the full story with mingled feelings of amazement and pity; amazement at the attitude of the brother's immediate Superior in the face of these developments, pity for the luckless religious who lost his own vocation and seriously compromised his Community by his failure to observe the safeguards with which Basil Moreau had surrounded both the spiritual and the temporal interests of his subjects.

The failure of the Ternes administration to make the regular financial reports required by the Rules of the Congregation had forced Father Moreau to ask for an explanation at the time of the General Chapter, in August of 1860. The best he could then secure was the promise that the steward at Ternes would make known his transactions to his immediate Superior. The Chapter ended, the weeks slipped by, finally in the following January, 1861, the Superior of Ternes informed Father Basil he could secure no information from the econome on the administration of the latter's office. It was from other members of the Paris house that the Founder was obliged to gather details of the irregular transactions of the hapless religious.

The report which Father Moreau made to the Provincial Chapter of France in 1861, sums up succinctly the manner in which he had responded to this new and crushing trial. He writes:[2]

> At the request of the Vicar-General of Paris and of his Grace, the Bishop of Le Mans, I went to Paris, and after having listened in silence to the contradictory advice of the civil council assembled at the College and the ecclesiastical council in session with the Archbishop, after having passed the night

[2] Vie, Bk. IV, p. 173.

in deliberation and heard for a last time the unhappy brother, not without misgivings I decided to treat at once with those of the creditors who were already prosecuting me, then with the others, and I engaged myself by note to pay the tradesmen of the College who should bring me their unsettled accounts. My concern was the greater becaue I was at the time unaware of the total indebtedness and during several weeks I went through a veritable agony.

When at last the Founder had before him all the debts contracted by this scandalous administration, he found himself faced by engagements totaling some 200,000 francs. In keeping with the spirit that had permitted, at least by omission, this sad abuse of office, the administration of the Paris house now looked to Father Moreau for the assumption and liquidation of these obligations.

Heavy as these debts undoubtedly were, they were not sufficient in themselves to shake the financial stability of Holy Cross, and consequently it would be wrong to seek in them the real cause of the embarrassment of Father Moreau's administration.[3] The occasion of his ultimate defeat they certainly became, but the cause was more crucifying to him in that not one religious but a small clique of priests and brothers were ultimately responsible for his final downfall. Where Father Moreau had a right to find support, he was to find only opposition; in place of assistance, these religious would give him but additional cares. Bravely the Founder bent his energies to this new burden. On the third of May, 1861, he addressed to the Congregation a circular letter from which we quote at length:[4]

MY DEAR FATHERS AND BROTHERS:
As some members of the Congregation were surprised at my consenting, with my Council, to take over the crushing debt

[3] Vide Cir. Letter of June 11, 1861. Gen. Archives, C.S.C., and others of this period.
[4] Gen. Archives, C.S.C.

contracted by ex-Brother ——, I hereby inform them that unless I did so, I should have exposed the Congregation to utter ruin by scandalous and unsuccessful lawsuits. Let those who still doubt my words read the following passages from a letter just received:

"At a time when, in the mind of all the government officials it seemed impossible to condemn us without doing violence to justice, the President of one of the courts received us couched on his ottoman, with his feet in the air and a cigar in his mouth. At our first reply he shouted back: 'Peter's Pence is at the bottom of it all,' and without further ado he ordered the continuation of proceedings against us, and that without any warrant. It was ex-Brother —— alone who had been summoned and condemned by default, so that by this judicial farce, the magistrate transferred to us a charge of which another was guilty. As a result of this decision the College of Ternes was liable to be seized and we were forced to pay 7,000 francs to a rogue who perhaps had not given 1,500 francs to the unfortunate brother."

You see, then, Reverend Fathers and dear Brothers, to what I would have exposed you had I consented to appear before the courts in place of the steward and the Superior of our College at Paris. I will go no further into the matter just now, as I intend to give a report on this frightful tragedy to the General Capitulants and to exonerate my administration so cruelly wronged by those who forget our Constitutions and Rules on Accounts.

Besides this heavy trial, it has pleased Providence not to take away as yet the cross which has so long rested on my shoulders.

The trial which Father Moreau here refers to concerned a lawsuit arising from the contesting of a will made by Miss Dubignon, sister of one of the Founder's most faithful friends. Though no less than three judicial decisions had been rendered in Father Moreau's favor, a further appeal to the court at Angers brought an adverse decision. The result had been anticipated by reason of the known anticlerical bias of the chief officer of this tribunal, yet the loss was the more keenly felt because of the financial obligations weighing upon Father Moreau at this precise moment. Nevertheless the sentiments with which he responded to this great disappointment prove that his soul was securely founded in the practice of abandonment.

If humility is the cradle of sanctity then surely holy abandonment is its ultimate goal, fusing the will of the creature with the adorable Will of God. The harassed Superior who penned the following letter to his spiritual family was surely nearing this goal:[5]

> Our Lady of Holy Cross,
> June 7, 1861.
>
> REVEREND FATHERS AND DEAR BROTHERS:
> May the grace of God and the blessing of His Mother conceived without sin, with the protection of St. Joseph, be ever with you!
> At last I know the will of God in the decision appealed from the court at Angers and while it is repugnant to nature I adore it, I bless it and I conjure you not to be saddened by this new trial which while depriving me of money which I had in no way asked for detaches me from earthly things and gives us all an opportunity of suffering for the love of Jesus Christ. My conscience, moreover, bears me witness that I have done my duty by my testrix, and although I have been urged to take the matter before a higher court I refuse to do so. I willingly make the sacrifice imposed upon me by the rejection of my suit by the Court of Cassation, against the judgment of the Chambre des Requêtes.
> Doubtless it would have been a pleasure for me to be able to offer to the Congregation property whose value surpassed the debt loaded upon us so unjustly some months ago. This should have put an end to all our anxieties concerning the finances of our Congregation: but God was pleased to deprive us of this consolation in order to arouse in us greater confidence

---

[5] Cir. Letter of June 7, 1861, Gen. Arch., C.S.C.

in Himself and to oblige us to abandon ourselves to His Providence in this matter as well as in eternal concerns.

May this temporal loss, therefore, procure for us a greater detachment from the world, a fuller renunciation of ourselves, and a more absolute abandonment to the designs of Heaven on our Congregation. O, if it pleased God to establish us in these holy dispositions how advantageous to us the loss of Chatelier would be. Then in very truth the old adage "Losers win" would be verified in our case.

Let us live in such thoughts, dear Fathers and Brothers. Let us enter into these sentiments, and far from permitting our confidence in God to be shaken by these happenings which run counter to man's views, let us put in practice the words which fell from the mouth of Him Who, although Lord of the Universe, had not whereon to lay His head:[6] "Seek ye therefore first the kingdom of God, and His justice, and all things shall be added unto you. Be not solicitous for your life, what you shall eat, nor for your body, what you shall put on. Behold the birds of the air, for they neither sew, nor do they reap and gather into barns; and our heavenly Father feedeth them. Are not you of much more value than they? And which of you by taking thought, can add to his stature one cubit? And for raiment, why are you solicitous? . . . Consider the lilies of the fields, how they grow: they labor not, neither do they spin. But I say to you, that not even Solomon in all his glory was arrayed as one of these. And if the grass of the field which is today, and tomorrow is cast into the oven, God doth so clothe: how much more you, O ye of little faith? Be not solicitous, therefore, saying, what shall we eat: or what shall we drink, or wherewith shall we be clothed? For after all these things do the heathens seek. For your Father knoweth that you have need of all these things."

I would not, however, Reverend Fathers and dear Brothers, have you believe that the Lord herein forbids foresight and human industry, for, as a matter of fact, He bids us be laborious, orderly, economical in the use of things earthly, but He forbids all anxiety as hurtful to His paternal providence. In a word, be not solicitous for the life that is, and have greater care for

[6] Matthew VI.

the life that is to be. This is what our Lord would have us do—contrary to what the world does. I ask of Jesus Christ through His holy Mother to give us all the grace to understand and to practice this important truth while always observing our Constitutions and Rules in the temporal administration confided to us.

And there is another fruit which we must gather from the decision which deprives me of an inheritance I did not seek. It is this: never to go to law, however just our case may be, unless we are obliged to do so, as I was in the case just settled, since a Prince of the Church and two bishops told me I could not but plead in court my right to the Dubignon legacy, "without doing violence to my conscience, betraying the piety of Miss Dubignon, and playing the coward." If such were not the case I would have no more gone to law in the case of Miss Dubignon's will than I did when her brother made me his universal heir.

In this latter case, of my own accord, though some of my enemies declared the contrary, I shared the 70,000 francs willed to me with the party threatening a lawsuit. It was in connection with this same decision that I abstained from all business transactions after the decision given in my favor at Laval even though I was warned that I would certainly lose at Angers. I congratulate myself today, because I prefer to lose everything rather than oppose the formal will of one who had so solemnly declared "that she excluded from her will" the very one who nevertheless inherits everything. How easily we can be deceived when putting our trust in the judgment of men.

It is an added reason for observing our Lord's counsel: "And if a man will contend with thee in judgment, and take away thy coat, let go thy cloak also to him." (Matt. V., 40.) May Heaven grant us such dispositions; for then Divine Providence will shower us with new blessings and if we are deprived of what is ours, God's goodness will find a way to inspire those blessed with His temporal gifts to come to our aid.

But to assure ourselves of this bounty, we must please God by an exemplary fidelity to our Rules, by a perfect fulfillment of our Vows, by exactness in our exercises of piety, by a spirit of faith, of mortification and of devotedness in all our conduct.

If we enter into the spirit of what I have just said and if each of you aids me as best he can, either by paying up what he still owes to the Mother House, or by advancing money, or by borrowing from individuals small sums payable in six months or a year, the storm the devil has let loose against the work of Holy Cross with such fury, especially since the last session of the General Chapter, will serve but to consolidate it and to sanctify each of us.

The sentiments thus expressed must certainly serve to strengthen the impression of Father Moreau as a priest dominated by grace and guided by the spirit of the gospel. In some lives the truths of Faith seem to exercise a vitalizing activity of peculiar intensity. These are the souls that may be truly said to live by Faith; and from their ranks come the great servants of God and His Holy Church.

We should remember, moreover, that while God's holy ones live by Faith, this very fact casts a wealth of supernatural light and warmth across their pathways. God's grace is the sunshine of the world of the spirit, and though at times clouds seem to wrap this world in impenetrable darkness yet those who live therein are sustained by grace, and are ordinarily conscious of the ceaseless activity of God within their very souls.

Living by Faith, Father Moreau had, it is true, much to suffer for His Divine Master—much more indeed than we can here speak of—but Father Moreau had as well some very deep consolations, some rare days of spiritual sunshine. It is of one of these consolations we shall now treat.

On the twenty-fifth of November, 1860, Father Dufal, Vicar Apostolic of eastern Bengal and a member of the Congregation, received episcopal consecration in the conventual church of Our Lady of Holy Cross at Le Mans. Archbishop Guibert of Tours was the consecrating prelate, and he was assisted by Bishop Nanquette of Le Mans and Monseigneur de la Hailandière, former Bishop of Vincennes. Bishop Dufal thus became the first of the sons of Holy Cross to be raised to the episcopal dignity. To one as sensitive to the activity of Divine Providence as Father Moreau such an occasion could not fail to elicit overflowing joy and gratitude. On the first of December, 1860, the Founder gave expression to his feelings in a letter to the Congregation from which we quote:[7]

> My dear Sons in Jesus Christ:
> Hardly had the Archbishop of Tours[8] assisted by Monseigneur de la Hailandière and the Bishop of Le Mans, finished the ceremony of the consecration of our Vicar Apostolic, Father Dufal, than I felt the need of thanking God for the remarkable favor thus conferred on our Congregation in the person of one of its members.
> My purpose in writing this Circular is to have you share my gratitude, because shared in common it will pay better the debt of Holy Cross; its homage will become for us more agreeable to the Lord, and a source of new blessings. . . .

Continuing in this vein, Father Basil asks of his spiritual sons a corresponding spirit of gratitude and faithfulness in thanksgiving, "for this new mark of the infinite mercy," and then visioning the apostolic character of Christ's priesthood, he points out that it is "for the unfortunate people of eastern Bengal who are living in darkness and the shadow of death spiritual and perennial, and not solely for Our Lady of Holy Cross, lovely though she be, that the episcopal dignity has been conferred on a member of our family": and then as his own apostolic soul glimpses that multitude of India's teeming plains, he adds a thought natural in a heart that felt habitually with the Heart of the Master:

> Our joy decreases, notwithstanding; our heartstrings tighten, when we think of the fifteen millions of infidels we are com-

[7] Gen. Archives, C.S.C.
[8] Mgr. Guibert.

ORATORY OF SAINT JOSEPH, MONTREAL. CENTER OF DEVOTION TO SAINT JOSEPH IN THE NEW WORLD AND PROVINCIAL HEADQUARTERS OF THE CANADIAN PROVINCE.

missioned by the Pope to bring into the fold of the One Shepherd, and of the fewness of subjects at our disposal, and the scanty resources at our command.

The consolation of seeing one of his spiritual sons receive the fullness of the Priesthood through episcopal consecration in November of 1860, was followed, as we have seen, by the depressing financial trials arising from causes beyond the Founder's control. Yet these very adversities while serving to refine Basil Moreau's soul furnished members of his spiritual family an opportunity to manifest their loyalty and devotion to their spiritual father, and he in turn responded with his habitual spirit of gratitude. On August 27, 1861,[9] the Founder wrote:

> For the rest, many have already acted as I suggested and I remember them particularly. I will not speak of Father Shiel's generosity,[10] or of that of the Sisters' Council of New Orleans, of the Sisters of St. Laurent, and of the haste with which Father Rezé paid all his debt to the Mother House.

And again on November 2nd of the same year:[11]

> If the indifference and negligence of some cause me sorrow, I must show sincere gratitude to most of the members of the Congregation, not excepting the dear Sisters, for their never-failing devotedness to me. I intend at some later date to include in a Circular letter and make known to all our family what each house will have done to aid me tide over the worst days Holy Cross has ever experienced.

How merciful are the ways of God in veiling from the eyes of our mortal frailty the panorama of the future! Could Father Moreau have visioned that future would he have had

[9] Gen. Archives, C.S.C.
[10] Father Shiel, Vicar of New Orleans, had sent Father Moreau 15,000 francs in response to the latter's appeal.
[11] Gen. Archives, C.S.C.

courage to go on? For "the worst days Holy Cross had ever experienced" were but the first phase of an assault upon Basil Moreau's lifework that would be consummated only after his valiant and pure soul should have found rest in the eternal arms.

XXIII

RESIGNATION—1862-1866

> *Impenetrable are the designs of Providence and we must bow our heads in resignation under the most painful blows.*
>
> —FATHER MOREAU.

IT is one of the paradoxes of Christianity that when God loves a soul He permits its crucifixion. In the spiritual life this process of crucifixion constitutes possibly the surest pledge of the acceptableness of a soul to God. So surely have His real lovers grasped this truth that they are fearful when not suffering, and in the end, rest contented only when permitted to drink daily of the chalice of their Master. Basil Moreau was undoubtedly beloved of God. Therefore we must expect to find in his life a configuration to the suffering Christ, a mystical participation in the Master's death as well as in His life. We have seen Father Moreau carrying his cross, now we are to witness his crucifixion.

In January, 1862, there remained to Father Moreau a decade of years. He was to spend them within the shadow of the Cross, a fitting last decade for a life consecrated to the Heart of Jesus and the Sorrows of the Blessed Mother. At their completion his soul would be ready and worthy of the eternal embrace of God.

What we have just written will serve as an introduction to the most trying ordeal of Father Moreau's entire career—the opposition which came to him from a small group within his own Congregation. Opposition from one's own carries bitterness of a special character, and when not tempered by the exercise of the Christian virtues engenders a fratricidal hatred of whose fruits the Spain of our day offers so pathetic an illustration. Our Blessed Saviour experienced this withering force as he passed through the streets of Nazareth-town, and rarely has he exempted His chosen servants from the unique anguish it engenders. Those whose life work consists of laying the foundations of apostolic works are by the very nature of their labor exposed to the criticism of their fellows and the life of Basil Moreau offers no exception to the rule.

At the General Chapter of 1860, Father Moreau, aware of the opposition to his superiorship on the part of some members of the Congregation, had willingly offered his resignation in the interests of peace and community concord. The welfare of the work God had given him to do was ever uppermost in his mind and heart, and as formerly in his own dark night of the soul,[1] he had cried out "My God, I consent provided the Congregation be saved and You glorified," so now he was ready to sacrifice all personal interests for the sake of Holy Cross.

In 1860, Father Moreau's proffered resignation was refused but the words in which he made this self-effacing offer deserve to be recalled. Concluding his report to the capitulants, the Founder declared:[2]

> I bring these words to a close by begging you not to permit me to be any longer an obstacle to peace, to the union of hearts in the work of Holy Cross and the development of our Order. Kindly then, accept my resignation as Superior General, or if you will not consent to this, grant that I may place it in the hands of the Vicar of Christ who would be able to convoke extraordinarily a session of the General Chapter at the close of this session. Besides no one feels more keenly than I the urgent need of solitude and silence in preparation for the great summons before another tribunal, as well the good I could accom-

[1] Vie, Bk. III, p. 39.
[2] Vie, Bk. IV, p. 151.

plish for the Congregation should I serve as Master of Novices. But whatever is the outcome of your deliberations, dear Brothers, be assured in advance of my deep gratitude for your devotedness, and that far from being discouraged, I thank God that He has permitted me to taste of the chalice of contradiction and humiliation in the foundation of Holy Cross.

In 1860 the work of undermining Father Moreau's position had made little progress but neither could it be halted by the magnanimity of its victim. Once little minds have determined upon an object they are apt to pursue it with the feverish persistency of ants provisioning their citadels of sand. How limited were the real number of Basil Moreau's opponents is revealed by the result of the secret ballot on the same question of his resignation taken three years later at the General Chapter in August of 1863. On this occasion the Founder having again offered his resignation to the Chapter, was refused by a vote of twenty to three; only three members of the entire Chapter being ready to accept the proposal of the Founder.

However, what the opponents had failed to obtain directly they did not hesitate to gain indirectly. At Rome the authorities at the Propaganda were the recipients of numerous letters signed and unsigned, representing the venerable Founder as an autocrat, despot and fool.[3]

This epistolary barrage in the end provoked from Rome a response in the form of a summons to Father Moreau and two of his priest accusers. The Founder left Le Mans on the twelfth of December, 1863, and reached Rome a few days later in the company of the priests who were his opponents.

Both at the Propaganda before Cardinal Barnabo and at the feet of the Holy Father it was not difficult for Father Moreau to give a satisfactory account of his stewardship, while his willingness to release the reins of government [4] was sufficient proof

[3] Cir. Letters #175, January 16, 1864, Gen. Archives, C.S.C.
[4] Father Moreau at this time offered his resignation both to the Prefect of Propaganda and to the Holy Father.

of his disinterestedness. From St. Bridget's, Rome, in January of 1864, the Founder penned the following beautiful letter to the Congregation.[5]

St. Bridget, Rome
January 16, 1864.

REVEREND FATHERS AND DEAR BROTHERS:

The Mother House and the Superior General have regained the confidence of His Holiness, Pius IX, and of Cardinal Barnabo, after having lost it by the false reports of some of our own members, who have represented me to Rome as an autocrat, despot and fool. Let us prove ourselves, now, more and more worthy of this regained confidence, and while blessing Divine Providence which has saved His work for the second time, let us observe our Rules and Regulations and our Constitutions more faithfully. Lack of fidelity to Rules, be assured, has brought down upon us all these dreadful misfortunes.

For myself, my happiness is complete, for I experience nothing but consolation from the audiences I am favored with at the Vatican and at the Propaganda. And yet withal, I am always fearful lest some false brethren shall again step in to end the blessings which the worthy Vicar of Christ is bestowing upon us. These unworthy members by their lack of religious spirit compromise the whole Congregation.

I conjure you, then, in the name of God and of His Church, in the name of the souls confided to us and of our own dearest interests, to no longer withdraw from the path set by authority governing our financial administration and the regular discipline. This is the wish I form from the bottom of my heart for each of our houses and for each one of you, dear Fathers and Brothers, at this the beginning of the New Year. This is the wish of the Holy Father with his blessing, a blessing at the same time for our benefactors, our relatives and our students.

I desire that for spiritual reading you read all my Circulars from the first to the last, then the Letter of St. Ignatius on Obedience.

MOREAU S.S.C.
Superior General

---

[5] Cir. Letters #175, Gen. Archives, C.S.C.

The spirit of Father Basil finds peace even amid such trying circumstances in the imitation of the meekness of his Divine Master; though fearful of the future by reason of the malice of his opponents, yet he refuses to be resentful, and hence he can write: [6]

> I assure you I am not animated by any resentment against those who obliged me to make so long a journey and who thus caused the Congregation unnecessary expense.

Moreover beneath the reasonable fears engendered by the knowledge of the character of the opposition there was in Father Basil's soul the deeper current of his Christian optimism; thus he can declare: [7]

> Must we despair of the future? God forbid! And since His work has withstood these deplorable catastrophes and the blind opposition carried to the Holy See, the very source of our moral strength, let us on the contrary reanimate our hope and our courage.

The concluding paragraphs of this Circular Letter of Father Moreau throw so much light both on his character and the needs of his foundations that we shall quote them at some length:

> While awaiting better times, let us continue to have recourse to Jesus, Mary and Joseph by our daily prayers made with more exactitude and fervor; let us thank Heaven for what has just happened to thwart the visible and invisible enemies of our Congregation; let us embrace with gratitude the means that are presented to us to repair the past, to save the present, and to assure a better future. Let not one among you, dear Fathers and Brothers, refuse to execute the measures taken by the Sacred Congregation of the Propaganda, and by the Chapter or the General Council, however much this may

---

[6] Cir. Letters #176, January 31, 1864, Gen. Archives, C.S.C.
[7] *Ibid.*

hurt self-love, but submit with as much readiness as fidelity, assured that in obeying you record victories rather than humiliating defeats.

Unite then, in the same spirit of obedience, not only with the Holy See, which still deigns to protect us, but with all the Superiors regularly elected to govern you. Strengthen the general authority, too often misunderstood, by surrounding it with your respect and your docility. Attach yourselves to the Mother House, in place of separating yourselves from it. The religious who are in authority there, have been elected canonically, two excepted whose nomination is, however, regular, and they have, no matter what is said, rights to your confidence by their age, their experience, and the grace of their election. Not one of them, besides, has done anything contrary to the interests of the Congregation but all have rendered it important service, something we could not say of some of those very ones who have calumniated Our Lady of Holy Cross. Address yourselves to them in all your administrative difficulties. Take inspiration from them. Let the rules and principles followed in the Mother House be the soul of your conduct in business affairs and you will see that God will bless your devotedness to His work.

Reverend Fathers and dear Brothers, may faith show us the Lord in each of our respective Superiors, and may the Mother House become so dear to us that no one can say aught against it without wounding us to the heart. When real disorders are pointed out to us let us address ourselves immediately to the General or to the Assistants to remedy them, just as when the heart or the head are threatened, all the members rise up to defend them. As to what regards myself, I promise to receive with joy, all the monitions that will be given me in this spirit by anyone whomsoever and I will be grateful for them.

Let us love sincerely, therefore, this cradle of our Congregation; let us attach ourselves to it as the branches of the vine to the vine-stock, always sharing in its trials and its combats, its joys and its sorrows, its fears and its hopes. Let us not limit our interests to the narrow confines of a particular house, province, or country; this would be egotism and self-seeking.

Let us identify ourselves with all our houses, regarding none as a stranger to the one we dwell in. May Our Lady of Holy Cross be to each house what the head is to the body. Instead of withdrawing from her influence, remain intimately united with her. Live her life, praying, weeping, battling, triumphing with her, as you promise each year in the hymn which ends the renewal of vows. Then Heaven will be with you, and the general administration meeting everywhere with the desired subordination will accomplish its mission in a way that will console the heart of the glorious Pontiff whom we have saddened; will reassure the illustrious Cardinal on whom depends our lot; will give to our Institute its reputation and to all those who form a part of it, peace and confidence.

This is why, Reverend Fathers and dear Brothers, I conjure you in the name of the sacred interests entrusted to us, and for which we are responsible; in the name of Jesus Christ and the ten thousand students confided to our care; in the name of the Divine Mother, Our Lady of Holy Cross, whose adopted children we are; in the name of St. Joseph, our patron and our model; in the name of our eternal salvation and of all we have done or suffered until the present time in responding to our vocation—for the sake of all these sacred things, let us forget our past wrongs, keeping in mind the reply of Our Divine Lord to St. Peter, who having asked how many times he ought to pardon, received from the Sacred Lips, the equivalent of these words: always and ceaselessly.

As for myself, I would remember only the devotedness of each one of you, and the consolations that they who brought me to Rome have procured for me contrary to their expectations.

It is true that here [at Rome] one finds wisdom that comes from on high, and a spirit of calm that is calculated to shed light on the most complicated questions and to bring peace to souls. Such at least has been my experience during my stay in this serene and tranquil atmosphere, removed from the rumors and fears which stir men's souls elsewhere; and how greatly I desire that the salutary influence which I have undergone may be felt by all the members of our Family! Then peace and cordial agreement will be established among us, and those sweet sentiments will fill each member with a new ardor in the performance of his obedience. This I urgently ask of the Lord, this I beg you all to ask, the brothers, by offering a Communion, and the priests, by saying a Mass for this intention.

This will gain for us, if we know how to profit by it, the apostolic blessing of Christ's Vicar, the Common Father of the faithful whom we cannot approach without feeling ourselves penetrated with the liveliest filial piety, and the most profound veneration. Would that it had been allowed you as it was me to see him with his face expressing paternal kindness and unalterable calm and radiant with a smile of ineffable sweetness which fills the soul with joy. Would that you had heard the Pope as I have now heard him in three private audiences, in one of which he chided me in the most touching manner for not having caused our Rules to be respected; or, again in the presence of those of our Congregation who accompanied me to the Vatican. On one of these latter occasions when four of us were present, His Holiness caused us to line up in front of him and recalled to us the four cardinal virtues, leaving to each of us the duty of seeing them practiced. He graciously called down the blessings of Heaven on our houses, our relatives, our benefactors, our friends, and on all the souls confided to our care. Oh, if you had seen and heard all this, never, oh, never, would you dare to trouble the mind of so holy and so good a Pontiff by bringing about a return of our past misfortunes! You would, likewise, fear to cause new embarrassments to the Prince of the Church, so worthy of the confidence of so great a Pope, to whom we owe the approbation of our Rules; and before entering into discussions which arise among us, you would do your best to arrange matters within the community.

Let us re-enter this road which we never should have left. Let us not continue to make known to strangers what would not be of a nature to edify them and to beget their esteem. Let us ennoble our minds by following the light of faith. Let us lift up our souls by purifying our intentions. Let us keep ourselves free from injurious suspicions and sad want of confidence in one another, but without ignoring whatever would be indicative of bad dispositions. Let us, on the contrary, have an eye to whatever could compromise the spiritual and temporal interests of the Congregation. Let us be ready to suffer something for it, and let us not complain at the least privation or contradiction. Otherwise we would be neither religious nor even Christians, much less children of Our Lady of the Seven Dolors and of the Cross. Alas! What is our life compared with that of the saints whose names we bear, and particularly with that of the Apostle who wrote from the very prison which I have had the happiness of visiting, "Even unto this hour we both hunger and thirst, and are naked, and are buffeted, and have no fixed abode. And we labor, working with our own hands; we are reviled, and we bless; we are persecuted, and we suffer it. We are blasphemed, and we entreat; we are made as the refuse of this world, the offscouring of all even until now." (I Cor. IV., 11-13.)

At least, Reverend Fathers and dear Brothers, let us bear the trials inseparable from our vocation fulfill our vows, follow our Rules, respect the decrees of the General Chapter and of the Holy See, without ever again doing or allowing others with whom we live to do anything which would renew past financial and moral scandals. I must add here, moreover, that if the spirit of intrigue, of cabal, and of ambition, again raises its head, I will denounce its principal authors to the whole Congregation and I shall beg them to withdraw from our Institute and let us continue in peace.

May my words be understood and received with docility by each of you, Reverend Fathers and dear Brothers, and may the blessing which His Holiness, Pius IX, gave me so cordially for you, for our students, our relatives, our benefactors and our friends, be a guarantee of our fidelity in the accomplishment of all our duties, and of our eternal union in God. May the Apostolic Blessing descend upon each of you, fructify your works and give a new life to all the members of Holy Cross.

In finishing, I want to thank all those who have accompanied me with their good wishes on my journey, and who were kind enough to express them at New Year's. Accept, then, my heartfelt thanks, with the sentiments which dictate these last lines, in life and in death.[8]

[8] Then follow several particular regulations for the Congregation.

We have quoted so extensively from this letter penned from Rome at the end of January, 1864, because it so fully demonstrates the beautiful spirit of forgiveness which was perhaps the supreme grace vouchsafed to Father Moreau in these closing years of his life. Like unto His Master, even in the hour of deepest anguish Basil Moreau would pray for his persecutors and be ready to excuse and forgive their actions.

The Founder's appeal for peace and unity, however, though received with proper reverence and obedience on the part of the majority of the priests and brothers of Holy Cross, fell on deaf ears where there was most need of its being heard and heeded. Those who are capable of formulating and propagating false charges against their superior officers will rarely be big enough to either forget or forgive. To forgive is perhaps the most divine of virtues, measured by the difficulty of its exercise by men. And, besides, Father Moreau's accusers had at least one real cause for forgiveness above those engendered by their own minds—and that was his success. Had the Founder really been guilty of their charges, possibly these misguided souls might have pardoned him; his innocence, added to his success in defending his administration at Rome, made forgiveness on their part impossible. So while Basil Moreau worked and prayed for the strengthening of the foundations of Holy Cross, his enemies continued their attack.

Father Moreau's letters of this period are filled with fervent pleadings for the maintenance of fervor and religious discipline in the houses of the Congregation. It will not be amiss to quote briefly some of these truly apostolic appeals:

In June, 1864, while announcing the completion of the final revision of the Rules, the Founder does not fail to point to their special role in the sanctification of the individual religious:[9]

> But these Rules, such as they are, Reverend Fathers and dear Brothers, I send you with the confidence that whoever

[9] Cir. Letters #178, Gen. Archives, C.S.C.

will practice them faithfully and with the sole desire of pleasing God, will strengthen his vocation, satisfy eternal justice for his sins, edify all who will be witnesses of his conduct and contribute to the salvation of countless souls. Besides, on our fidelity to them depends the whole future of our Congregation—its honor and its glory, as also the peace and union of its members.

In November of the same year, the Founder writes again to his spiritual sons, describing the spirit in which the decisions of the Sacred Congregation of the Propaganda relative to Holy Cross should be received. His words need no comment; their spirit is self-evident.

> With gratitude then, let us grasp this plank of salvation offered us, and if the decrees I am going to have read impose upon our pride some sacrifice, let us hasten to accept it nevertheless, bearing in mind that the grain of wheat cannot take root and bring forth fruit unless it has been buried in the ground. In like manner, let minds at variance be reconciled and hearts embittered be sweetened by the voice of our Holy Father, the Pope. Let us entertain the same thoughts, the same affections, and be of the same mind and heart; let us close our ranks against the common enemy, and let us seek our vengeance on him for having tried to destroy us by making this sad occasion an epoch of entire renewal in the spirit of our vocation.[10]

Again in December of 1864, we find the Founder pleading for the detailed observance of the Rules and insisting on the true value of the religious life:

> Do not forget that it is neither money nor talent which effects God's works, but faith, prayer, and fidelity to Rule. This is the unique way of obtaining vocations, the need of which we feel so much more now than ever before.[11]

With the New Year of 1865 came the usual greetings from his spiritual children, and Father Moreau answers their expres-

[10] Gen. Archives, C.S.C., #179.   [11] Gen. Archives, C.S.C., #180.

sions of filial devotion and loyalty in the following beautiful letter from which we quote.[12]

>Our Lady of Holy Cross
>January 10, 1865.

REVEREND FATHERS AND DEAR BROTHERS:

I am availing myself of these first spare moments since the close of the Provincial Chapter of France, to thank you for your New Year greetings and to reanimate your confidence in the future of our Congregation and that, in spite of the many trials she has undergone during the past year, trials which have greatly worried you.

Besides it is my essential duty to encourage you to stand firm and faithful in your vocation, so that resisting the devil's illusions, the seductions of the world and the flesh you may obtain the recompense promised to virtue.

Be not surprised then at the violent storm the enemy of all good has stirred up against the Congregation of Holy Cross; and be not frightened either at our financial condition which is perceptibly improving, or by the scandal given by some of our members. Do not be frightened at the departure of certain subjects who have in a cowardly way abandoned the Master after having so long enjoyed His blessings; nor at the incredible facility with which several have blackened and calumniated in Rome's eyes the Congregation which received them into her bosom, instead of upholding her honor and reputation by word and example. Ungrateful children they have disemboweled their own mother and deserve to have applied to them the words of Isaias (I. 2): "I have brought up children and have exalted them, but they have despised me."

As for myself, Reverend Fathers and dear Brothers, I am not at all surprised at all these trials, and, thanks be to God, they have but caused me to increase my confidence in Him Who alone has founded and sustained our Congregation and Who will cause it to develop more and more if we do not play into the hands of the devil who would destroy it because he sees the souls we are snatching from him. How, in fact, could it be

---

[12] Gen. Archives, C.S.C., #181.

a matter of indifference to him to see the ten thousand students confided to our care as well as so many other souls snatched from hell by our apostolic ministry? Hence, I am in no way surprised to find the devil laying snares for our faith. But the Saviour is faithful and He will not permit you to be tried beyond your strength. If we but know how to awaken Him from His apparent sleep by our prayers He will command the storms and the tempest to subside, and the calm of other days will be ours. Even in the Chapter that I recently presided over, this peace of mind and heart was felt and its members thus found new light and encouragement.

Be convinced that Divine Providence, having willed that its greatest works begin in humility and abjection, has also decreed that they shall develop only through difficulties and contradictions, crosses, contempt, slanders and calumnies, so that the cornerstones of these spiritual edifices be tried as gold in the fire. Does not Bethlehem, the feast we celebrate, exemplify this forcefully? What do the stable, the crib, the swaddling clothes, the poor shepherds teach? Did not persecution receive this Infant God into a world He was to save by dying on the Cross, after having been satiated with opprobrium? Did not the Apostles, too, drink of the bitter chalice of His passion? And is not the fruit of all this suffering, the founding of the Church and the conversion of the Gentiles?

Now, though the trials that Holy Cross has undergone have been as cruel as they have been numerous, yet far from destroying or uprooting this newborn plant they should but strengthen and foster it at the same time that they should purify the virtue of those who do not allow themselves to become discouraged while increasing their knowledge of God.

Realizing that to bear joyously the trials and sacrifices of the religious life one must maintain and deepen his spiritual life, we are not surprised to find Basil Moreau insisting on the importance of meditation, and this with a clear intuition of the varying needs of individuals. In his Circular Letter of February 8, 1865, he writes:[13]

[13] Cir. Letters, #182, Gen. Archives, C.S.C.

I conjure you, Reverend Fathers and dear Brothers, never to neglect your prayer and that you may succeed in it memorize what the directory teaches on this subject. I entreat all superiors and directors of houses to have this read to their subjects once a month and to have them report once a week on the thoughts and sentiments with which God inspired them during meditation. If some should find the method of St. Ignatius too complicated they may reduce their prayer to certain very simple acts, as for example, adoration of Jesus Christ, the practicing of any special virtue, the offering to Him of our admiration, joy, love, or compassion, our gratitude for favors received, requests for the help one needs to conquer self, to be faithful to God's inspirations or to bear patiently daily trials.

But nevertheless the fruit to be gained from the method described in the directory will repay the efforts you make to observe it. To help you to do this I enclose with this Circular a brief analysis of the method in question.

However, while the Founder of Holy Cross was thus engaged like Zorobabel and Josue [14] in building anew the walls of Jerusalem, there were those who were busily engaged in nullifying his efforts. Father Moreau was painfully aware of their activity, and felt constrained to warn the Congregation of this deleterious influence.[15]

In October of 1865, he writes:

Finally, Reverend Fathers and dear Brothers, I would urge you to be on your guard against the spirit of detraction of which the Mother House does not cease to be the object and the calumnies that are uttered with appalling facility.

The warning of the poor afflicted Founder was impotent, however, to stop the vigorous campaign being waged to undermine his authority in the Congregation and his good standing at Rome with the Sacred Congregation of the Propaganda and the Holy Father. I think it is Voltaire who is credited with

[14] I Esdras, IV.
[15] Cir. Letters, #187, Gen. Archives, C.S.C.

declaring that if one throws enough mud some of it will stick. The Papal Authorities yielded at last to the epistolary bombardment.

Once again Father Basil was invited to Rome.

The remainder of this particular chapter can best be summarized by utilizing the last three Circular Letters Basil Moreau addressed to his spiritual children, and therefore I have thought it well to let them tell their own pathetic story. In January of the previous year, 1865, Basil Moreau had penned the following words vibrant of his faith in the ultimate triumph through suffering of Justice and of Holy Cross:[16]

> Be glad, then, Reverend Fathers and dear Brothers, to have been found worthy of suffering in body and soul and to have shared in the passion of this Institute. Be glad and reassured in proportion as I personally suffer tribulations, since these trials are a sure guarantee of the Divine Will in our regard and in regard to our Institute whose instruments we are.

Surely the priest who wrote these lines was on the side of the angels, surely God must reward such living faith. God has, indeed, but at the moment the path of Basil Moreau was leading into the depths. On January 13, 1866, Father Moreau addressed the following Circular Letter to the Congregation:

> REVEREND FATHERS AND DEAR BROTHERS:
> If the year just passed was full of trials for me, that which begins promises no diminution in their number or gravity. But the marks of affection of which I have been the recipient and your devotedness to Holy Cross soften the bitterness of my sorrows, without, however, relieving my soul crushed by the spirit of division which the demon of discord has sown among us.
> In the midst of so many trials, we can do nothing but beg God to give us His peace; and to deserve it, we must renew

[16] Cir. Letters, #181, Gen. Archives, C.S.C.

our fidelity to vow and rule. Hence I beg you to walk more and more in the path of obedience, while strengthening the bonds of fraternal charity and frequently meditating on the share of responsibility which each of you has in the future of Holy Cross. For me, advanced in years as I am, I tremble at the thought of the account I shall have to give; and while thanking you for your good wishes for my happiness, I cannot but implore the aid of your prayers and your forgetfulness of the faults by which I have saddened or disedified you.

Believe me, Reverend Fathers and dear Brothers, when I tell you that, to my last sigh, I shall be all yours with the most tender affection in Jesus, Mary and Joseph.

MOREAU.

Well might the patient Founder have premonitions of trials to come. The persevering efforts of his enemies had once again forced Rome to take action and once again the harassed Father of Holy Cross found himself in Rome.

From St. Bridget's [17] February 11, 1866, Father Basil, once again vindicated yet saddened, writes:

REVEREND FATHERS AND DEAR BROTHERS:
Knowing that my departure from France is causing anxiety to certain minds, and not being sure when I shall be able to return to the Mother House, I want to reassure you of my journey which I have happily completed by land and of my arrival in Rome on the feast of the Purification of the Blessed Virgin.

I have found here the same friends and the same kindness as during my last visit. Be assured and have no anxiety in this regard. But pray and be regular in your observance of discipline. Close your ranks and face the enemy of Holy Cross by uniting yourselves to God, by flying from sin, by frequenting the Sacraments; and by uniting yourselves to your Superiors by obedience and to your brethren by charity, for the demon of discord has done us immense harm.

Do all you can toward paying the annuity due April first

---

[17] Cir. Letters, Gen. Archives, C.S.C.

to the creditors of the ex-econome of the College of Ternes and count on my affectionate devotion in Jesus, Mary and Joseph till my last breath.

B. MOREAU.

The demon of discord had indeed done Holy Cross great harm for Father Moreau's enemies had at last succeeded in bringing about the setting aside of the cornerstone of Holy Cross. Father Moreau's last Circular Letter succinctly tells the story.[18]

Holy Cross of Le Mans, June 21, 1866.
REVEREND FATHERS AND DEAR BROTHERS:

While thanking you for your greetings on my feast day I am happy to inform you that after having refused to accept my resignation on my arrival in Rome, and again at my departure, His Holiness has since deigned to accept it and to name as Vicar General, until the next Chapter, Reverend Father Chappé, whom henceforth you should obey as you obeyed me, and with whom you should treat of all matters. At the coming Chapter we must consider the organization of all our civil corporations.

That you may fully understand my dispositions in the turn which affairs have taken, I believe it my duty to give here the following extract from my letter to His Eminence, the Cardinal Prefect of the Propaganda, a few days before the meeting of the Sacred Congregation, as well as the reply I have just received.

St. Bridget, May 27, 1886.
YOUR EMINENCE:

That the Sacred Congregation may have no doubt about the dispositions I manifested to your Eminence in the conversation in which you honored me yesterday with such paternal goodness, I believe I ought to declare here before God, your Eminence, that I am ready to hand in my resignation either to His Holiness or to our General Chapter, provided I be then freed from all financial responsibility, promising in consequence to use all the means judged most apt to facilitate the

[18] Cir. Letters, Gen. Archives, C.S.C.

free action of my successor, and promising as well an exemplary obedience to the Superior General who will be canonically elected.

Your Eminence, etc.,
Signed: MOREAU.

The response from His Eminence Cardinal Barnabo reads as follows:

Rome
The Propaganda
June 14, 1866.

VERY REVEREND FATHER:

In the last general meeting of June 4, the affairs of your Institute were examined, and His Holiness has approved all the deliberations taken by this same holy assembly.

The Holy Father, on the advice of the most Eminent Fathers, has deigned to accept the resignation offered by Your Paternity on the twenty-ninth of last November. He has also decided that the General Chapter shall be convened as soon as possible, and that it shall be presided over by the Bishop of Le Mans, who shall have all necessary and proper powers; and in order that in the interval the Institute may not be without government, He has named as Vicar General Apostolic of the Congregation until the next Chapter, the Very Reverend Father Chappé.

Surely, Reverend Fathers and dear Brothers, I can but bless Providence for this news and I like to believe that everything will pass off at the next Chapter in accordance with our Rules and the prescriptions of the Holy See.

In the meantime, let us pray, and count always on my devotedness to the work, as also on the affectionate interest with which I shall live unto death, Reverend Fathers and dear Brothers,

All yours in Jesus, Mary and Joseph,

MOREAU, C.S.C.

P. S. I commend to your prayers the Curé of St. Pierre d'Entremont of whose death I have just learned. He was one of Holy Cross's best friends. Remember him prayerfully;

also do not forget to say a word to God for the repose of the souls of Sisters Mary of the Compassion and Mary of Saint Julia who died last month at the Mother House.

Is there not a poignant revelation in this final postscript of the Founder's? His final word as he bravely relinquishes the guidance of Holy Cross is a plea for the remembrance of benefactors. Thus ever-thoughtful of the gratitude due to others, Basil Moreau tread closely in the footsteps of his Master resigning himself to the ingratitude of men and the just judgments of Almighty God.

XXIV
DEEPENING SHADOWS—1866-1867

> *God has accorded me a most profound peace, and relieved me of all preoccupation for the Institute. I pray that He will in the end convert to Himself the evil-minded.*
>
> —FATHER MOREAU.

IT was at spiritual reading on the evening of the twenty-first of June that the last Circular Letter of Father Moreau was read to the assembled Community of the Mother House. When the reading was finished, Father Moreau addressed his spiritual sons in the following terms:[1]

> Reverend Fathers and dear Brothers, what you have just heard comes without doubt as a surprise to the majority of you; but it ought not to disturb you because it has been foreseen and wisely planned. It is besides a precious grace for me, as it will be for you if you know how to profit by it. It happens sometimes in the works of God that there are names so compromised by the struggles inseparable from their foundations that it is of advantage that they disappear in order that passions may be quieted and the opposition of the enemies of good may cease. That is why during the last nine years, I have often offered my resignation to various General Chapters, to the Sacred Congregation of the Propaganda, and last November to the Holy Father himself. The responsibility, moreover, I have carried frightened me as I thought of eternity and the account I must soon render of my charge. His Holiness, after having refused many times to relieve me has finally deigned to grant my wishes, and has chosen Father Chappé, one of the two religious I was permitted to suggest to replace

[1] Vie, Bk. IV, p. 254.

me. He is given you as a bond of union between those who sympathized with my spirit in heart and action, and those who have not understood my administration. The letter by which God sent me this good news was addressed to me on the Feast of Saint Basil, and thus becomes the most precious gift of my feast.

I have felt for a long time past that some necessary contribution was lacking on my part in the work, and I bless Providence which has now made this contribution possible. Up to now because of my position, it has been impossible for me to command and obey at the same time; but from this very hour I hope, with God's grace, to give you all an example of submission and obedience. And now, before inviting the Reverend Father Chappé to take my place here, it only remains for me to beg pardon of the members for the poor impression that I have made on you during my long administration, and for the obstacles I have placed in the way of your sanctification and the development of God's work.

Do not these words convey the impression of a man whose self had long since been lost in the greater-self of Christ? With what simplicity he grasps the interests of God in this painful situation, with what humility he begs pardon for his faults, with what courage he faces the future, with what meekness he speaks of "those who have not understood my administration!" The gold in the fire already gleams fair to our eyes, but the Divine Goldsmith had not yet finished His work. Basil Moreau had yet many things to suffer for the Lord and Holy Cross.

The spirit in which Father Moreau undertook his new life of a simple religious may be deduced from the testimony of the acting Superior General, Father Chappé, who informed Cardinal Barnabo that "far from impeding my action, the Father Founder seconds it by a humility and obedience that confounds us all."[2] But do what he would, it was impossible

[2] Vie, Bk. IV, p. 258.

for Basil Moreau to escape the suspicion and veritable persecution of those who in the charity of Christ he had described as "not understanding my administration."

The unvarnished truth seems to be that the opponents of the Founder were determined to erase his work and to rebuild upon the ruins a new edifice in which Basil Moreau would be but a pitiful memory. I do not say that this course of action was determined upon with malicious motives. Centuries ago Our Blessed Lord with His divine knowledge and prophetic vision gave warning of that mysterious complex by which even murder would at times be considered a service of God. Of the interior dispositions of men there is One who searcheth and knoweth. But whatever the subjective integrity of Father Moreau's persecutors, objectively their policy was one of attrition, and despite the withdrawal of the Founder from office, there was no noticeable break in the continuity of its execution.

Sensing the reaction of this group to his presence at the Mother House in view of the approaching General Chapter, Father Basil retired forthwith to The Solitude of St. Joseph, the Novitiate of the Josephites, and sought for that peace which the world cannot comprehend, in the exercises of the annual retreat.

One desire the Founder had, however, quite understandable in men of integrity, that the rectitude of his financial administration should be looked into and recognized; and certainly to this scrutiny as a legally-responsible administrator leaving office he was entitled. When, therefore, the General Chapter had been assembled, Father Basil submitted a carefully prepared account of the administration of the temporals of the Mother House and general administration, together with his humble petition that after due examination their correctness should be certified and himself relieved of further responsibility for material affairs in which he no longer had part. Since the Founder's management, despite the exactions created by the debts of subordinate houses, was in good order and revealed the financial solvency of the Mother House, it would never have done for his enemies to recognize this fact so damning to their alleged assertions.

As a result, Basil Moreau pleaded in vain for the examination of his financial record, and was left civilly responsible for an administration in which he had not the slightest part. This was obviously a cruel injustice, and, perhaps better than any other single fact, bears witness to the fact that Father Moreau's opponents were aware of the weakness of their case.

To this cruel thorn in Basil Moreau's crown of thorns was added still another when, the Vicar General of the Congregation evidently misled [3] by a slanderous charge that the Founder had denounced him at Rome, changed in his attitude toward Father Basil, and would not permit the latter even to communicate his accounts rendered to the former assistants or the members of the Chapter. The reasons given the Founder for this prohibition are quite illuminating: [4]

> That the majesty of silence alone was becoming the new status of the Founder; that it would be useless to treat again of accomplished facts; that no justification was possible for him before the Holy See which had lost all confidence in him; *that his opponents would never recognize their wrongs* [italics the author's]; and that by the provoking of a new recourse to Rome he would be responsible for the dissolution of the Congregation.

The majesty of silence then was the role assigned to Father Moreau; did they remember who else had played that role? Even the Gentlest Saviour had asked for the evidence against Him, and had been answered in terms of brutality!

Yet other configurations of the disciple to his Divine Master were to follow in due process of time. Calvary had witnessed

---
[3] Vie, Bk. IV, p. 264.
[4] Vie, Bk. IV, p. 265.

the Saviour stript of all possessions, and even His disciples dispersed. During the months and the years yet to be unfolded Father Moreau was to watch in anguish while the successful College and substantial Mother House of Our Lady of Holy Cross were first dismantled and then sold, the religious and the students dispersed and even his own personal effects sacrificed in the futile effort to eradicate his work and name. Writing to the newly elected Superior General, Bishop Dufal, Father Seguin, former Secretary General and one of the three chosen for the revision of the Rules declared:[5]

> Your Reverence will not be apt to think that I insist too much if you had seen for yourself the feverish desire for a clean slate and innovation which is manifest: if you had heard the demand, for example, that we burn at this session the registers of the administrative acts of Father Founder.

Meanwhile in the seclusion of the Solitude Basil Moreau strengthened his soul for the trials of the morrow, and in long hours spent before the Blessed Sacrament renewed the twin flames of faith and love that burned so brightly despite the encircling gloom. To Mother Mary of the Seven Dolors, Mother General of the Marianites Sisters, his steadfast and understanding spiritual daughter, Father Basil entrusted the following simple but touching verses to be sent to the sisters of New Orleans in appreciation of a gift:[6]

> Why tarry I on earth, so far from Thee, my Saviour?
> Cruel the war that rages within my heart yet ever,
> Unceasing would I love Thee,
> Tasting at Life's each stage,
> The bliss in pain's endeavor,
> When of myself I strive
> Some tiny good to do,
> In that same hour, I learn

[5] Vie, Bk. IV, p. 269.
[6] Vie, Bk. IV, pp. 270-271, Translation, author.

My nothingness, anew:
The world has been unleashed,
The devil prowls,
Without the price of pain,
Where all things are destroyed,
Nought can I hope to gain.
Be Thou, my Light,
Sole Author of all good
Direct my course aright,
And furnish me Thy aid:
Sustained by Thy grace,
Hell even will I brave,
Disgrace before the world,
The axman's blade.
Submitting to the course
Of the infernal plan,
For this, Thy work,
To suffer I consent;
And ready should it be—
The price required,
This self to immolate,
Till Life's last day be spent.
My glory be Thy Cross,
There rest my happiness,
To victory aspiring
Despite my earthiness.
Yearning Jesus, for Thee,
Each hour, more and more,
Certain am I in death,
To have Thee, evermore.

It is true these lines, even in the original French, do not approach the heights of literature, but when we reflect the circumstances under which they were penned, must we not recognize that elevation of heart and soul that constitutes the unique physiognomy of God's saints? What a picture for the brush of a great artist,—the ex-Superior General pausing from his preoccupations to respond to the charity of his distant spiritual daughters by a little message rhythmic with faith divine. Shadows were deepening around the lonely figure of Basil Moreau, but clearer and clearer through the thickening gloom shone the light of his beautiful soul.

XXV
LIGHT IN DARKNESS—1866-1868

> *I am able to assure you, my dear Sons and Daughters in Jesus Christ, that I have not forgotten you at the holy altar nor will I forget you in the future; for though my heart tells me that I bear no feeling of resentment toward anyone, yet I have a living gratitude for all who wish me well.*
>
> —FATHER MOREAU.

IT is when the darkness thickens over the sky-line that lights gleam brightest; the darker the setting, the better the jewel-facets gleam; that is why Calvary made such a perfect setting for the rubies of the Precious Blood, and that is one of the reasons why Jesus consents to the night of trial in the lives of His holy ones. And thus it is that the darkness of tribulation, gathered about the foundations of Holy Cross and the figure of its Founder, served but to emphasize the grandeur of his character and the stability of his work.

Finding himself set aside from his labor of love in the up-building of his Institute, Father Moreau with that logic characteristic of true zeal turned to the one field of labor still open before him. He began again the exhausting apostolate of a parish missionary. With what spirit and with what results the following extracts from his letters will reveal:

Writing from Coulombiers to one of his sisters, he declares:[1]

> The mission of Coulombiers has effected some remarkable conversions; poor sinners in great numbers have approached

[1] Vie, Bk. IV, p. 276.

the tribunal of Penance from which they had been away, fifteen, twenty, thirty, forty or fifty years. I have been obliged to ask the assistance of two neighboring pastors for the confessions.

And again:

At last I have finished the mission at Coulombiers and I shall leave in a few hours for St. Christopher's of Jambet, full of gratitude to God who has deigned to renew this parish which I leave now in the hands of a poor sick pastor. I am tired, but I hope to return to you alive on Easter Monday. Truly I did not think myself capable of so much work. Yesterday, I was able to speak to the women at six-thirty, to the men at quarter past eight, to both groups at ten-thirty, to the women at two o'clock, to the men at four o'clock, and to all at six-thirty; each time I spoke for almost an hour and always to a full church. They tell me I look tired, but if I do not lose my voice, I will begin another mission this evening.

Thus it goes with the real laborers in the Master's Vineyard, the flame of Christ's Spirit drives them on and on and they can find no rest on earth save in the Will of God. During the year 1867, Father Moreau gave missions or retreats at Flee, Coulombiers, St. Christopher's of Jambet, a second one at Flee, and one at Chateau-Loir. His missions were thoroughly organized and embodied all the essential features that are today characteristic of the parish mission apostolate of his priestly sons. Congregational singing was encouraged and provided for by a collection of popular hymns which Father Basil had printed. The renewal of the baptismal vows was given fitting solemnity and the solemn blessing of the little children of the parish emphasized the complete character of Basil Moreau's service for the salvation and sanctification of souls. Many have been witness to the effectiveness of Holy Cross missionaries; few have realized that the ultimate source after God of this efficiency is part of the precious heritage of Basil Moreau to His spiritual family.

While the rejected Founder was thus engaged in fulfilling as best he might the exactions of his zeal, the Heavenly Father was preparing for His faithful servitor a chalice of consolation. Early in 1867 the Sacred Congregation of the Propaganda completed its scrutiny of the Constitutions of the Marianites of Holy Cross and recommended their approval to the Holy Father. The abiding graciousness of Pope Pius IX to Father Moreau and his works found herein another chance for expression; and, under the date of February 19, 1867—in that year, the commemoration of Our Lord's prayer in Gethsemane —the decree of approbation was signed.[2]

This singular grace of seeing both his foundations receive approbation from the Holy See during his lifetime occasioned a fresh outpouring of gratitude on the part of the Founder. In a note to Mother Mary of the Seven Dolors, Father Basil writes:[3]

> I would go at once to thank you for the attractive little volume of your Constitutions, my dear Mother and Daughter in Christ Jesus, did hoarseness not warn me against going out because of the cold and my coming mission at Mamers. During the rest of my days I will bless the Divine Goodness that has granted me the sublime consolation of seeing your Congregation approved together with the Rules which I submitted to the Holy See.

The chaliced consolation of the approval of his Marianite Daughters was destined, however, to be bitter-sweet, for by that process of growth and division, at once so natural and so painful, he was soon to witness the separation of the Sisters of the Indiana Province from the administrative unity of the Marianites. The Founder was possessed of too keen a mind not to have anticipated this development, and too paternal a

[2] Vide Appendix.
[3] Vie, Bk. IV, p. 285.

heart not to have suffered while continuing to cherish all his Daughters in Christ Jesus.

June of 1867 found Father Moreau seeking a respite from his missionary labors at the Trappist Monastery near Mortagne. It was here that thirty years earlier he had settled upon the fundamental structure of his Congregation; it was here he returned to seek that quiet peace so dear to apostolic hearts drawn by the Charity of Christ into the vortex of humanity.

In the lives of God's chosen ones how often we find these two cross currents of love of souls and love of solitude. From St. Paul to the little Pastor of Ars, all God's saints have felt the twofold tug of the Christ of Tabor and the Christ of the hearts of men.

Father Moreau writes from his retreat: [4]

> The aspect of these silent walls, the recollected and mortified appearance of the religious, the order and cleanliness which one finds everywhere, the gracious reception one receives, the air so soft and pure, the touching chant of the Salve Regina which was being sung as I arrived, all these things produce in one's soul a more intimate and habitual presence of God.

Even in retreat, however, Basil Moreau could not be unmindful of the needs of his spiritual children, and he must needs preach to them the virtues he, himself, had so constantly the occasion to practice. His customary spirit of faith dominates the painful circumstances of the moment, and so he can declare: [5]

> Bless you and thank you again; but do not weep over me; in place of condolences, congratulate me on having been relieved at last of a frightful responsibility. This is a great grace in the eyes of faith and a sweet consolation to my aging years; I feel this keenly in leaving my retreat, and if I would express a regret it is that you have not shared with me the charm of this attractive solitude.

[4] Vie, Bk. IV, p. 293.   [5] Idem.

It was at this moment that Father Basil composed the following spiritual will or testament whose spirit is so plainly that of another and better world:[6]

This is my spiritual testament, which I make, this second day of my retreat, at Grand-Trappe, near Mortagne, in the name of the Father, and of the Son, and of the Holy Ghost, Whom I humbly beseech not to allow me to insert in this testament anything that might be dictated by human nature, being intent in this as in everything else, on listening to the voice of grace.

I thank Almighty God, and I hope to have the happiness of thanking Him throughout eternity, for the great grace of being born in the Roman Catholic Church, to the decisions of which I humbly submit, as a son to a Mother, all that I have written, published, and done up to this day, as well as all that I shall say, do, write, and publish in the future.

I ask, and I shall continue to ask pardon of the three Divine Persons for all the sins committed against the Blessed Trinity, in thought, word, action, and omission; humbly supplicating the Father Who created me, to re-establish in me His divine image, disfigured by sin; supplicating the Son Who redeemed me, to apply to my soul the fruits of the Redemption, in order to make up for the insufficiency of my good works; and, finally, supplicating the Holy Ghost Who has sanctified me through the Sacraments, to perfect His work by giving me His seven gifts, with the theological and the cardinal virtues.

I pardon in all sincerity all those persons who have harmed me in the exercise of the holy ministry, by slander, which, undoubtedly, must have been unintentional. I beseech Almighty God to pardon all those of our household who have imprudently paralyzed the growth of Holy Cross, by having had recourse to means as contrary to the spirit of our Constitutions and Rules as they were to the virtues of obedience, truth, simplicity, and religious abnegation. If they could read the feelings of my heart, they would find therein no bitterness, but tenderness and love for all the members of my religious family.

[6] On the King's Highway, p. 91.

I would suffer willingly a great deal more, if I could consolidate the work shaken to its very foundation. May Heaven grant that the observance of the Constitutions and our primitive customs be re-established, and that the salutary maxim of St. Bernard be no longer forgotten: *Major omnium persecutionum quas patitur Christus est ab iis qui alios ad remissius agendum induant.* "The saddest persecution that Christ endures comes from those who lead others into wrongdoing." Let this be understood without reference to anyone in particular, but let the past be a salutary warning to all those who would in the future plot or enter into any intrigue in view of satisfying their ambition.

Moreover, I ask pardon of all those whom I have unintentionally saddened, offended, or scandalized. I entreat them to forget all that in word or in act appeared to them unworthy of my priestly character and of the mission which I had to fulfill, to the prosperity of which I am aware that I placed many obstacles. Hence, I beg Our Lord Jesus Christ to efface by virtue of His Precious Blood, the faults that I might have occasioned by disedification; and in His divine mercy, I ask Him to supply what was wanting in my ministration to souls during my long years of apostleship.

The interest bestowed on my spiritual family is closely united to that which I feel for those near and dear to me. I congratulate you, my dear relatives, on your spirit of faith which helps you to understand that I did not enter the priesthood to enrich you. You were proud of the institutions that were founded under my direction, although their prosperity added nothing to your resources. May you live and die in the faith you practice with so much fidelity, and may you leave your children the admirable examples that were bequeathed to you by your parents and mine.

I sincerely thank the persons who have seconded my efforts in the several foundations that constituted my life work. I recommend myself to their prayers, promising not to forget them before God, if, as I hope, through His infinite mercy, He will deign to grant me to live and die in His Heart.

But my last word is for you, my dearest friends, Fathers, Brothers, and Sisters of Holy Cross, dear Sons and Daughters in Jesus Christ, who have stood by me throughout the crucial period of my life. You never ceased to show me the deepest interest, the most tender attachment, and the most generous devotedness. Accept then the last expression of my gratitude, my esteem, and my affection.

Although separated in body, let us remain united in mind and in heart. We shall then merit by the constant practice of our Rules, by our devotion to the Sacred Heart of Jesus and the Immaculate Heart of Mary, to enter the eternal union of God with His elect. There we shall be reunited, after our adieus to this earth, if, faithful to our vocation, we become daily more perfect in the practice of the spirit and the virtues of our holy state. To attain this end, keep faithfully the three vows of your religious profession, read and meditate on your book of Rules and my Circular Letters. Then, may I request your prayers for the humble priest who, on earth, was your father, and whose last benediction before death closed his eyes was for you, his devoted children. *Fiat. Fiat.*

BASIL MOREAU.

On the twenty-second of September, 1867, Monseigneur Dufal, the newly elected Superior General, reached Le Mans and took over the administration at Our Lady of Holy Cross. Some nine months had passed since his election, and during the interim, Father Moreau, though a stranger to the financial affairs of the Congregation, was nevertheless civilly responsible for the administration. Though refusing to undertake the detailed examination of Father Moreau's accounts, which the Founder so ardently desired, Monseigneur Dufal did grant him on the twenty-first of November, the Feast of Our Lady's Presentation, a certified release from further financial responsibility, and thus, after these long months of uncertainty and anguish, yet another heavy burden was lifted from the shoulders of the Founder.

XXVI
BLACK HORIZONS—1867-1868

> *God knows what I suffer in this state of affairs; however, one must submit and see in this rain of blows God's mercy rather than His justice.*
> —FATHER MOREAU.

A PASSAGE taken from a letter of filial homage addressed to the retired Founder for his Patronal Feast of St. Basil, in June of 1868, will serve as a fitting introduction to this chapter. Written by a member of the Paris Community and signed by all the religious of the house—Father Moreau's opponents having left for Rome [1]—it bears eloquent testimony to the deep appreciation of the rank and file of the Congregation for their distressed Father in Christ Jesus.

"We recall," they declared,[2] "those happier hours when we loved to press around you as infants about their father in testimony of our gratitude and to open our hearts made joyful by the bright hopes of the future. Today the tempest threatens and the black horizon is prophetic only of shipwreck and disaster. In the midst of our anxiety, we offer you with deep anguish our reflections on the unjust treatment that has been accorded you, and the pain which the sale of the Mother House to which you have consecrated a lifetime of labor, sacrifice and love, must cause you."

Well might these sincere priests and brothers visualize as black the horizons which at the moment rimmed the existence of the Founder and the whole Congregation of Holy Cross.

[1] To attend the General Chapter, June, 1868.
[2] Vie, Bk. V, Chap. IV, p. 312.

Monseigneur Dufal, but lately returned from Bengal to assume the duties of Superior General, had recognized by March of the following year, 1868, the futility of his administration, and resigned. It is in general easier to start a fire than to extinguish its flames. The adversaries of Father Moreau had enkindled the fires of discord and destructive criticism. They had not been able to direct the devastating flames exclusively toward the person and reputation of the Founder. To the latter, Monseigneur Dufal wrote at this time:[3]

> You sense, my Very Reverend Father, why I abstain from entering into a detailed discussion of the grave step I have taken: the Congregation ought to know enough on this point. I desire only to let you know the nature of one of the accusations brought against me, to which I made reference in my Circular and which deeply humiliated and disgusted me. They have had the audacity to accuse me, by letters from Paris and Le Mans, of seeking here at Rome the means of driving you and M. ——[4] from the family of Holy Cross. I had already heard other accusations against my brief administration, and I had borne them in silence; but this one made silence impossible.

The immediate result of the resignation of the second Superior General of Holy Cross was the convocation of an extraordinary General Chapter of the Congregation which was summoned to meet at Rome on the eighth of June, 1868. The sessions actually began on the fourteenth of the following month, with seventeen members in attendance.[5] The Constitutional rights of election having been set aside by means of a tortured interpretation of a special papal indult permitting the summoning of others besides the regular delegates, the enemies of Father Moreau were at last in control and lost little time in

[3] Vie, Bk. V, p. 301.
[4] Probably Fr. Charles Moreau, the Founder's cousin and former Assistant-General.
[5] The Province of Canada was not represented.

renewing their purpose of destroying the Founder's work and reputation. The sale of the Mother House at Le Mans together with the College and the Mother Church and the two novitiates [6] was settled upon, and a slanderous attack upon the Founder and his administration drawn up by a subcommittee.

One thing, however, the General Chapter at Rome accomplished that was to be for the ultimate good of the Congregation. It brought to the General Superiorship, in the person of Father Edward Sorin, Provincial of the Indiana Province, a strong man who for more than a quarter of a century had visioned and directed the destinies of the first American foundation at Notre Dame du Lac.

It would be futile to maintain that Father Sorin saw eye to eye with Father Moreau. Nevertheless the new General of Holy Cross was an apostolic priest possessed of many admirable qualities, two of which, his love of Mary and of country, he would leave as a priceless inheritance to the great University forever associated with his name. From the first moment of his arrival on our shores Father Sorin had been enthralled by the grandeur and possibilities of the United States. His was the spirit of the pioneer, and the pages of our country's history will reveal few figures who equal Edward Sorin, the priest-son of France and Holy Cross, in the completeness and ardor of their devotion to the land of their adoption. The greater greatness of Basil Moreau was recognized and acknowledged by Father Sorin himself,[7] and being the greatness of sanctity casts no disparaging shadows but only the light of God's grace.

However, the point one would here emphasize is that in placing the general administration of the Congregation of Holy Cross in these virile hands, God was in reality answering the deepest prayer of Father Moreau's soul. Basil Moreau had

[6] Both specified gifts to Father Moreau.
[7] On the King's Highway, p. 35.

FATHER EDWARD SORIN, C.S.C. PIONEER OF HOLY CROSS IN AMERICA. FOUNDER OF NOTRE DAME UNIVERSITY, AND THIRD SUPERIOR GENERAL OF THE CONGREGATION.

never desired to escape personal suffering; the draught he trembled to lift to his lips was that of the dissolution of the work he felt so profoundly God had used him to create. And that cup the Founder was not ultimately asked to drain for during the next quarter of a century Father Sorin would hold firmly in his patriarchal grip the sadly compromised interests of the Congregation.

In the wake of the General Chapter concluded at St. Bridget's on the twenty-second of July, 1868, Father Moreau found himself summoned to the feet of the Holy Father. Clearly foreseeing the hostility of the Chapter by reason of the arbitrary method of the selection of capitulants, and questioning as well he might the legality of its convocation, the Founder had declined to attend the General Chapter. He had every reason to believe his presence thereat could affect nothing of good. Moreover his absence at such a distance from Le Mans would make possible the rapid disintegration of the material resources of the Mother House, resources which Father Moreau felt a duty to defend in view of his legal responsibilities and the trust that had been reposed in him by the creditors of his administration.

Having respectfully submitted to the Holy See his reasons for declining the invitation to the Chapter and having received through Bishop Fillion,[8] the information that his presence in Rome was nevertheless required, the Founder made what arrangements he could for the defense of the material interests of the creditors, and left for the Holy City on the night of August the tenth. At that very moment the city of Le Mans was being circulated with a libelous attack upon his character and administration, yet the defamed Founder could find the courage and grace to write:

[8] Bishop Fillion had succeeded to the See left vacant by the death of Bishop Nanquette in the fall of 1861.

I crush in my soul all the reflections that rise therein, in order to say to you, before leaving Our Lady of Holy Cross, that I forgive all those who have striven to ruin my reputation, and I will never forget those who have without ceasing showed their devotion to me in my most painful trials.[9]

Forgiveness and gratitude! What an inspiring echo of words spoken from Calvary's summit, bespeaking the soul of a true disciple of the Master.

At Rome unexpected consolations awaited the harassed Founder of Holy Cross. We shall permit Father Moreau to tell the story in his own words:[10]

> Monday, the first day of September, was the day of my papal audience. At eleven o'clock I entered and prostrated myself at the feet of His Holiness, having left my companion in the throne room. Instead of an angry judge I found a father.
>
> "How is Abbé Moreau!" he said, as he offered me his ring to kiss. As I remained kneeling, he said, "Arise, and come here before me." Then continuing in the same friendly manner:
>
> "Ah, well, Abbé Moreau, you have not been obedient enough, I have been pained. And besides, you have wished to have too much of a hand in the administration since your resignation."
>
> "Most Reverend Father, does Your Holiness permit me to speak?" "Yes, yes, speak."
>
> Then the Pope rested his head on his left hand, his elbow supported by the arm of his chair while I spoke with hands clasped.
>
> "Most Holy Father, Jesus Christ, of Whom Your Holiness is in my eyes the living image, is my witness, and I would swear it on the Holy Gospels, that I have not had the idea of resisting your august will for a single instant; but I waited to have positive knowledge as to what you desired and to know whether the reasons of excuse, which I had the honor of submitting to Your Holiness, were agreeable to you or not. I add, because it is the truth, that since my resignation I have said

---

[9] Vie, Bk. V, p. 354.
[10] Vie, Bk. V, p. 358.

or done absolutely nothing that supposed the least authority, but have given myself to the apostolate of preaching."

"You have some Philotheas? A princess has come here to plead your cause."

"Most Holy Father, it is not a Philothea, but a lady very devoted to the work of Holy Cross, a relative of the Bishop of Carcasson, who took upon herself the initiative in this matter."

(The Holy Father) "What has pained me more is what has been published about you."

"Since Your Holiness wishes to manifest this new mark of interest in me I ought to declare before God that the publication in question is a tissue of falsehoods and calumnies."

(The Holy Father) "I regret that; I did not know of it until after it was published."

"That which most hurt me, Most Holy Father, is that they have dared to write that in my preaching I forgot the respect due the Holy See, and your own person, and that I have braved canonical censures. Most Holy Father, after having taught during fourteen years pure Roman doctrine, I consecrated my life to founding the works which Providence entrusted to me, and in particular that of Vigna Pia,[11] how could I forget myself in so strange a manner! No, Most Holy Father, no, a hundred times no."

(The Holy Father) "No one said that to me of you!"

Then, having spoken of Vigna Pia, from which our religious had been withdrawn as a result of a discussion with the president of the Commission of Administration, I was hoping that the Pope would express his regret; but His Holiness, resting his eyes compassionately on me, was silent for an instant and then added:

(The Holy Father) "Your poor Congregation, it is faring badly?"

"Most Holy Father, it is unhappily too true; but if the Propaganda had been as enlightened as Your Holiness when you honored me by declaring that there was in our Institute

[11] Vigna Pia had been lost to the Congregation since Father Moreau's resignation. It was a loss most keenly felt by the Founder.

three or four troublemakers who disturbed all, I would not see such ruins about me today."

The audience continued at some length and finally terminated with Father Moreau's heartfelt declaration made on his knees after kissing the Pope's ring: "Most Holy Father, I will never forget the paternal goodness with which you have deigned to receive me." [12]

The fullness of the tide of opposition to the Founder had in fact but served to lift him higher in the esteem of thoughtful and influential observers both at Rome and elsewhere. Moreover the knowledge of the paternal understanding and esteem of Christ's Holy Vicar remained to the very end of Father Moreau's life, after the testimony of his own conscience, his deepest consolation.

The sixth of September found Father Basil back at Le Mans to the discomfiture of those who had not reckoned on so happy and prompt a conclusion to his Roman journey. His presence, however, could not halt or alter the determined program of liquidating the now rapidly mounting debts of the Congregation by the alienation of the very Center of its life and vitality. While the parties responsible for this policy proceeded to its execution, he who had most to suffer in these painful circumstances, returned to the exacting labors of parish missions and retreats. During the single month of November, 1868, Father Moreau preached missions in the parishes of Saint Corneille, Grey and Commerveil, and thus in works of zeal found means to stifle the anguish which the coming destruction of his foundations must have engendered in his soul.

From the neighborhood of Mamers where he was giving a retreat, the distracted Founder writes on December 6th, of this year: [13]

[12] Vie, Bk. V, p. 360.
[13] 1868, Vie, Bk. V, p. 371.

I understand that they intend to sell Our Lady of Holy Cross for four hundred thousand francs. I wish to doubt this until I have fuller information; for it does not seem to me to square with honesty, probity and even the justice due our creditors, that they make themselves masters of the deplorable situation which has been brought about since my voluntary resignation by proposing the question of sale without any regard for the real value of the property.

Not infrequently we find the souls of God's servants who are, of a truth, the wheat of Christ, being prepared for the consecration of sanctity between the millstones of the moral and theological virtues. At this period of Father Moreau's life one of the deepest sources of his sufferings was the knowledge of the injustice being wrought to the creditors of Holy Cross by the unwarranted dissipation of the material resources of the Mother House. Basil Moreau willed by God's grace to be both charitable and just, but the human difficulty of reconciling these virtues in practice added greatly to his suffering at this moment. Writing to the Mother General of the Marianites, he declares:[14]

> I am thinking continually concerning the reimbursement of your deposits, and I hope that the dissolution of the civil society will hasten this or at least prevent a more total loss.

Then lifting his vision to higher altitudes, the Founder adds:

> My mission goes well, thanks to God, and my health is very good. I would I were able to give half of it to your three invalids, but it seems it is better for them to drink of the chalice of the sufferings of Christ Jesus. Let us adore the Divine Will while begging their convalescence if this be pleasing to God.

Whatever the Divine Will for the sick Marianites, for Basil Moreau it was that he continue to drink of the mystical chalice of his Divine Master while waiting for the break of light athwart black horizons.

[14] Vie, Bk. V, p. 386.

XXVII

CONSUMMATION—1869

> *Despite all the troubles showered upon us by Divine Justice, it is not necessary that we be disquieted concerning temporal things, but only that we apply ourselves to serve Him well Who feeds the birds of the air and never abandons those who love Him.*
>
> —FATHER MOREAU.

WHEN disaster falls upon a home or enterprise, one of the pathetic dramas following in its wake is to be found in the reactions of the elder parties involved therein. Youth is not tied so firmly to its brief past by those kindly strands of nature that grow stronger and stouter with the passing years. Young men and young women can begin anew, while their elders must be contented to salvage amid the ruins of the present the precious relics of the past. When the long-impending blow fell upon the Mother House of the Congregation, and the cries of the auctioneer began to echo through the silent corridors and halls of Our Lady of Holy Cross, others of the distressed religious departed for the various residences of the Congregation but the grief-stricken Founder chose to remain amid the ruin.

Doubtless a fine sense of honesty inspired in part the Founder's action; he would do what he could to protect the interests of the legitimate creditors of his betrayed institution; yet deeper still and woven into the very fibers of his priestly heart was a love for these sturdy walls that had become the visible symbol of all he had wished to accomplish for his Master. As a result, though Father Sorin, the new Superior General, had long since offered him asylum amid the expanding loveliness of Notre Dame du Lac, at the moment we treat of, the community residence of Saint Brieuc had been designated for his retreat. But Father Moreau, utilizing the gracious permission which the Holy Father had granted him of choosing his own place of residence,[1] selected to remain in Le Mans. Toward the end of April, 1869, he writes:[2]

> Everyone will have left Holy Cross in three days, and tomorrow I go to give a little ten-day mission near Saint-Calais. Thus Divine Justice passes upon us, and those who had wished to cast me out are themselves rejected. On my return, I shall retire to the home of my two sisters while waiting the final despoilment. I shall follow my rules as best I can.

At number 20, rue de Notre Dame de Sainte-Croix, separated from his beloved establishment by a narrow street, two of Father Moreau's own sisters, who had assisted him in the earlier days of the Congregation, had lodgings. Here in a cell-like room Father Basil chose to dwell, and here on the twenty-eighth of April, he moved his simple belongings. His nephew and ever-faithful disciple, Father Charles Moreau, assisted in the transfer. Only two trips were required to transport by hand the few paltry possessions consisting of some articles of clothing, a number of books, his framed certificate of ordination, and a thousand hymn cards for mission use.

Availing himself of a legal right, Father Moreau claimed and received the bed of his deceased friend and confessor, Canon Fillion,[3] who had spent his last years at the Mother House and whose earthly remains rested in the mortuary

---

[1] Vie, Bk. V, p. 360.
[2] Vie, Bk. V, p. 405.
[3] Canon Fillion was the uncle of Bishop Fillion and had been formerly Superior of the little Seminary of Tesse.

chapel of the Community. The Founder's claim, however, was motivated by reasons of sentiment rather than of utility, he, himself, thanks to the thoughtful charity of his Marianite daughters, being enabled to continue in possession of the armchair which had served him exclusively for a bed during the past twenty years.[4]

The gracious charity of the Marianites revealed itself in an even more practical manner by their proposal to supply the meals both for their spiritual father and for his aging sisters. On the nineteenth of this same month of April, 1869, Mother Mary of the Seven Dolors had addressed to the Founder the following note:[5]

> My Most Reverend Father, if I am not mistaken, it is tomorrow that the religious dwelling at Notre Dame de Sainte-Croix are to leave. I come, in the name of all your daughters of the Mother House, to pray you to permit us to bring you your meals in whatever place you will designate. We will consider as a favor, Most Reverend Father, this privilege that we so desire you to grant us. In courtesy you will not refuse this favor to your daughters who have a prior right. We wish and desire to do the same for your sisters.

To this note the Founder's reply was in his typical spirit:[6]

> Although I am unaware when the cuisine at Holy Cross will cease, I do not wish to delay to thank you, my dear Daughters, for your farsighted and generous offer to me and my sisters. I am conscious of your good will, and long experience does not permit me to doubt your eagerness to come to my aid in need. I have counted upon this, and your letter gives still another proof that I have reason to do so. However I do not wish to trouble you before time and become an expense to you when I am so desirous of reducing your poverty and of making amends for your privations if not for the loss

[4] The Sisters bought this armchair for Fr. Moreau at the auction.
[5] Vie, Bk. V, Chap. XII, p. 406.
[6] Vie, Bk. V, p. 406.

of the funds you confided to my administration. God knows what I suffer by reason of this state of affairs; but it is necessary to bow one's head, and to see in the blows that rain upon us rather God's mercy than His justice. For me I wish always to kiss most lovingly His paternal hand and to engage myself solely with the accomplishment of His always adorable Will. I pray that you may profit more and more by your own trials, that He may put an end to our misery and make all worthy of a better life.

The priest who could pen these lines at the very moment when flagrant injustice had deprived him of all things but his personal honor; could write them in answer to the proffered alms of his daily bread, had certainly accomplished successfully that most delicate of spiritual operations, the substitution of the Divine Will for the will of self.

Basil Moreau had need of this heroic refuge in the Will of God as the despoliation of his foundations continued. June of 1869 witnessed the auctioning of the belongings of the Brothers' Novitiate, The Solitude of St. Joseph, and the following month the sale of the property itself together with The Solitude of the Saviour, the Novitiate of the Salvatorists. But the spirit of the Founder arose by God's grace to meet every new exaction with the steadiness of a staunch vessel in a storm. In July of this same year, 1869, he writes:[7]

> The two Solitudes are to be sold on the 17th. While I was away on a mission they sold everything in my room.[8] Let God's Holy Will be done.

God's Holy Will often becomes more discernible, sometimes only discernible when viewed from the higher altitudes of the supernatural. From this vantage point we may now reverently surmise what the Divine Master was accomplishing through the medium of human limitations.

[7] Vie, Bk. V, Chap. XII, p. 409.
[8] The Founder had held his room at the Mother House during the auctioning.

It is the profoundly precious gift of the Incarnate Word to His mystical bride, the Church, that she should share in His Passion and Crucifixion. It was the precious gift of Christ Jesus to the Congregation of Holy Cross that she, in the person of her Founder, should partake of the Master's sufferings. As they stript Jesus so they stript Basil Moreau; as they parted among them the garments of the Saviour, so they parted the possessions of Holy Cross; and one in spirit with the gentlest and most merciful of masters, Basil Moreau looked on and bade his Father forgive.

October, the second, brought the final and concluding scene in this painful drama. On that date the Mother House, Conventual Church and College of Our Lady of Holy Cross with adjoining land were first offered in parceled lots, and then bought collectively by the Marquis de Nicolai with the intention of the establishment of a College under the direction of the Society of Jesus. With the news of the sale, the suffering Founder could at last whisper, "It is consummated."

XXVIII
WINTER SUNSET—1869-1872

> *I would fear to be lacking in the acknowledgment before God of the great graces He has heaped upon me since that memorable day whose anniversary we celebrate.*
>
> —FATHER MOREAU.

IF success serves to test the caliber of a soul's humility, certainly failure furnishes us with a deeper revelation of its courage and faith. The reactions of Basil Moreau amid the apparent dissolution of his work perhaps more than anything else in his career are able to furnish us with a decisive argument as to the heroic measure of his sanctity. The lesson of the one thing necessary which Our Blessed Lord inculcated in the little home at Bethany had been well pondered and its meaning assimilated by the Founder of Holy Cross. Having done, therefore, all that lay within his power to secure the just rights of the creditors of his wrecked foundation, Father Moreau committed the future into the hands of God, and directed his seemingly exhaustless energy into the channels still open for its exercise, the work of the home missions and the apostolate of the press.

At an age when most men would feel justified in releasing themselves from the more arduous fields of priestly activity, we find Father Moreau pressing ever forward, seemingly only mindful of the crying needs of immortal souls and of that night in which no man can labor. During the year 1869, he conducted missions at Saint-Mars of Lacquenay, at La Bosse, at Foultourte, at Parigné-le-Polin, at Préval, at Vinsontiers, at

Ivré-l'Eveque, at Saint Corneille, and at Spay. From the last parish he wrote:[1]

> The harvest is going to be abundant here and the church too small. I have written to two pastors—the local pastor being sick—to come to assist me with the confessions. Yesterday at seven o'clock in the evening, before a considerable crowd, filling the church for the third time, I had to leave the pulpit to take care of an urgent baptism, the child being in danger of death. I had them sing hymns during my absence, and then took up again my instruction. . . .

He concluded this note with one of those exquisite touches that only Divine Love can inculcate, "May you be cured of your neuralgia and may you be sick only from love of God in whom I love you always with all my heart."

Midsummer of 1870 was to bring to France the terrible ferment of war and to witness the humiliation of her arms before the new-found might of Prussia. But before those eventful days and out of his own defeat, a valiant French soldier of Christ rose up to preach the way of peace that the Jubilee message of Christ's Vicar had pointed to the world.[2] Before the storm broke over France, Father Moreau had renewed the spirit of faith in the parishes of Saint Julian of Champagne, Saint Aubin of Locquenay, Fillé-Guécélard, Parigné-le-Polin, Grand-Lucé, Teillé and Coulans. Let it be remembered that some of these missions were of three weeks' duration, and one's amazement grows at the capacity, physical as well as spiritual, of this white-haired veteran of Christ's priestly hosts.

Nor must it be thought that this apostolic labor of Basil Moreau ceased at the foot of the pulpit or the door of the confessional. Not infrequently the coming of the missionary was utilized by the parish clergy as the occasion of relieving

[1] Vie, Bk. V, Chap. XIII, p. 423.
[2] Proclaimed by Pius IX, 1870.

themselves temporarily from the responsibilities of their office; and the fulfillment of Father Moreau's chosen apostolate of assisting priests, was thus happily accomplished. Fortunately the Founder has left us a glimpse of this more intimate servicing of souls. In a letter of the 28th of March, 1870, addressed to Mother Mary of the Seven Dolors, he writes:[3]

> Yesterday evening I remarked to the servant at the rectory, "I have a strong feeling I will be called to the sick tonight," and sure enough at eleven they called me. It was a woman of the village who had been speaking with her neighbors at 9 o'clock, and two hours later was in eternity.

Then as the thought of the heavy responsibilities of priests directly charged with the care of souls swept in upon him, the Founder adds a thought well-calculated to make those bearing this weighty burden pause for reflection:

> The more I advance toward the end of my course, the more I realize I should bless God for not having made me either a pastor or curate.

Strange words these for an indefatigable hunter of souls, if we do not pause to weigh, as do the saints of God, the insufficiencies of self against eternal responsibilities.

A ministry, which though more indirect was nevertheless most beneficial to others and consoling to Father Basil, was the fruit of the general esteem manifested by the diocesan clergy for this valiant and venerable priest who could always be relied upon to respond so generously to their needs. By reason of his mission activities, passing from parish to parish, the priests of the countryside were enabled to visit and confer with Basil Moreau more frequently than formerly. The result was inevitable; to the memories that many of them cherished of an ardent, white-faced young professor were added now the unique spectacle of a white-haired missioner eloquent both

[3] Vie, Bk. V, p. 432.

by word and example in the preachment of the Word of God, yet even still more eloquent by reason of the sweet charity of silence which locked his lips against all recrimination of those who had worked him ill. Priests constitute no exceptions to the general law of the superior value of example in the inculcation of the virtues, and Basil Moreau's abiding charity but served to emphasize the supernatural character of his way of life.

So into the winter of his life Basil Moreau labored on ever faithful to those ideals of priestly and religious decorum he had adopted in life's springtime.

The tenth of January, 1871, found the armies of Prince Frederick Charles confronted at the gates of Le Mans by Chanzy with 150,000 French troops. For three days the fighting raged before the French commander was forced to withdraw leaving 6,000 dead and wounded behind. Father Moreau's spiritual daughters responded nobly to the needs of the wounded and dying. The college buildings were converted into a vast hospital, and the venerable priest who had raised these walls in the cause of Christian education now returned to exercise therein among the wounded of both armies the beautiful ministry of the Catholic priesthood.

One result of this sudden turn of events was especially consoling to Father Moreau; it brought him back to offer the Holy Sacrifice every morning in his beloved Church of Our Lady of Holy Cross. It was thus that his courageous and zealous character became known to the Jesuit Fathers who since the tenth of the preceding May had taken over at Le Mans the apostolate of higher education so rudely torn from the hands of Basil Moreau.

The unsettled conditions that followed upon the humiliating terms of peace signed at Frankfort, on May 10th, made inadvisable the solemn celebration of the Founder's golden jubilee of priestly ordination in the summer of 1871. The jubilee was, however, celebrated the following year, by simple yet heartfelt services in the little chapel of the Marianite Sisters.

Father Moreau began the celebration of his jubilee by offering the Holy Sacrifice assisted by Father Charles Moreau, at 7 o'clock. At its close the venerable jubilarian turned to the congregation composed of his spiritual daughters, and a few of his relatives and friends, and addressed to them a touching discourse treating of the sublimity of the priestly vocation and tracing the gracious mercies of God in his own life and work.

A true priest lives ever in humble wonderment of the greatness of God's gifts; the priesthood of Jesus Christ is too immense and mystical a gift to be capable of human comprehension; yet every priest must seek to fathom his own sacramental character, and at such times as anniversaries give expression to his findings. Let us pause for a brief space to listen to the priestly soul of Basil Moreau giving utterance to its depths:

> Yes, O Mary, my Good Mother! Your humility drew the Word of God but once into your virginal breast, while every day the Priest draws the Word of God down on the altar by virtue of his all-powerful words: "This is My Body, This is My Blood." O my God! shall I dare to lift my gaze yet higher? An angel was flung into the abyss for having dared to say: "I will be like the Most High." Nevertheless I will dare my God, since the faith has taught me how sublime is the priestly vocation. Penetrate, then, into the bosom of the Eternal, and see God calling forth from nothingness the magnificent spectacle of infinite numbers of creatures both living and inanimate: yet is it not greater to command the Creator, Himself, and to change the bread and wine of the Sacrifice into the Body and Blood of the Man-God? O, yes, Lord, my soul glorifies you, because in me Thou hast wrought such great things.[4]

Such were the exalted sentiments of the soul of Basil Moreau in the golden glow of his heart's gratitude for more than

[4] Vie, Bk. V, p. 456.

fifty years of sacerdotal sacrifice and sanctification. Need we be surprised that the ever-kindly Providence of the Divine Master saw to it that before this day of happy memories and brimming gratitude had passed, the ever-paternal hand of Christ's Vicar upon earth should be raised to give this humble French priest the most treasured of graces—the apostolic benediction?

Sometimes of a winter's day, out of the grim cloud-barriers of the West, before night comes, the sun looks forth and pours upon the earth, for one brief instant, a molten stream of glory. So, in the lives of God's servants, there is oftentimes, before the night comes wherein no man can work, a moment filled with exultation, prophetic of a glory yet to be. Such a moment we have witnessed in the life of Basil Anthony Moreau.

XXIX
WAITING FOR THE MASTER—1872

> *Those who have persecuted me have rendered me a great service, and I have today the consolation of resting in peace in my little solitude, outside of the time of my missions, and assured of the favor of the Pope.*
>
> —FATHER MOREAU.

WITH the return of peace to the trampled fields of France, Father Moreau, despite his aging years, took up once more his apostolate of parish missions. He preached during the Lent of 1872, at La Bosse and at Saint-Symphorien. From Pentecost till Trinity Sunday, he was at Ecommoy preparing the children for their First Communion, a work very dear to his priestly heart because of the intensity of his devotion to Our Lord in the Blessed Sacrament.

In July of this same year we find him rendering his customary tribute of gratitude to God in these lines which reveal the constant character of his labors:[1]

> My health continues to hold out and I thank the good God for having made it possible for me to continue my retreats and missions for three consecutive months.

Preaching four or more times a day, and each time for upwards of an hour, adding to this the long hours spent in the confessional cleansing and binding the wounds of our common humanity, and this, week after week, for months at a time, are we not face to face here with the exercise of heroic zeal?

[1] Vie, Bk. V, p. 462.

But even these labors were not sufficient to consume the spiritual energies of Father Moreau. Indeed true zeal cannot be exhausted for though the channel is finite, the source of the stream is to be found in the unfathomable depths of Divine Charity. That is why we find the aging Founder in the silence of his little room bending himself to still another task of love: he wished above all things to gain souls for Christ, and when he could not reach them with his living voice he would reach them by the medium of his pen. The result was a third edition [2] of his "Christian Meditations" enlarged and adapted to the needs of the diocesan clergy and the laity. The purpose of the author is thus stated in the preface: [3]

> The truths of religion have noticeably decreased in the eyes of the children of men and if this continues much longer one might think that the prediction of the Saviour were accomplished, "Think you, when the Son of Man shall come He shall find faith upon earth?" Then will take place that terrifying seduction of the AntiChrist, from which not even the elect would escape were not its duration shortened.
>
> This is why now more than ever it is important for the faithful to meditate upon Christian truth, the ignorance or forgetfulness of which causes the loss of many souls and all the upheavals in human society. To aid souls to preserve and reanimate their faith the author, encouraged by two venerable prelates, offers this new edition of his "Meditations." He is persuaded that thus he may help to preserve souls from the seductive doctrines of our age while helping them to advance in piety.

In the midst of these varied activities Father Basil was too practical a Christian not to remind himself that his own life must presently have its ending. Indeed, this very thought serves as the spur to his zeal; foreseeing this eventuality he

[2] The other editions had been issued in 1855 and 1858 and were intended primarily for his religious sons and daughters.

[3] This translation is made from a new edition issued at the Oratory of St. Joseph, Montreal, 1932.

wished his book of "Meditations" "to continue to make religion known and loved when he can no longer either write, or speak, or act."[4]

When not engaged in his apostolic missions, the Founder said Mass each morning in the little chapel of the Marianite Sisters. In the afternoon he would return for his visit to the Blessed Sacrament, recite his office and make the stations of the Cross, the last being a devotion he had practiced for many years. And the evening would find him returned yet once more, for spiritual reading, the recitation of the rosary and night prayers. The regularity and isolation of this manner of life far from breaking Father Moreau's spirit, served merely to tighten that loving union with the Master which is at once the beginning and the end of the spiritual life. Thus he could write:[5]

> That is why, O Lord, I will bless You even unto my death for having released me from the preoccupations inseparable from the foundations of which You have seen fit to make me the instrument, and have granted me at last to live alone with You alone.

The thought of death appears not infrequently in his writings of this year destined in the designs of God to be his last on earth; and, as if in preparation for it, his spirit of forgiveness and abandonment become more striking.

"It is not necessary," he declares, in a letter of this time,[6] "to extinguish the smoking wick. As for calumnies, I have read so many of them that I do not trouble myself nor preoccupy myself about them, having abandoned all to Divine Providence." And again, writing to Father Séquin, his former Secretary General, he declares of a religious who had injured their reputations: "I am surprised that —— has dared to go to

---

[4] "Meditations," edition of 1932, p. 445.
[5] "Meditations," edition of 1932, p. 29.
[6] Vie, Bk. V, p. 467.

you after what he has said against you and against me; but if he has done it to make up for the past, I am very pleased for his sake. Whatever it be, I do not doubt you have received him graciously; this is a time to render good for evil. Thanks be to God, there is in my heart no bitterness toward him." [7]

These sentiments, simple though they be in their expression, open to us the casements of a soul becoming daily more and more identified with the Heart of Christ, ever more fully released from earthly values and hence prepared for an eternal evaluation. Nor could such a spirit fail to arouse in other hearts sentiments of a kindred nature, and even as the Good Thief sought forgiveness of the dying Saviour, so, more than one of Father Basil's spiritual sons sought and received from his venerable hand and loving heart a pardon registered in Heaven. Thus advancing in sanctity as well as age Basil Moreau toiled and prayed on in the service of the Master.

On the 19th of November, 1872, we find his naturally cheerful spirit regarding optimistically the limitations age is slowly placing on his shoulders. To the Superior of the Marianites of Louisiana he writes: [8]

> I am not dead yet, and I still hope, despite my seventy-three years, to preach the Lenten services next year in one of the parishes of our diocese. However, old age warns me that I am getting close to the end, and I am longing to see God and to be no longer capable of offending Him. Beg this grace for me, and count even to death on my tender devotion.

Though longing for the Divine Union, Basil Moreau like a faithful soldier held himself relentlessly to his chosen line of duty. In the little notebook where he was accustomed to record his missionary engagements we find the following notes for 1873: [9]

[7] Idem.
[8] Vie, Bk. V, p. 469.
[9] Idem.

Maresché, solemn adoration of the Most Blessed Sacrament, the 26th of January. Eight days of preparatory services.

Mont-Saint-Jean, first Communions, Thursday within the Octave of Corpus Christi.

There is something of arresting impressiveness in these records of engagements destined never to be fulfilled. They stand mute witnesses to the limitations of human contracts that rest upon a contingent future. But they stand, as well, as an abiding proof of the spirit of the zeal of him whose pen traced here the willingness of his heart to labor on and on for the glory of God in the salvation and sanctification of immortal souls.

The Master was a long time coming, but He would find when He came, a faithful servant waiting, yet not idly waiting, at the gates.

XXX
THROUGH THE GATES—1873

Yes, to all—benediction, absolution, all that I can give.
—FATHER MOREAU.

IT is in keeping with the paradoxical character of Christianity that the most vital moment of life should be the one in which earthly vitality ceases. As a consequence, this mysterious moment, hidden from our eyes in both the Justice and Mercy of a Heavenly Father, must ever remain the object of our deepest personal solicitude and most reasonable ambition. For to die well is to save one's soul and to save one's soul is the primary and basic part we each must play in the promotion of God's eternal glory. In this chapter we shall witness the blessed death of one who in life and in death belonged wholly and unwaveringly to God.

New Year's eve of 1873 found the slight figure of Father Moreau turning away from the friendly warmth of the New Year felicitations of his relatives and his spiritual daughters to hasten to the aid of the sick pastor of the little village of Ivré-l'Eveque. As Father Basil made his way through the early dusk of the dying year, did he know that he, too, was dying? For some months now he had been suffering physically, but never a word of complaint. Or did his thoughts turn back the memory-pages of fifty years to that night, when with the holy oils still moist upon his palms, he had responded to the call of another sick priest and sped through the night with the Light of the World to cheer his soul, and a dim lantern to guide his feet?

Whatever Basil Moreau's thoughts were that New Year's

eve, before morning swift and cruel pains were racking his poor body. When morning came, he dragged himself to the altar and managed to say Mass for the assembled parishioners. The brevity of his sermon served notice that the venerable missioner, whose eloquence was a household word throughout the district, was a sick man. When he left the altar that New Year's morning he had offered his last Mass, he had completed the last apostolic service of his priestly years.

Father Moreau returned the same morning to Le Mans, and was placed at once under the care of a physician. Sick as he was, and with his sufferings augmented by reason of the treatments he was forced to undergo, it was only on the fourth day he could be persuaded to abandon the reclining chair in which for upwards of twenty years he had taken whatever sleep his labors and prayers permitted.

This was his descent from the Cross. From this moment he gave himself into the hands of his attendants, accepting with gratitude whatever their loving hearts could devise to lessen his sufferings. He was moved from his own cramped quarters into a larger and more airy room. He even asked to have a fire lighted—a concession to nature he had denied himself for many years. It would seem, at times, as if the Master willed His faithful servants should receive services akin to those that came to Him when Mary at Bethany broke her alabaster box of spikenard and prepared His Body beforehand for burial.

Grateful to all, appreciative, as was his nature, it was to God the sick priest turned habitually and constantly, using the words of the liturgy and of the Holy Scriptures, and familiar ejaculations in honor of God, God's Mother, and the saints. When for a few days it seemed a rapid convalescence might be expected, his thoughts returned at once to the missions he had engaged himself to undertake in the New Year. For a while he even anticipated resuming his apostolate on the nineteenth of the month.

When, however, the development of his condition postponed definitely the possibilities of his offering or even assisting at the Holy Sacrifice, the dying Founder prepared himself, with all the fervor of his lifelong devotion to the Eucharist, to receive the hidden Master he had loved and served so long. Before communicating, his lively faith prompted an apology to Jesus for his inability to receive the Sacred Host prostrate upon his knees.

"You are my witness, O my God!" he declared,[1] "my soul is constrained by my body at this solemn moment, and if pain did not prevent me I would not be seated in an armchair. I would receive You on both knees and with my head bowed low."

Basil Moreau's fundamental spirit of humility was evidenced in this inspiring scene which left a lifelong impression on those who were privileged to be its witnesses. Faith, a faith that burned with a steady flame and threw an unwavering light across his pathway was leading the dying Founder into the valley of the shadow.

By the seventeenth of January, Feast of St. Anthony, one of the Founder's principal patrons, and thus a day of special commemoration for him, it was evident to the watchers in what direction the sickness of their beloved Father was conducting him. That evening the entire Community of the Marianites were permitted to gather about the bedside, while their chaplain voiced their sentiments and last wishes:[2]

> My well-beloved Father, the Community of your spiritual daughters, to whom you have given the religious life, are come to offer you their devoted sympathy in your sufferings, together with the homage of their unending gratitude for all the benefits of your devotion and example. They are on their knees, asking your benediction as their Founder and their Father;

---

[1] Vie, Bk. V, p. 472.   [2] Vie, Bk. V, p. 472.

they promise you the assistance of their prayers and an inviolable fidelity to the Rule which you have given them.

The reply of the dying priest was couched in that simplicity that so well becomes souls upon the brink of eternity:

> Yes, with all my heart, may God bless you by my hands in the Name of the Father, and of the Son, and of the Holy Ghost.

They then asked him to extend his benediction to the whole Congregation of Marianites scattered afar, and again, the Founder responded with words:

> Yes, to all. I begin again to bless them: benediction, absolution, all that I am able to give.[3]

All that Father Moreau could give to his Divine Master was already given; it remained only for the sacramental sealing of the gift. On the eighteenth he received Extreme Unction, and in the evening the apostolic benediction and plenary indulgence. There followed a day and a night of slowly dimming faculties, through which, as through a veil, the dying priest seemed graced to follow those venerable prayers to the chanting of which the Christian soul goes forth to meet her Bridegroom. Finally on Monday, the twentieth, at about mid-afternoon, the labored breathing eased away, the mortified body relaxed its grip, and the pure soul of a noble and faithful priest passed through the gates into life.

On Wednesday, the twenty-second of January, they laid the Founder to rest in the little mortuary chapel he, himself, had erected in his faith-guided reverence for the one-time earthly temples of the Holy Ghost. In the interval between his death and burial, crowds thronged to view for a last time the calm and peace-inspiring face of this humble yet ardent servant of the Adorable Trinity. The parish priest celebrated the Mass

---

[3] Vie, Bk. V, p. 473.

and gave the final absolution. The dean of the Canons of the Cathedral together with superiors of the various religious communities of Le Mans, the Marianite Sisters, former students of the College and his own dear family were present for the services. By the Providence of God, some of the Josephites learned of their former Superior's death in time to be present, and at least two of Father Moreau's priestly sons were likewise in attendance.

A marble slab was placed upon his grave and thereon one may read the following brief tribute: [4]

IN THIS CHAPEL, ERECTED BY HIMSELF,
AND, UNDER THIS SLAB,
PROOF OF THE LOVE OF HIS KINDRED,
OF THE GRATITUDE OF THE SISTERS MARIANITES,
AND OF THE FAITHFUL REMEMBRANCE OF HIS STUDENTS,
RESTS UNTO THE LAST DAY
THE DEVOTED SON AND SERVANT OF THE CHURCH,
BASIL ANTHONY MOREAU,
APOSTOLIC MISSIONARY,
ELOQUENT IN WORD AND IN WORKS,
FORMER ASSISTANT SUPERIOR OF THE GRAND SEMINARY
AND HONORARY CANON OF LE MANS,
FOUNDER AND ECCLESIASTICAL SUPERIOR
OF THE MONASTERY OF THE GOOD SHEPHERD AT LE MANS,
AND OF THE HOUSE OF OUR LADY OF HOLY CROSS,
OF THE RELIGIOUS INSTITUTE OF HOLY CROSS
APPROVED BY ROME IN 1857,
AND OF THE RELIGIOUS INSTITUTE OF THE SISTERS MARIANITES
APPROVED BY ROME IN 1867,
BORN AT LAIGNÉ-EN-BELIN, THE 11TH OF FEBRUARY, 1799,
DIED AT LE MANS, THE 20TH OF JANUARY, 1873,
BLESSED BY HIS HOLINESS, PIUS IX.

Thus in a silence suggestive of God's Peace and expectant of another and kindlier spring rests the earthly all of a nobleman of both grace and nature.

[4] On the King's Highway, p. 90.

XXXI
A PRECIOUS HERITAGE

> *Heart of Jesus, speak to our hearts and convert them to Thee forever. We ask this by the wound given Thee on Calvary, and by that counter-thrust which at the same time pierced the living heart of Mary, Thy Mother.*[1]
>
> —FATHER MOREAU.

THE same instinct of faith that makes men pause in reverence at the crib of a little child, makes them bow with reverence before the couch of death. In both cases there is mystery; in one of life beginning, in the other of life just fled. The Marianite Sisters keeping vigil beside the strangely silent figure of their spiritual father in the hours before his burial felt this second mystery but slightly. In the tranquil light of the candles the white face of the dead priest seemed set in lines of peace, and when a vagrant air current stirred the black draperies and set the taper-flames dancing, it was easy to imagine that he was smiling in his sleep. Meantime, the devotion of the faithful who thronged the little convent chapel eager to pay a final tribute of homage to this priest they had known and loved, confirmed the conviction of their own hearts, that their Founder had been very dear to God.

Sanctity in the eyes of God's Church is fundamentally not a question of miracles but of virtue,—of virtue carried to heroic heights. Grace and nature work together in the process of

---
[1] From Sister Eleanore's beautiful translation of Father Moreau's Conferences for Religious, "Our Light and Our Way," Bruce, 1936.

sanctification, and Peguy's simile of the "two hands clasped" is perhaps truer of this co-operation than of the union of body and soul to which he referred.[2]

In Basil Moreau's soul, from earliest childhood God, like unto a placer-miner, had been busy washing away the sand of imperfection in the stream of grace until at last nothing remained in the divine hands but flakes of purest gold. That is why amid the apparent dissolution of his foundations, the soul of Father Moreau could remain unchanged, unperturbed by the reversal of fortune, at peace with itself and God. Whence, we may ask, was the source of this peace?

Holy Scripture supplies the answer. "When a strong man, armed, keepeth his court, those things that he possesses are in peace." Basil Moreau was a strong man armed by faith and the spirit of prayer. The most superficial study of his life reveals the evidence of his faith. From childhood he not only believed, he preached. The naïve sermonettes of the little Basil most certainly amused the elder members of his family,[3] yet they served as well to give notice of that earnest apprehension of the things of God that is born of the gift of faith. Between the little lad preaching to his sisters in the warmth of his mother's kitchen and the aged missioner preaching with pain-taut lips in the cold of a country chapel, on New Year's day, 1873, there stretch more than sixty years of laborious pilgrimage; yet there is abundant evidence that every step of that arduous journey was motivated by faith.

Basil Moreau had, however, more than the virtue Faith; he possessed those gifts of which Faith is the sure foundation, the virtues of Hope and Charity. It is true these sweet infusings of God's Holy Spirit are the baptismal gift of the Adorable Trinity to the souls of the children of men, but what barren

[2] Oeuvres Completes, Vol. V, p. 329.
[3] Conference of Frere Marie-Antoine, C.S.C., Saint-Laurent, August 3, 1920.

soil they ofttimes find within the breast of humanity, and what rich soil they found in the heart of Basil Moreau!

Hope, the virtue of the strong, finds its most obvious expression in the reactions of a soul to the trials and difficulties of life. Few of God's servants in modern times have faced more persistent trials and greater difficulties than Father Moreau; few of God's servants have surpassed him in the buoyant resurgence of their spirit amid the waves of adversity. His life, especially in its final phases, became a veritable passion.[4] "My life has been but a long agony," Father Moreau wrote on the first day of January, 1863—yet three years later when his trials had increased rather than decreased we find him writing:[5]

> I am appreciative always of your good wishes—but I desire to see you more resigned and abandoned to God in the midst of your trials which are likewise mine.—Hope against all hope—.

The sentiments of Father Moreau which we have just quoted serve here a further purpose, for in them we find the inculcation of the practice of abandonment to the Divine Will which when reduced to constant practice constitutes a most convincing witness to a soul's perfection. Perfect charity not only casts out fear, it literally casts the soul itself into the arms of God. "Into Thy hands, O Lord, I commend my spirit" was the cry of the Divine Redeemer on Calvary, and must ever remain the ultimate expression of His servants' adherence. Basil Moreau practiced abandonment in a manifestly high degree. At a time when he had been unjustly deprived of an inheritance which would have greatly relieved his concern for the financial security of his Institute, impaired by the folly and disobedience of subordinates, and when his own actions were

[4] Cir. Letter, January 1, 1863, Gen. Archives, C.S.C.
[5] Vie, Bk. V, p. 272.

already the objective of slanderous tongues, we find him writing:[6]

> Oh, how sweet it is to abandon ourselves to the love of Our Father who is in Heaven by seeking His most holy Will and His alone. And what is more reasonable, Reverend Fathers and dear Brothers? So in the midst of the critical circumstances that face us still, our chief thought must be to know what God exacts of us, and then to give ourselves entirely to His service.

The abandonment born of perfect charity must not be conceived of as conducive to a state of inaction. Just the opposite is true, for the soul in uniting itself to the Divine Will enters more intimately and completely into union with the Divine Activity, and sustained by God's graces gives itself with the utmost ardor to the accomplishment of God's Will upon earth. That is why the saints are the greatest benefactors of their fellowmen whether their activity be the hidden labor of a Saint Therese or the public service of a Curé of Ars. That is why we find Father Moreau carrying on literally into the shadows of the valley of Death his priestly ministration to souls. That, too, is why we find no pause for prolonged recreations or vacations in the routine of this hard-driving missioner, who sleeps in an armchair in order "to be more ready to note the thoughts that come to him in sleep,"[7] and who as early as 1853, utilizes a period of enforced idleness "to put in order the Rules, the Directory, and to complete his Manual of Prayers."[8]

Moreover as Divine Love draws the Eternal Word to seek in Mary's virginal bosom an ineffable union with our humanity, so the soul that is united to Christ will have no deeper desires,—indeed, eventually no other desires,—than those of the

---

[6] Cir. Letters, #168, Gen. Archives, C.S.C.
[7] Vie, Bk. V, p. 470.
[8] "Meditations Chrêtiennes," Montreal, 1932, p. x.

Sacred Heart. And the Sacred Heart had pleaded in the tragic setting of the Last Supper,[9] "That they all may be one, as thou, Father, in Me, and I in Thee; that they also may be one in Us. . . ."

Basil Moreau had been for half a century a priestly lover of the Sacred Heart. To that Heart he had consecrated the priests of his nascent Congregation, asking them to make It both the model and the center of their lives. It was inevitable then that he should place an especial emphasis on the spirit of union among the members of his religious family. A holy family it was to be, in imitation of that Holy Family of Nazareth wherein God had revealed to an astonished world the aristocracy of humanity and the democracy of God.

Small wonder, then, that Basil Moreau would never cease to plead for what Christ so desires, the union of hearts in His. In his letter of August 22, 1863,[10] to the Congregation, Father Moreau thus reveals his sentiments on this subject:

> He [Christ] earnestly asked that His disciples be united with one another, as are the Three Divine Persons of the Trinity—making them all as one. Oh! who will give us such union with authority and among ourselves, union begotten of the indissoluble bonds of obedience and of charity? With this union we shall triumph over the enemy of each of us and of the Institute of Holy Cross which is entrusted to our care. Let us close our ranks instead of separating them and disbanding; and let us be so united that beholding the members of our family the world can say of us as the pagans said of the first Christians: "See how they love one another."

Where the love of God is authentic it cannot fail to reveal itself in charity toward His creatures. Moreover of all the expressions of fraternal charity none is more difficult in practice than the forgiveness of injuries. Yet we witness in the

[9] St. John, Chap. XVII, v. 21-22.
[10] Gen. Arch., C.S.C., #172.

life of Father Moreau the constant exercise of this rare virtue. The letter from which we have just quoted continues:

> —I declare that I forget all that was done to sadden me and to those who did so I give once again the assurance of my affection and confidence.

Basil Moreau was ever ready not only to forgive but to forget as well, not only to forget but to restore both affection and confidence even to those who had failed him so cruelly in his hour of direst need.

In his love for humanity, Father Moreau turned with that simple logic to which grace added supernatural ardor to devotion to God's Most Holy Mother and St. Joseph. The special attractions of his devotion to Our Lady were her Immaculate Conception and her Seven Dolors. In Mary Immaculate the purity of his own soul found its ideal imaged, while in the Sorrowful Mother his ready sympathy discovered a subject of abiding worth and inspiration.

His devotion to St. Joseph, truly suggested that of St. Theresa of Avila. His confidence in the Foster-Father of the Incarnate Son knew no bounds and found expression with consistency in his correspondence and conferences. In his Circular Letter of March 27, 1860, Father Moreau wrote:[11]

> When I recall how twenty years ago the worthy Spouse of the Mother of God was so little known and invoked by our students, and when I behold them now so attentive every evening to the preacher of St. Joseph's virtues and greatness; when I behold these same students invoking Mary's Spouse and offering him the homage of their studies, I am forced to conclude that the time spoken of by a celebrated writer has come: The Holy Ghost will not cease to speak to the hearts of the faithful until the whole Church more especially honors St. Joseph.

[11] Vide, Cir. Letter of Very Rev. James W. Donahue, C.S.C., January 18, 1937.

FRÈRE ANDRÉ, C.S.C.

THE MODERN APOSTLE OF ST. JOSEPH

In our own day these words have received a remarkable confirmation through the life and labors of Brother André of Mount Royal, the modern apostle of devotion to St. Joseph. In the simplicity of this humble coadjutor-brother of the Canadian Province of the Congregation of Holy Cross the Heavenly Father would seem to have found a fitting mirror for the image of the ever faithful Guardian of His Only Begotten, while through Brother André's untiring zeal Our Lady's Divine Spouse has seen fit to give a mighty impetus to devotion to her Virginal Consort.

After Our Lady and St. Joseph, Father Moreau's devotion went to all God's saints and to the holy angels, in particular to his holy patrons, Saint Basil and Saint Anthony of Egypt, and the founders of religious communities: Saint Vincent de Paul, Saint Ignatius Loyola, Saint Alphonsus Liguori, and Saint Francis de Sales. One cannot truly love God without loving His works and the greatest of these are the souls of His elect.

Moreover as in God all things have their source in Love, so in man, it is love, though diverse of character, that ultimately determines the course and development of the individual. Father Moreau's life was dominated by love,—a love of God, unselfish and all-pervading. Love of Jesus in the Sacrament of His love, love of Jesus imaged in His Holy Face, love of Jesus in the person of His Vicar, love of Jesus in His Mother and His saints, love of Jesus in the Holy Souls, love of Jesus in the souls of his relatives and religious brethren, love of Jesus everywhere and always—these were all characteristic devotions of Basil Moreau. These were his virtues, consonant notes of his spirit, and by consequence, the priceless heritage of his priests, his brothers, and his sisters in the Family of Holy Cross.

The grace of God falls upon the prisms of immortal souls and effects the colorful spectrum of the virtues. God's grace rested upon the soul of Basil Moreau and was refracted in the radiant virtues of Christian living. We who are his spiritual children are confident that someday Holy Mother Church will assure us that the grace of God has woven for Father Moreau a crown of everlasting glory.

EPILOGUE

SOMEWHERE in the world at every moment it is morning and the low-hung mists that have enveloped in their chilling shrouds the landscape retreat with seeming reluctance before the hosts of light. Somewhere in the world at every moment, I love to think of Truth as playing Light's eternal role; of pushing back the mists of prejudice, of tearing asunder the clouds of error and superstition and warming into friendlier concepts through juster observations the hearts and the minds of men. Under this innate impulse of Truth, and guided by God's grace, nations must learn to revalue nations, and men to revalue men. And when this process shall have retrogressed to the France of the last century and come upon the slim cassocked figure of Basil Anthony Moreau, I am sure the final verdict will bespeak the gracious virtues of a knightly priest of Mary who stood with her beneath the Cross.

APPENDIX

I. FUNDAMENTAL ACT, 1837
II. FATHER THEINER'S REPORT, 1850
III. BISHOP NANQUETTE'S LETTER, 1856
IV. THE CONSTITUTIONS, 1855-1857
V. APPROBATION OF THE MARIANITES, 1867

APPENDIX

I

FUNDAMENTAL ACT, 1837

PREAMBLE

On March 1, 1837, the Council being assembled, Father Moreau, Superior of the Association of Holy Cross, wishing to obviate, as far as possible, the serious inconveniences that would result, if, in case of separation, the two Societies (the Auxiliary Priests and the Brothers of St. Joseph) should wish to know their respective rights and if in their opinion the financial accounts were not correct, and wishing, moreover, to stabilize the still precarious Institute of the Brothers of St. Joseph whose money derived from the sale of their property in Ruillé is about to be devoted to the constructions of Our Lady of Holy Cross, the equity in which cannot, by unanimous declaration of the Brothers of St. Joseph, yield them the right to a sum exceeding forty-five thousand francs ($9,000), including the earnings accruing from their various Houses (the property of Our Lady of Holy Cross with its appurtenances and the country house at Charbonnière belonging exclusively to Father Moreau, to whom the above gifts were made long before the transfer of the Brothers of St. Joseph from Ruillé to Holy Cross), a deduction is made of said sum of forty-five thousand francs and the chattels belonging to the Brothers, as listed in an inventory. Desiring, finally, to strengthen the union between the two Societies, while still leaving the Brothers in dependence on the Auxiliary Priests, to whom Father Moreau wished the direction and government of their Society to be confided, on a basis fixed by common agreement, among the members of the Council representing the two Societies, he proposed the following resolution which was agreed upon and accepted by the Council.

Article I

To get a just idea of the state of the receipts and expenses of the three establishments of Holy Cross; viz., the Auxiliary Priests, the

Brothers of St. Joseph, and the Boarding School, there will be opened, beginning March 1, 1837, a Book of Receipts and Expenses for the exclusive use of each of these three Establishments, and it shall be called the General State of the Receipts and Expenses of Each of the Said Establishments up to this time. This Book shall be kept by a Brother of St. Joseph, who is a member of the Council of Administration, under the supervision of an Auxiliary Priest who shall present it every eight days to the Council for examination and verification.

Article II

There shall be opened a Cash Book stating the amounts received or disbursed by each of the said Establishments respectively. This Book shall be kept by the Treasurer who will present it at each meeting of the Council.

Article III

The "Safe" shall be locked by three different keys, one of each of which shall be in the possession of the three members of the Council: these three members of the Council shall be present each time the Safe is opened.

Article IV

Abbé Moreau and the Auxiliary Priests unanimously grant to the Brothers of St. Joseph, on the property adjacent to the House of Holy Cross, formerly occupied by Abbé Delile, a right equivalent to 45,000 francs ($9,000), comprising, besides the money received from the actual or possible sale of their property at Ruillé, all the furniture already bought by them, or to be transported to Holy Cross, all the disbursements made even up to the present day, by their various Establishments, and finally all the work done or to be done by their working Brothers. The Brothers of St. Joseph who are Members of the Council, representing the entire Congregation, unanimously recognize that the sum of $9,000 exceeds rather than falls short of the real estimate of their share of capital in the said building.

Article V

Abbé Moreau declares that he wishes to take measures necessary to assure the Brothers of St. Joseph a right equal to that of the Auxiliary Priests on the property of Holy Cross and its belongings so that if, for example, the said property with its belongings were valued in the future at two hundred thousand francs ($40,000) the Brothers would have a right to claim fifty-five thousand francs in addition to their forty-five thousand francs.

Article VI

Abbé Moreau in proposing this decision wishes and intends that the profits already received or about to be received from the Boarding School annexed to the work of Holy Cross, shall be equally divided, at the end of each year, between the two Communities— the Auxiliary Priests and the Brothers of St. Joseph, whatever be the number of the said Auxiliary Priests or said Brothers of St. Joseph residing at Holy Cross.

Article VII

Wishing that each of the two Congregations be equally interested in the mutual existence and preservation of the other, Abbé Moreau declares that it shall be his will, if one of the two be dissolved before the other, the members of the dissolved Congregation preserve a right to their personal support out of the property and revenue of the surviving Congregation which would administer the property and revenue of the extinct Congregation until such time as it would be possible for the dissolved Institute to revive and then enter upon all its rights, without, however, being able to claim in any way acquisitions made during its dispersion or its dissolution.

Article VIII

Unable in the actual condition of political society to assure legal existence to the Establishments of Holy Cross, and because of the great inconveniences which would result from their dissolution and wishing nevertheless to preserve the said Establishments from the harm which the infidelity of one of its legatees would bring about, Abbé Moreau wishes each of the members of the two Establishments to sign, on the day of his definite admission, an authentic agreement by which he will consent, if he voluntarily withdraws from the Congregation, or is dismissed by the Superior with the consent of his Council, either in conscience or before a civil tribunal, not to lay claim to any rights which have been granted on the goods of the Community by will, by a sealed letter, or by any other act.

II
FATHER THEINER'S REPORT, 1850

To His Excellency the Most Reverend Monseigneur Alexandro Barnabo, Secretary of the Sacred Congregation of the Propaganda:

YOUR EXCELLENCY:

Although living in retirement in the solitude of my hermitage of St. Francis at Mounte Mario, I do not hesitate for an instant to obey the command with which your Excellency honored me by your kind letter of the 23rd instant.

You desire to know my humble judgment of the pious Institute of the Brothers who are so aptly called "The Brothers of St. Joseph"; what advantage the Church can reap from this Institute; and finally if this Institute is really deserving of some testimonial of esteem from the Holy See.

I will answer briefly each of the above questions:

1. In the second decade of this century, a worthy and venerable Priest and Curé in the diocese of Le Mans, France, founded the pious Institute named the Congregation of the Brothers of St. Joseph. Its members, though laymen, vowed themselves to the service of all classes of society in the primary schools of cities and country towns. They were to do this under the supervision of the respective curés and with the Bishop's permission. They taught the elements not only of Christian Doctrine, but also of the sciences.

From the beginning, this Institute made such marvelous progress that it would not be easy to enumerate all the testimonials of praise which it received. Its members were so progressive that Louis XVII at the urgent request of the zealous Bishop de Le Myre of Le Mans, gave it his approval for several departments of the Kingdom of France by a Royal Ordinance of June 25th, 1823.

The pious founder had arrived at extreme old age, and had consequently lost the vigor requisite for the direction of such a holy and beneficent work, which the Revolution of 1830 had almost annihilated. On August 31, 1835, the Bishop of Le Mans replaced him in this high office, by appointing the excellent priest, Abbé

Moreau, who on previous occasions had zealously loaned his aid to the Abbé Dujarié and who was at the same time the Vice President of the Episcopal Seminary. Bishop Bouvier in a circular address to his clergy on the following 27th of September praised him in the highest terms. Abbé Moreau left nothing undone to perfect the work which had been inaugurated under such favorable auspices. With this in mind, he introduced simply temporary vows which the Brothers had not taken. Moreover, he founded after the model of the already existing congregation of the Brothers, another Congregation of Auxiliary Priests who loaned their services to the diocesan clergy; and he then associated with them a third congregation of Sisters who took their name from the sweet name of Mary and followed the Rule and the constitution of St. Joseph.

The new director was not satisfied with having enlarged the restricted field of the primitive Institute, as we have noted, but he desired, moreover, to give to its spirit and to its end the greatest possible development through the Congregation of priests which he himself had just founded. The Association consequently aims at giving both religious and scientific instruction in colleges and in the Little Seminaries conducted by the bishops.

The entire Institute takes the general name of "The Association of Holy Cross." This title was given by the Founder himself to the Mother House, situated in a town called Holy Cross.

Let me cite on this point the very words of the printed Constitutions: "The Association of Holy Cross is made up of three very distinct Societies, although they are all governed by the same Superior General. The members of the Priests' Society, or Salvatorians, are so named because they are consecrated to the Sacred Heart of Jesus, the Saviour of mankind. The members of the Society of the Brothers, or Josephites, are so named because of their devotion to St. Joseph, their Patron, whose most pure and most faithful heart they especially honor. The members of the Society of the Sisters or Marianites are so named after Mary, the Mother of God, whose most pure heart pierced with the seven swords of sorrow is the object of their special devotion."

The Society of the Salvatorists is made up of clerics whose special end or aim is to preach retreats and missions, and to teach in universities and colleges. The Society of Josephites is made up of religious laymen, whose special aim or end is to conduct parochial and industrial schools. The Society of Marianites is made up of religious laywomen, whose special aim or object is to teach girls, and to render domestic service in the houses of the Association.

The three Societies, as we have already stated, are united, are helpful to one another in accordance with the inspirations of Christian charity, and are all governed by the one Superior General.

All members of the Association of Holy Cross depend entirely on their respective bishops in whatever is not contrary to their statutes, and depend absolutely upon the Holy See, as the unique and true center of Catholic unity.

Incredible and really marvelous has been the progress of this Institute, especially so since the actual superior took over its direction, and he can in all truth, for he has every title thereto, be called the real founder. The special visible blessing of heaven seems to have descended on all three societies of the Association of Holy Cross. In France alone, it has already almost sixty houses; in the United States, in New Orleans, in Algeria and in Canada it has a goodly number; and in England it is negotiating a new foundation.

Not only have more than forty bishops of France heartily praised this Institute, but also several of them have fully approved the Association, as well as its constitutions, and also I, who write this report, have in my possession their personal letters of approval. Here I shall quote only a few lines from the letters given by the Bishop of Chartres, dated March 10, 1842: "These Rules and Constitutions breathe the Spirit of God. They cannot fail to aid those who shall observe them to attain religious perfection whilst at the same time they devote themselves to the salvation of souls by their prayers, by their teachings and example."

Louis Philippe's government, quite hostile to religious, gave its approval to the Institute by a Royal Ordinance of March 3, 1843, by introducing it into Algeria.

2. What advantage can the Church reap from such an Institute? Its entirely unforeseen and wonderful expansion within so brief a period, its approval by all the bishops of France, of America, and of other countries convincingly prove that the Church has great advantages to reap from this Institute. Indeed, to be frank, among all the pious and religious institutes charity has caused to be founded for the relief of humanity in these our times, I know of not another of its kind that can render more invaluable service to

the public at large, and which is so well prepared to offer a cure for the ills of our unhappy epoch. I do not believe that I belong to that class of men of our day called visionaries, for I abhor them, yet I frankly acknowledge that this Institute, once all its Societies are developed, if the Lord continues to bless it in the future as He has abundantly blessed it up to the present, will, in the course of time, attain to an extraordinary importance, and will be thus enabled to exercise such an influence as I can neither imagine nor describe. The Church has not had, in these our times, such an extensive and salutary lay association which is so immediately and essentially devoted to her service, and which is directed by herself. The Association of Holy Cross will be a new glory for the Church of God.

It is especially on the Foreign Missions and across the Atlantic in the midst of the forests, that this Institute shall render service, nay, even if Heaven so wills, it will work marvels. Hence in the XXIII Constitution (first edition) it wisely and earnestly invites all its members to devote themselves to the Missions while disregarding whatever hardships and sacrifices are thereby entailed. We cannot, indeed, read without the deepest and loftiest emotion, without being moved to tears, the touching letters of Father Sorin, Superior of Notre Dame, and of Sister Mary of the Five Wounds, Superioress of another house in New Orleans, who wrote, the former on March 1, 1849, and the latter on March 4, 1849, giving descriptions of the progress which this Institute has already made during the two years they spent among the Indians and the heretics of that faraway land.

3. Is this Institute deserving of some testimony of esteem from the Holy See? What has been said above in Nos. 1 and 2 might serve as a reply to this third question, since it follows clearly that if ever there was a pious Institute which deserved to be encouraged by the Holy See, and to be honored by some testimony of esteem as well for services already rendered, as for future services which it is naturally able to render, it is surely the Association of Holy Cross.

That the Holy See ought to show the Association of Holy Cross some testimony of esteem, I consider not only meet and just, but even obligatory. And for this reason chiefly (even if we disregard all other reasons), since His Holiness in His wise solicitude to advance the interest of morality and of agriculture among the poor and abandoned classes, has called the members of the Institute to Rome and has dowered them with his fatherly protection. For (I take the liberty of speaking quite frankly) the excellent Father Moreau has told me in all loyalty and candor that certain parties wished to prevent him from founding a house of his Institute in Rome. They gave as reasons (the risk of failure apart) that he would incur opposition, raillery and insults, as if Rome opposed like pious works. The desired testimony of esteem I would have the Head of the Church grant this Institute, will have the further effect of destroying such evil prejudices against Rome. I will add that since this Institute is eminently suited to the Foreign Missions, where it will find its greatest expansion in the future, it would be more fitting that the desired testimony of esteem should be given through the Sacred Congregation of the Propaganda rather than through the Congregation of Bishops and Regulars.

Besides, this testimony of esteem should cover the entire Institute of the Association of Holy Cross, and in the Brief or Rescript, distinct mention should be made of the three parts or branches (Societies) of which the Association is made up, the Priests or Salvatorians; the Brothers or Josephites; and finally the Sisters or Marianites; for these three Societies form the one Association of Holy Cross, and are under the government of one Director or Superior General.

Whilst humbly submitting to your Excellency's consideration these findings which are all that lack of time and fuller information have permitted me to collect, I have the honor to declare myself with profound respect,

Your Excellency's very humble and very devoted servant

AUGUSTINE THEINER, *Priest of the Oratory.*

III

BISHOP NANQUETTE'S LETTER, 1856

Most Eminent and Most Reverend Seigneur:

As the Reverend Father Moreau, founder and superior of the Institute of Holy Cross, is now on his way to Rome in the interests of his Congregation I take this occasion to recommend this foundation to Your Eminence. This Congregation has come into being and developed in the midst of innumerable obstacles. In spite of these it has succeeded, nevertheless, from the financial point of view in establishing itself solidly and its situation today is prosperous and flourishing.

The Congregation, moreover, is animated by a truly religious spirit and by filial devotion to the Holy See. It has already rendered educational and missionary service and could render still more if the approval of the Holy See were to favor its development and draw to it a greater number of subjects remarkable for learning and virtue.

Deign to accept the homage of the profound respect with which I remain the most humble and most obedient servant of Your Eminence.

✠ James, *Bishop of Mans.*

In conformity with the original in the Archives of the Propaganda, *Acta S.C. de Prop. Fide,* page 133.

Giuseppe Monticone, *General Archivist.*

IV

CONSTITUTIONS
OF THE
CONGREGATION OF HOLY CROSS

Approved

by the decree

of the

SACRED PROPAGATION OF THE PROPAGANDA

dated

May 13, 1857

Pius IX

Sovereign Pontiff

Gloriously Reigning

(Seal)

In the General Assembly held on June 18, 1855, the Most Eminent Fathers Mattei, Patrizi, Amat, Franzoni, Barbarini, Brunelli and Marini decided to answer as follows the questions proposed: *On the petition for approbation of the Institute of Holy Cross and of the Rules or Constitutions of the same:*

As for the first question: there is reason to approve the Institute in its first form and limits; as for the other points the decision is

APPENDIX 305

postponed, and the remarks of the Consultor who has drawn up the Report as well as those made by the Most Eminent Fathers in the course of the discussion, will be communicated to the Procurator General resident in Rome.

As for the other questions: the solution contained in the preceding answer.

Place of the Seal.

Conformable to the original existing in the archives of the Sacred Congregation "de Propaganda Fide," *Acta S.C. de Propaganda Fide,* for the year 1855, p. 517.

(Signed) GIUSEPPE MONTICONE, *General Archivist of the Propaganda.*

N.B. This document constitutes the first official approbation of the Congregation of Holy Cross by the Holy See. Nevertheless, at the request of the Very Reverend Father Moreau, who feared that its brevity might pave the way to false interpretations, it was not published. The Sacred Congregation of the Propaganda resumed the examination of the question in its General Assembly of June 17, 1856, and published the following Decree, which is a confirmation as well as an official and authentic interpretation of the decision of June 18, 1855.

DECREE OF PRAISE

In the general Congregation of the Propaganda on May 19, 1856, there were proposed the following doubts:

1. If there is reason for some new decision regarding doubts of the "Position" of June, 1855; *On the desired approbation of the Institute of Holy Cross and of the Rules or Constitutions of the same? And in case of an Affirmative Answer:*

2. If and in what degree it is proper to amplify the approbation already granted *Juxta Primaevam Formam* (according to its first form) to the above-mentioned Institute?

3. If and what changes and modifications recently proposed by Abbé Drouelle are to be inserted in the Constitutions already submitted to Their Most Reverend Eminences (position of June, 1855) and in the respective doubts, that they may merit the good pleasure of the Sacred Congregation?

4. If and what modifications are to be adopted regarding the section of the Marianites?

The Most Eminent Fathers answered:

1. As regards the complete separation of the Marianites, what has already been decided upon must stand, and more: as for the other doubts, their solution will be contained in the following answers:

2 and 3. Praise is due the Institute consisting of Priests and Brothers, who are nevertheless to be so united among themselves in a friendly union that while preserving the nature of each Society, neither one may dominate the other, but that both may co-operate in the best possible manner to the attainment of their respective ends; the approbation of the Constitutions being deferred until after an examination has been made by one Consultor according to the following norms: let the form of government be rendered more simple; let greater authority be given to the Sacred Congregation in more serious matters; let it not be easy for the Brothers of St. Joseph to ascend to the priesthood; let the community of goods between the various houses of the Institute be not indefinite and too far-reaching; let there be sought out a method of providing for the more pressing and necessary needs of the Congregation without harm to the good order established between the two Societies, and this according to our intention which is "that the Most Eminent Cardinal Recanati be pleased to take upon himself the duty of coming to an agreement with the representatives of the Institute, to induce them to carry out these and other similar modifications before handing over the entire matter to the new Consultor for the drawing up of his Report.

Thus it is.

P. C. MARINI, *for Most Em. Altieri, Relator.*

In the audience of May 25, 1856, His Holiness confirmed and approved the decision of Their Eminences.

AL. BARNABO, *Secretary.*

N.B. This Decree approved the Congregation of Holy Cross as an Institute, but not its Constitutions. That is why the Sacred Congregation of the Propaganda issued, on May 13, 1857, the following Decree, which approves the Constitutions.

DECREE OF THE SACRED CONGREGATION OF THE PROPAGANDA

The Rules and Constitutions of the Institute or Congregation called of Holy Cross and erected in the city of Le Mans, having been, upon the presentation of the Reverend Father Mary Basil Moreau, Superior General of the said Congregation, submitted a first and a second time to a serious examination in a general session of the Sacred Congregation of the Propaganda, to the end that the Apostolic See might deign to approve and confirm them, the Most Eminent Fathers, who had already, with the consent of our Most Holy Lord, Pope Pius IX, sanctioned the approbation of the above-mentioned Institute, on June 18, 1855, have likewise decreed the approbation and ratification of its Rules and Constitutions, after the following corrections have been introduced and inserted therein, that is to say:

The concession of the permission requested in No. 17 of Constitution III, to confer Sacred Orders on clerics under the title of *mensae communis,* must be understood as being made for ten years only and only for those cases where the candidate has not the patrimony which he must have according to rule; in which regard there is a grave obligation in conscience on the part of the Superior.

1. Local Superiors should not be chosen exclusively from among the Salvatorists or in the class of Priests; consequently, reply in the negative to the propositions contained in articles 36 and 37 of Constitution VI.

2. In the Chapters, whether general or particular, the vote of the respective Major Superior should not have that preponderant force whereby, in case of a tie vote, it would suffice to settle the question, according to the opinion of the Very Reverend Father Consultor expressed on page 20, as on the enclosed sheet.

3. No. 52 of Const. VIII, should be corrected as follows: He is eligible to the charge of Superior who has finished his eighth year of profession; whoever has completed his fourth year of profession can be promoted to the office of Assistant.

4. Those paragraphs of the Constitutions wherein there is ques-

tion of founding new houses or of giving up houses already founded, should be understood in such wise that in all these cases the permission of the Sacred Congregation is necessary.

5. As regards the alienation of real estate, of which there is question in No. 9 of Const. II, the Bishop has given faculties to authorize alienation up to the sum of 5000 French francs, and the Superior of the house up to 1000 francs.

6. Let there be in the Institute or Congregation a general Economate, understood in this sense, not that the property of the Institute is held in common, but only the surplus of the revenues; nevertheless, the General Econome shall take care to note in his account-books the special accounts of each house.

7. In the course of this coming year there shall be presented to the Sacred Congregation the Constitutions or Rules to be followed in the foundation and directions of schools.

8. The above-mentioned corrections or modifications having been introduced and inserted, we testify and witness that the said Rules and Constitutions, by virtue of this present Decree, are approved and ratified by the Sacred Congregation; all things to the contrary notwithstanding.

Given at Rome, in the Palace of the Sacred Congregation of the Propaganda, May 13, 1857.

Signed: AL. C. BARNABO, *Prefect,*
CAJETAN, *Archbishop of Thebes, Secretary.*

V
APPROBATION OF THE MARIANITES, 1867

The Constitutions of the Sisters Marianites of Holy Cross having been submitted to the Sacred Congregation of the Propaganda, the Most Eminent Fathers in the General Assemblies held the eighteenth of March, 1865, and the twenty-fourth of September, 1866, after a searching examination, have unanimously approved and confirmed for ten years, on trial, the practice of the Constitutions above mentioned, an exact copy of which is subjoined, with the corrections indicated. The undersigned Secretary of the Sacred Congregation, having presented this decision to His Holiness Pius IX, by Divine Providence, Pope, in audiences given the third of April, 1865, and the thirtieth of September, 1866, His Holiness graciously approved it, in all its details, and he ordained that in proof thereof, the present Decree be forwarded to the Congregation of Holy Cross.

Given at Rome, in the Palace of the Sacred Congregation of the Propaganda, the nineteenth of February, 1867.

AL. CARD. BARNABO, *Prefect,*
A. CAPALTI, *Sec.*[1]

[1] Copy in St. Mary's Archives, Notre Dame, Indiana.